A series of student texts in

CONTEMPORARY BIOLOGY

General Editors:
Professor Arthur J. Willis
Professor Michael A. Sleigh

To our parents (J. C. H., J H., J. E. P., R. J. P.† 19 XII 1976) with thanks and gratitude

In Deo Fidemus

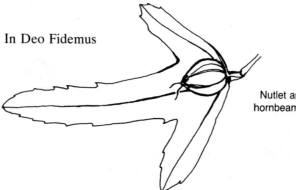

Nutlet and trifid involucre of hornbeam (*Carpinus betulus*)

Ecology of Woodland Processes

John R. Packham
M.Sc., Ph.D., F.L.S.

Senior Lecturer in Plant Ecology,
Department of Biological Sciences,
The Polytechnic, Wolverhampton

and

David J. L. Harding
M.A., Ph.D., M.I. Biol.

Senior Lecturer in Zoology,
Department of Biological Sciences,
The Polytechnic, Wolverhampton

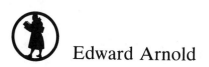 Edward Arnold

© John R. Packham and David J. L. Harding, 1982

First published 1982
by Edward Arnold (Publishers) Limited
41 Bedford Square, London WC1B 3DQ

British Library Cataloguing in Publication Data

Packham, John R.
   Ecology of woodland processes.—(Contemporary
   biology)
   1. Forest ecology
   I. Title II. Harding, David J. L. III. Series
   574.5′2642   QH541.5.F6

ISBN 0 7131 2834 8

Text set in 10/11pt Linotron 202 Times, printed and bound
in Great Britain at The Pitman Press, Bath

Preface

This book is designed primarily to provide undergraduates and teachers with a concise account of woodland ecosystems and how they operate, particular attention being paid to the inter-relationships between the various plant and animal populations which make up woodland communities, and also to the flow of energy and cycling of nutrients.

As trees clearly dominate woodlands, their establishment, replacement, and influence in modifying the environments of associated plants and animals are of primary importance. Recent studies of the physiological ecology of trees and other plants have provided much information concerning the roles of light and shade, water regime and soil type, as well as competition and other biotic factors in primary production and plant distribution. Emphasis is placed on the dynamics of woodland ecosystems as revealed by modern research, including the International Biological Programme. Included are such topics as succession and zonation, selection strategies, and species diversity, rather than descriptive details of various types of woodland of which there are good accounts elsewhere.

The primary production of the autotrophs provides the materials necessary to support the immense populations of heterotrophs found in forests. Many of these, including the plant pathogens, are involved in the grazing chain while others form part of the decomposer chain. Both chains are concerned in the cycling of mineral nutrients which makes possible the continued growth of trees and other green plants. Different members of the same taxonomic group of organisms may play different parts, for example certain fungi act as parasites,

whereas others are saprophytes or are involved in mycorrhizal relationships that have particular importance in the mineral nutrition of forest trees. Many species of plants have evolved together in such a way that they can associate in apparently well adjusted communities. The timing of the periods of active growth and flowering of different plants is an essential part of this mutual co-existence: phenology is an important facet of woodland studies. Plants and animals have also co-evolved, sometimes to the advantage of both, for example with respect to pollination, seed dispersal and food supply. In other instances plants have avoided excessive vulnerability to attack; some have developed chemical defences against defoliating animals.

We have had numerous discussions and communications with other woodland ecologists; we are very grateful to them and to the authors and publishers who gave permission for the reproduction of many of our illustrations. In a few cases it proved impossible to obtain a reply to copyright enquiries, but the origins of all non-original illustrations are given. Much of the book has arisen from our woodland ecology courses at the Polytechnic, Wolverhampton; the stimulating queries of students and the support afforded by the Department of Biological Sciences are gratefully acknowledged. Mr A. R. Hare, of the library staff, has drawn our attention to many interesting papers and answered numerous questions with unfailing good humour. The Forestry Commission staff at Cannock Chase, Staffs, have been similarly helpful and courteous. Dr O. Rackham read the drafts of several chapters and his constructive comments resulted in a number of noteworthy improvements. We are similarly grateful to Dr E. W. Jones who read and commented on the whole manuscript. Dr D. E. Coombe went to considerable trouble over the hemispherical photograph (Fig. 2.8). Discussions with our editor, Professor A. J. Willis, throughout the production of the book, have been most valuable, as has been the support of the Publisher. Finally we thank our wives and families for their patience and understanding.

Department of Biological Sciences,	J. R. P.
The Polytechnic,	D. J. L. H.
Wolverhampton.	1982

Contents

PREFACE v

1. INTRODUCTION 1
 1.1 Ecology and trees 1
 1.2 The spatial framework and the changing seasons 4
 1.3 Woodland ecosystems 9
 1.4 Decomposition and renewal 14
 1.5 Population stability, selection and strategy 16

2. PRIMARY PRODUCTION: THE AUTOTROPHS 22
 2.1 Plant life forms 22
 2.2 Biological spectra 26
 2.3 Processes of primary production and the light climate 31
 2.4 Sun and shade plants 39
 2.5 The water relations of forest plants 46
 2.6 Evergreen and deciduous 'strategies' 53

3. SOILS, CLIMATE AND ZONATION 56
 3.1 Soils and trees 56
 3.2 Roots and competition 67
 3.3 Zonation: distribution in space 71
 3.4 Diversity in communities of woodland plants 78

4. REPRODUCTIVE STRATEGIES OF WOODLAND
   PLANTS   86
   4.1 Reproduction and fruiting   86
   4.2 Masting   91
   4.3 Influence of animals   95
   4.4 Seasonal changes and aspect societies   99
   4.5 Silviculture and the replacement of trees   104

5. SUCCESSION   108
   5.1 Succession and cyclic change   108
   5.2 The maintenance of species richness in woodlands 116
   5.3 Forest change and seral woodlands   120
   5.4 Origin of British woodlands and their floras   132
   5.5 The ecology of coppicing   139

6. THE EXPLOITATION OF LIVING AUTOTROPHS   144
   6.1 The role of heterotrophs in woodland ecosystems 144
   6.2 Epiphytic microorganisms   145
   6.3 Forest pathogens   146
   6.4 Dutch elm disease   150
   6.5 Woodland herbivores   154

7. BALANCED COMMUNITIES?   162
   7.1 Population fluctuations: key-factor analysis   162
   7.2 Regulation   166
   7.3 Dynamics of specific woodland animals   167
   7.4 Changes in community structure   178
   7.5 Diversity and stability   179

8. DEATH AND DECAY   183
   8.1 Decomposition: resources and processes   183
   8.2 Degradative successions   186
   8.3 Divers detritivores   196
   8.4 Relative roles of agents of decay   201

9. ENERGY FLOW AND NUTRIENT CYCLING   207
   9.1 Biomass and productivity of autotrophs   207
   9.2 Secondary producers: the herbivore subsystem   215
   9.3 The decomposition subsystem   221
   9.4 Energy flow through woodland ecosystems   228

9.5 Nutrient cycling in temperate, boreal and tropical
     woodlands   230

10. WOODLAND MANAGEMENT AND RESOURCE
    POTENTIAL   242

    FURTHER READING   245

    REFERENCES   247

    INDEX   257

    ENGLISH AND LATIN NAMES OF SOME COMMON
    WOODLAND ORGANISMS   262

1

Introduction

1.1 ECOLOGY AND TREES

Woodland ecologists are interested in pattern and process in ecosystems dominated by trees. They seek to discover how woodlands are organized and how they function. In order to find how various species fit into a particular community, studies can be made of their inter-relationships and roles, while function at the ecosystem level involves such processes as the flow of energy and the cycling of nutrients, which feature prominently in reports of the International Biological Programme (I.B.P.). The ultimate aim of many of these studies is to identify the structure and processes characteristic of particular woodlands and to predict the likely outcome of disturbance to such a system, for instance by storms, epidemics or human interference. Because of the sheer complexity of most woodlands relatively few studies have progressed far beyond the descriptive stage. There has, however, been a steady increase in the number of predictive models which attempt to simulate such phenomena as pest outbreaks, succession, regeneration, and the relationship between stability and species diversity.

Trees vary greatly in shape, size and many other attributes, but all are large woody plants with a comparatively long life-span. Typically, though not invariably, they are single-stemmed whereas many shrubs are multi-stemmed. Their woody nature enables trees to grow far higher than herbaceous forms, allowing their leaves to receive more light than the shorter plants beneath them, effectively displaying flowers to pollinating animals or the wind, and increasing the distance over which the seeds can be shed. There are, however, concomitant disadvantages[108] to this life form in which a mature tree possesses a dead, though essential, skeleton (largely of heartwood) as well as large amounts of living cambia, phloem and wood parenchyma, which together form a major respiratory burden. The enormous accumulations of dead tissue within living trees may provide food for heterotrophs, including certain pathogens, while great height itself increases the possibility of damage by fire, lightning, wind or hurricane. In addition, as it grows older, the form and physiology of a tree must allow it to grow under the changing conditions of life associated first with the ground vegetation, then the shrub layer, and finally the tree canopy.

The *size, form* and *longevity* of a tree all influence the development of the community to which it belongs, as do the shade which it casts, the plant litter which it produces, and its ability to resist disease, water loss and fire. The characteristics of various species, especially with regard to initial establishment, competition and edaphic require-ments, fit them for a wide variety of habitats which they occupy for very different periods of time. Many British spoil tips abandoned soon after the beginning of the present century were colonized by birch, most of which are now mature or dying, and frequently a process of succession to oak, ash, sycamore or mixed woodland can be observed. Fifty years is a fairly typical life-span for the silver birch (*Betula pendula*) which casts a light shade, spreads widely and rapidly by winged seeds and often acts as a pioneer species. In contrast, the big tree (*Sequoiadendron giganteum*), a redwood from the Sierra Nevada, is so huge, long-lived and has such a dense shade that it excludes competitors for a period equal to several generations of smaller conifers. The heaviest living tree is an individual of this species known as 'General Sherman' whose estimated weight is 2030 tonnes, while the tallest is a coastal redwood (*Sequoia sempervirens*) estimated at 366 ft (111.6 m) in 1970. Records of even taller trees of Douglas fir (*Pseudotsuga menziesii*) and *Eucalyptus regnans* remain unverified. 'General Sherman' is known to be between 3500 and 4000 years old from a ring count made on a core drilled in 1931. The oldest recorded living tree, however, is a bristlecone pine (*Pinus longaeva*) which grows at 10 750 ft (3280 m) under bleak conditions on Wheeler Peak in California, U.S.A. Dendrochronologists found this to be about 4900 years old.

Ring count dating, which employs the characteristic patterns of stem rings which develop in response to the climatic patterns of succeeding seasons, has been extended to earlier than 6200 B.C. by the use of fallen bristlecone pine wood. Annual growth rings are particularly prominent in such trees as elm (*Ulmus*), whose ring-porous wood contains large vessels formed in the spring and much smaller ones formed later in the season. In contrast, the wood of birch (*Betula*), in which the xylem vessels are essentially uniform and fairly evenly distributed throughout, is diffuse-porous though the annual rings in this tree are also quite distinct. Examples of radial increment diagrams, which show variation in the width of the annual rings during the life of the tree, are shown in Fig. 5.1b.

Almost all conifers and some angiosperm trees are *evergreen*, their leaves lasting for several seasons so that the tree canopy casts a heavy shade throughout the year. Beneath *deciduous* trees, however, a far higher proportion of the available light reaches the forest floor in winter than in summer. The structure and chemical nature of leaves influence woodland processes when they are dead as well as when they are alive. Many conifers have needle leaves reinforced with sclerenchyma that keep their shape in droughts, possess thick cuticles and have stomata in grooves. Such leaves often take several years to decay, forming a thick litter which impedes the growth of herbs and the development of tree seedlings. They usually yield relatively little in the way of mineral nutrients and give rise to a discrete layer of humus. In contrast, the large pinnate leaves of elder (*Sambucus nigra*), a deciduous shrub or small tree which flourishes on soils rich in phosphorus, are much less rigid, rich in minerals and are decomposed and incorporated in the soil within a few weeks. The chemical content of leaves also affects their palatability to herbivores. The sparseness of herbivorous species living on elder leaves is presumably due to distasteful or toxic chemicals. '*Defensive compounds*' such as certain phenolics, terpenoids and alkaloids,[124] are widespread in the plant kingdom, and display their greatest diversity in the tropics. Toxic chemicals in trees may also lead to reduced competition from other plants. A number, including black walnut (*Juglans nigra*) and butternut (*J. cinerea*), produce a biochemical exudate, juglone (see below), with a herbicidal action. Both these species have rather sparse foliage, but few saplings and little understorey grow beneath.[114] The needles of pines and many other conifers contain phenolic compounds, which may be leached from their litter and which inhibit the germination of seeds.

Structure of juglone, an allelopathic chemical leached by rain water from the leaves of *Juglans nigra*. Juglone inhibits the growth of seedlings of many species, particularly those of black walnut itself. *Allelopathy*, in which chemical compounds produced by plants inhibit or depress growth in other plants, has frequently been demonstrated in the laboratory; the example quoted above is one of a small number shown to be of significance in woodlands.

Similarly the size, number and composition of the seeds and fruits influence not only the efficiency with which the tree reproduces, but also the organisms which feed on many of these structures. Most trees are *polycarpic*, seeding many times, but some such as the talipot palm (*Corypha umbraculifera*) are *monocarpic*, producing a single large harvest and then dying.

The form of the *root system* differs both between and within species; beech (*Fagus sylvatica*) has extensive shallow roots when growing on the chalk while Scots pine (*Pinus sylvestris*) develops very long tap roots on deep soils. The ability of certain trees to form *root nodules* containing symbiotic nitrogen-fixing microorganisms (*Rhizobium* bacteria in leguminous trees, actinomycetes in alder (*Alnus*), she-oaks (*Casuarina* spp.) and some other non-leguminous trees) makes a very important contribution to the amount of fixed nitrogen available in some forest ecosystems, for example the succession at Glacier Bay, Alaska (see Section 5.3). Soil erosion is often reduced by tree roots and avalanches prevented by planting protection forests.

Because of their economic importance an increasing proportion of forests and woodlands is planted by man, often leading to a loss of species diversity, and sometimes a danger of rare species or varieties becoming extinct. Ecological studies of woodlands are increasingly concerned with plantations and semi-natural communities, and can make a worthwhile contribution to forestry, one of the few primary industries dealing with a *renewable resource*.

1.2 THE SPATIAL FRAMEWORK AND THE CHANGING SEASONS

Trees form the most obvious feature of a wood; their aerial parts tower above the shrubs, herbs and bryophytes which form the other three layers or strata commonly present in temperate woodlands. In tropical rain forests—the most complex vegetation known[41]—some five strata, excluding bryophytes, may often be recognized. Tall plants modify very considerably the microclimate experienced by smaller organisms associated with them; trees are the dominant plants in woodlands, largely determining the conditions of life of the smaller plants. Temperate trees are commonly *sun plants* (see Section 2.4), with a fairly high requirement for light energy. Young trees compete very vigorously, particularly for light and water, so the number of saplings present in an area that has experienced an exceptionally good mast year, in which seed production is very high, falls rapidly and the survivors are often very drawn up unless the area is further thinned by a forester.

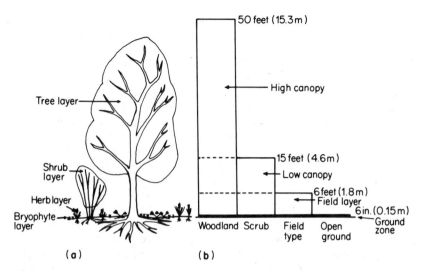

Fig. 1.1 Stratification of shoot systems. **(a)** The four strata commonly present in a temperate forest and the terminology often used in plant ecology. **(b)** Terrestrial formation-types and their vertical layers. (From Elton.[7]) All four formation-types can occur at the edges of forest glades. Note that this system, much used in animal ecology, is not completely compatible with that shown in **(a)**. Botanists frequently use herb layer and field layer as synonyms, though many would include low-growing shrubs within the field layer.

The *stratification* shown by the aerial systems of woodland plants (Fig. 1.1) is paralleled by the *layering* of their underground systems, those of the largest plants usually penetrating to the greatest depths. The deeper roots of trees absorb water and anchor the trunks securely, while the shallower or feeding roots absorb most of the mineral nutrients taken up by the tree, often assisted by mycorrhizal associations with basidiomycetes. Adjacent trees of the same species are commonly joined by *root grafts*, which occasionally enable a tree to take over part of the root system of a neighbour whose trunk has been cut down; grafts are also a means of transmitting disease. Herbs live in microhabitats where trees shade out much of the light and deplete the soil of water and nutrients; though root layering may diminish competition between herbs and trees it does not eliminate it. The bare areas of many young beechwoods often result as much from the permeation of the ground by their roots as from the heavy shading caused by a virtually unbroken canopy. On the other hand trees provide a windbreak and the microclimate of a forest is much better buffered than that of open country, temperatures are less extreme and relative humidity is usually high enough to encourage the growth of small herbs, liverworts and mosses. The development of the understorey is greatly influenced by the species, size and spacing of the trees present; that beneath English oak (*Quercus robur*) is much more extensive than beneath beech. There is normally a *mosaic* on the forest floor; variations in humus and nutrient contents, pH, soil moisture, soil aeration, and available light are reflected in the distribution of shrubs, herbs and bryophytes, which can often be used as *indicators* of environmental conditions.

The distribution of precipitation on the forest floor is locally very uneven; the ground becomes wetter under holes in the canopy, under the outer regions of the crown (from which it drips), and near the trunk. *Stem flow* is highest in trees with smooth bark whose branches are held at a steep angle to the ground. The amount of water infiltrating the soil at the bases of beech trunks can exceed that penetrating in open sites by over 50%. Usually only a small amount of the water intercepted by tree foliage is absorbed by the plant— most evaporates. *Interception losses* vary in response to changes in meteorological conditions, while trees with open crowns and large smooth leaves retain less precipitation than those with dense crowns and small, easily wettable leaves. As a first approximation interception losses can be taken as 30% in evergreen coniferous forests and as 20% in broadleaved deciduous forest.[142]

Moisture often influences zonation in woodlands, as on the north-west face of the Ercall, Shropshire, which is largely covered by oak with a moderately open canopy. Beneath is a heathy field layer and an extensive bryophyte cover in which *Plagiothecium undulatum* and the cushion form *Leucobryum glaucum* are common and widespread. The much smaller moss *Orthodontium lineare,* however, tends to form zones round tree bases. These are widest on the downhill side of the trunks down which water flows after rain; additional moisture clearly favours the moss, though it may also benefit from leachates in the water.

Figure 1.2 shows the *hydrologic cycle* of the Belgian mixed oak-wood whose primary production and nutrient cycling are discussed in Chapter 9. In summer losses caused by evapo-transpiration are high, those by drainage are low; the reverse is true in winter when stem flow is also higher. In sloping sites surface run-off and lateral drainage into streams are often large, particularly after winter rains.

One of the fascinating features of deciduous woodlands with rich herb communities is the sequence of flowers, many brightly coloured, produced by different species in spring and early summer (Fig. 1.3; see also Fig. 4.5). These form *aspect societies* in which the appearance of an area varies as the flowering periods of different species follow each other. Some of the herbs involved, for example bluebell (*Endymion non-scriptus*) and wood anemone (*Anemone nemorosa*),

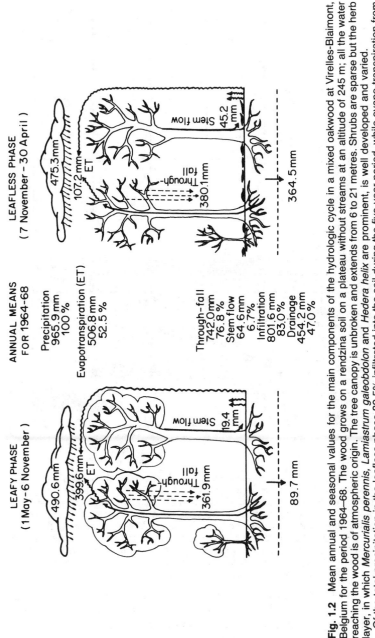

Fig. 1.2 Mean annual and seasonal values for the main components of the hydrologic cycle in a mixed oakwood at Virelles-Blaimont, Belgium for the period 1964–68. The wood grows on a rendzina soil on a plateau without streams at an altitude of 245 m; all the water reaching the wood is of atmospheric origin. The tree canopy is unbroken and extends from 6 to 21 metres. Shrubs are sparse but the herb layer, in which *Mercurialis perennis*, *Lamiastrum galeobdolon* and *Hedera helix* are prominent, is well developed and varied.

Of the total precipitation in the leafless phase 89.5% infiltrated into the soil during the five-year period, while evapo-transpiration from the soil and the foliage of trees, shrubs and smaller plants reached only 22.5%. The corresponding figures in the leafy phase were 76.7% and 81.4%; as a result of the high losses by evapo-transpiration the water content of the fine earth was low in summer. (Redrawn from Schnock and from Froment *et al.* in Duvigneaud.[6] © UNESCO 1971. Reproduced by permission of UNESCO.)

In the figure:

LEAFY PHASE (1 May–6 November)
490.6 mm
ET 399.6 mm
Through-fall 361.9 mm
Stem flow 19.4 mm
89.7 mm

ANNUAL MEANS FOR 1964–68
Precipitation 965.9 mm — 100 %
Evapotranspiration (ET) 506.8 mm — 52.5 %
Through-fall 742.0 mm — 76.8 %
Stem flow 64.6 mm — 6.7 %
Infiltration 801.6 mm — 83.0 %
Drainage 454.2 mm — 47.0 %

LEAFLESS PHASE (7 November–30 April)
475.3 mm
ET 107.2 mm
Through-fall 380.1 mm
Stem flow 45.2 mm
364.5 mm

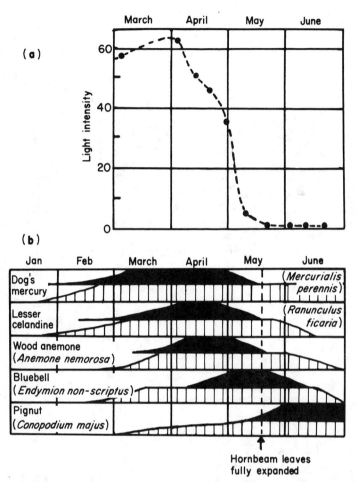

Fig. 1.3 **(a)** Seasonal changes in the intensity of diffuse light (measured at one spot in the wood and expressed as a percentage of diffuse light in the open) in an English oak-hornbeam (*Quercus robur–Carpinus*) wood in Hertfordshire. **(b)** The period of foliage (vertical hatching) and flower production (black) for common species of the shade flora based upon the average for several years. The diagram shows the onset of leaf and flower formation, followed by development to full leaf and bloom, and eventual senescence. In pignut flowering occurs only in the coppiced wood. Compare this diagram with Fig. 2.7 in which light is expressed in absolute units. (Redrawn from Salisbury,[200] by courtesy of the *Journal of Ecology*.)

are sun plants which use the relatively large proportion of the available light reaching the forest floor before the tree canopy expands to grow, reproduce and accumulate the food reserves that enable them to survive another year.

In temperate deciduous woodlands early spring growth by many of the herbs is followed by the expansion (*flushing*) of the leaves of the trees and shrubs, thus diminishing the proportion and absolute amount of solar radiation reaching the forest floor. This renewed activity in the spring is initiated by rising temperatures which cause the hormonal changes that break dormancy. Provided water availability is not limiting, the overall primary production of the woodland reaches its peak in mid-summer when temperatures and solar radiation are at their highest. With autumn comes the maturation and dispersal of seeds and fruits, followed by leaf fall and a period of relative quiescence. The aerial parts of many herbs now decay though some, such as wood sorrel (*Oxalis acetosella*) and yellow archangel (*Lamiastrum galeobdolon*), are wintergreen and may accumulate dry weight into autumn. Many other seasonal changes occur. The fruiting bodies of the larger fungi are a notable feature of the autumn (when a 'fungal foray' is held in many areas). Breakdown and ultimate mineralization of plant litter release nutrients into the soil from which they may be absorbed for spring growth.

Seasonal changes in climate can have a direct influence on animals; for example rut in fallow deer is stimulated by the effects of short day length. There are many other examples of the direct effects of climate on animals, but their activity is largely dependent on food availability which may vary seasonally. The reproduction of host-specific herbivores, such as sycamore aphids and bruchid beetles, may be closely geared to such aspects of plant phenology as leaf flushing or fruit ripening. More catholic species, for example the great tit (*Parus major*), vary their diets according to availability but may still show seasonality in breeding, related to an abundance of caterpillars or other seasonal herbivores. Similarly the breeding seasons of some litter-dwelling invertebrates may be correlated with temperature, day length or stage of decay of plant debris. Certain worms and millipedes avoid extremes of cold or drought by burrowing deeper into the soil; wider scale migrations by birds and mammals are more familiar avoiding strategies. Finally, unfavourable seasons may be endured in an inactive condition, as in hibernating mammals or in those arthropods which can enter a state of suspended development (*diapause*) at various stages in the life history.

1.3 WOODLAND ECOSYSTEMS

An *ecosystem* consists of all the organisms in a community, such as that of a woodland, together with the environment—particularly its chemical and physical features—in which the animals and plants are living. The dynamic nature of the term is emphasized by including the interactions between the various living and non-living components. Consequently it has been argued[156] that the ecosystem is the fundamental functional unit for ecological studies. This approach emphasizes the fact that the same general features, such as the very different fates of energy (which basically flows through ecosystems) and mineral nutrients (which are recycled; Fig. 1.4), are common to all ecosystems.

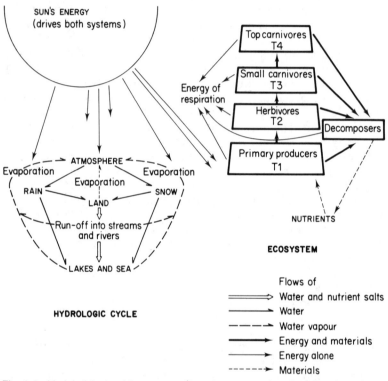

Fig. 1.4   Model of the trophic structure, flow of energy, and cycling of nutrients in an ecosystem together with the hydrologic cycle. Far more energy is used in evaporating water than in photosynthesis, but ultimately all energy received from the sun is radiated out into outer space. The nutrients are continually recycled, though there is a loss from the land via drainage systems. (Partly after Mann.[156])

Relationships which involve these fundamental ecosystem processes can be more readily understood by grouping the various organisms together according to their modes of nutrition (Figs. 1.4 and 1.5). The concept of *trophic levels* is used to indicate the number of feeding links between the original solar energy and a particular

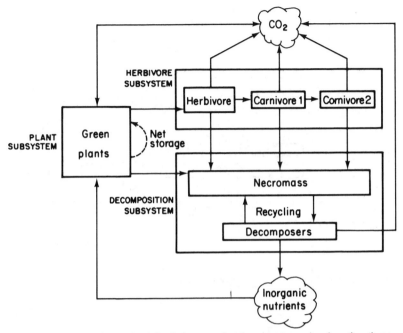

Fig. 1.5 A generalized model of the woodland ecosystem showing the three subsystems. Arrows indicate major transfers of matter between organic matter pools (rectangles) and to and from inorganic pools ('clouds'). (Modified from Swift, Heal and Anderson.[25])

organism. *Primary producers* (T1) are autotrophs; in woodlands these are almost exclusively green plants, which utilize in photosynthesis a small proportion of the incident solar radiation, forming organic compounds and releasing oxygen. The green plants use much of this trapped energy for their own metabolism, but the remainder is available to *heterotrophs*.

Herbivores, which subsist on living green plants, constitute the second trophic level (T2); in woodland many of these are foliage feeders, ranging from plant-parasitic fungi to grazing insects and mammals, including elephants. In their turn, herbivores may be devoured or parasitized by *carnivores* (T3) and these by *top carnivores* (T4). A simple progression through the trophic levels is a *food chain*; the example shown below is from Wytham Wood, near Oxford, one of the most fully investigated woodlands in the world.[7, 231]

Oak tree ⟶	Winter moth caterpillar →	Blue tit ⟶	Weasel
Quercus robur	*Operophtera brumata*	*Parus caeruleus*	*Mustela nivalis*
PRODUCER (T1)	HERBIVORE (T2)	CARNIVORE (T3)	TOP CARNIVORE (T4)

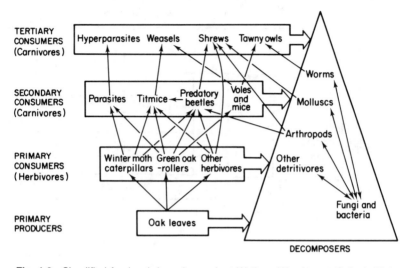

Fig. 1.6 Simplified food web based on oak at Wytham Wood, near Oxford. (Data from Varley.[231]) Note the two-way interactions among the decomposers.

This is a typical grazing chain, starting with herbivores, but, as shown in Fig. 1.6, it forms part of a more complex *food web*, which also includes decomposer chains, involving animals and microbes nourished by dead tissues. These various components can be considered as parts of three subsystems: plant, herbivore and decomposition (Fig. 1.5). Note that omnivores derive their energy and nutrients from several trophic levels; similarly certain fungi, such as honey fungus (*Armillaria mellea*), attack living trees, acting as herbivores, and then feed saprophytically on the tissues that they have killed. Furthermore, some carnivores feed on herbivores and on decomposers, and are not restricted to a single subsystem. In constructing energy flow diagrams (e.g. Fig. 9.9) attempts are made to allocate the various energy transfers among the appropriate trophic levels. Such studies indicate that in woodlands the decomposers are responsible for a much higher proportion of the total energy flow than are members of the herbivore subsystem.

There is a considerable loss of energy at every link in a food chain, since even if digestion is 100% efficient, the energy released in respiration is not available to the next trophic level. It is often stated that the efficiency of energy transfer between successive trophic levels, based for example on values for net production at the two levels, is about 10%. This figure is founded largely on freshwater studies made in the 1950s and 1960s, whereas more recent comparative studies[112] suggest a wide range of values; those for terrestrial grazing chains seem to be considerably less than 10%. Whatever the value, the storage of energy as *secondary production* in heterotroph tissues is necessarily far less than primary production.

Though energy may remain in an ecosystem for some time—comparatively large carnivores may satisfy their energy requirements by consuming small decomposer animals—the cycling of energy, as occurs with matter, is thermodynamically impossible. The input of electro-magnetic energy from the sun leads to a cycling of the various chemical elements, during which solar energy is degraded into heat and ultimately lost as longwave radiation. Much of the heat is, however, employed in the hydrologic cycle, in which water is transpired from vegetation and evaporated from the surface of the earth only to condense again and fall as rain or snow.

Cycling of nutrients is brought about by the activities of organisms and by geochemical processes, for example weathering of rocks, volcanic action and transport by wind or water. Within a woodland ecosystem the major *nutrient pathways* are from the soil to green plants and back again (Fig. 1.7). Such cycles are virtually closed and self-maintained, with usually minor inputs from rocks or the atmosphere (with the notable exception of carbon and, to a lesser extent, nitrogen), and with losses as wind- or water-borne material or in harvests. These cycles involve the uptake of nutrients by autotrophic plants and their incorporation, largely as organic compounds, into either incremental growth or ephemeral tissues such as leaves and flowers. Nutrients are returned to the soil as leachates and exudates from foliage and roots, and in the form of *necromass* (dead organic matter), especially litter. Nutrients are released from dead tissues by leaching and other abiotic agencies, such as fire, and by the catabolic activities of decomposers, the resultant release of inorganic nutrients from their organic, *immobilized* combinations, being referred to as *mineralization*. Autotrophs absorb most of their nutrients in inorganic form, commonly with the aid of mycorrhizal fungi, but availability may be reduced by leaching or soil adsorption, or by the nutrient requirements of other organisms. Heterotrophs are particularly important in perpetuating the major cycles, although these may be modified by certain herbivores or by human interference.

Characteristically, an ecosystem functions as a largely self-contained entity. Energy is imported as sunlight and exported as longwave radiation, but, with the exception of losses in harvests or in drainage water, there is usually only minimal transport of fixed energy or nutrients across ecosystem boundaries.

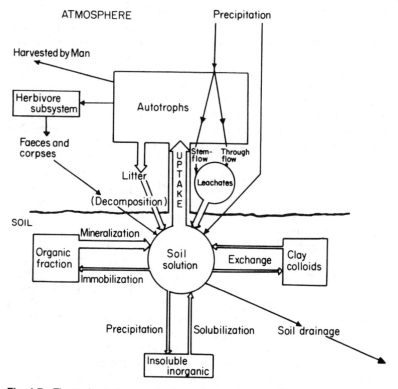

Fig. 1.7 The major pathways of nutrient transfer in a woodland ecosystem. (Partly based on Swift, Heal and Anderson.[25])

1.4 DECOMPOSITION AND RENEWAL

Much of the material produced by trees and associated smaller plants is consumed by herbivores. An even higher proportion is deposited on the forest floor as *plant litter*, whose subsequent fate differs from one woodland to another and is of great importance with regard to nutrient cycling, energy flow and fire risks. Plant materials which decompose to form humus are originally rich in carbon and poor in nitrogen, although the ratio between these elements varies according to species. The rates at which the carbonaceous and nitrogenous compounds in the litter are broken down differ; this has a major effect on the *C/N ratio* of the resulting humus. In many peats the microorganisms present are unable to attack cellulose, which has a high carbon content and forms the bulk of plant cell walls. Thus, despite the slow rate at which nitrogenous compounds break down in peat, the C/N ratio increases with time. The majority of soil bacteria and fungi are most active on substrates with a low C/N ratio, so their activities are further decreased by the fall in nitrogen and decomposition of the plant remains proceeds very slowly.

The litter of temperate woodlands on acid soils possessing few earthworms tends to accumulate as a thick organic deposit, in which three horizons may often be distinguished (Fig. 3.1a). The L horizon at the surface consists of intact litter with little visible sign of decomposition. The F (fermentation) layer beneath is of well comminuted (fragmented) litter; between it and the mineral soil is well decomposed humus (H layer) containing little or no mineral matter. This *raw humus* or *mor* has a high C/N ratio (*c*. 20) and is of low fertility. It frequently develops under conifers such as *Pinus sylvestris,* especially those planted on former heathlands. It can also develop beneath oak or beech when these trees are on acid soils poor in bases. Mor has thick L and F layers, and its pH varies between 3.0 and 6.5. *Mull* humus has a pH between 4.5 and 8.0 and has passed at least once through the gut of one of the larger soil animals, usually an earthworm, while most mor has not. Mull typically forms under deciduous or mixed forests on moderately well-drained soils containing adequate calcium, but can develop in forests of cedar or of those spruces whose litter has a high calcium content.

The absence of earthworms from acid soils has been shown to be due to the sensory responses which these annelids make to media of low pH.[208] Earthworms are, however, abundant in broadleaved woodlands on soils of higher pH in which mull is formed, and play a very active part in draining and aerating the soil. Many species feed on leaves from the surface, as well as on soil rich in organic particles. Their castings offer a substrate that can readily be attacked by smaller decomposers. Earthworms commonly deposit below the surface, but *Lumbricus terrestris,* and especially *Allolobophora nocturna* and *A. longa* also make castings above ground which provide excellent seed beds. In contrast to the relatively large lumbricid earthworms characteristic of mull the animals found in mor, which include mites, springtails and potworms (Annelida, Enchytraeidae), are small, though fungi are common. Mull, which is well incorporated in the mineral soil, has a low C/N ratio (often about 10). Soils which contain mull are often covered by a thin L layer, but the F and H horizons are scanty or absent. A more detailed account of humus forms and types is given by Russell,[198] while the processes of decomposition are considered in Chapter 8.

Large accumulations of inflammable materials including dead leaves, twigs, branches and trunks increase the risk of fire, a major forest hazard which severely damaged many British woodlands during the exceptional drought of 1976, but which usually causes damage on a much wider scale in America and Australia. Paradoxically, fairly frequent controlled fires of short duration and low intensity can often be employed to prevent major accumulations of forest trash, a technique formerly used by the North American Indians. Fire, which can also be employed to prevent valuable grassland reverting to scrub, has been an important factor in forest clearances since Neolithic times and is both a major hazard and a potential management tool.

Minerals are released from plant and animal materials by leaching and by decomposition brought about by the activities of hosts of organisms including fungi, bacteria, earthworms, insects, myriapods, mites, molluscs and nematodes. Death and decay thus precede renewal and when forest trees die and ultimately crash to the woodland floor the resulting glades are soon colonized by multitudes of plants, many of which were unable to grow beneath the shade of the living trees. When trees are healthy and closely spaced even their own seedlings are often shaded out, though there is frequently a positive correlation between the shade cast by a tree and the *shade tolerance* of its seedlings. Beech (*Fagus sylvatica*) and yew (*Taxus baccata*) both cast very heavy shade and have shade tolerant seedlings, whereas birch (*Betula*) gives light shade and has shade intolerant seedlings. Even beech seedlings, however, do not mature beneath the full shade of the parent trees and saplings arise either in the clearings or at the margins between individual tree canopies where light intensity is higher and root competition less. At any one time a natural forest usually represents a *mosaic* of trees of various species and ages, and of clearings in which herbs flourish and tree seedlings can come to maturity. Many forests, such as the English oakwoods, now seldom regenerate naturally. The causes of this failure are often complex, though in areas where the numbers of large predators have been reduced by man, tree seeds and seedlings are destroyed in very large numbers by voles, shrews, squirrels, rabbits, birds and other animals. In addition, successful tree seedlings have not only to overcome the difficulties caused by shading and plant pathogens, but also the attacks of defoliating and sap-sucking animals.

1.5 POPULATION STABILITY, SELECTION AND STRATEGY

The continuity of natural woodlands is one of their most reassuring features: from year to year the changes in the trees, shrubs, and woodland herbs, and in the seasonal patterns of activity within the woodland community often seem slight. Yet things are never quite the same, there is always a change of balance. As the environment changes, perhaps owing to management policy, one species will increase and another decrease. More than once in European pre-history the vegetation has altered as the climate changed from cold and dry to mild and wet, as at the beginning of the Atlantic period (*c.* 5500 B.C.) when oak, elm and lime were replacing the pine in Britain.[19] Such climatic changes often take a very long time; with plants it is usually reproduction that is first affected. As oaks live for three centuries or more, and redwoods for three millenia, the resultant changes in the populations of trees are not easily noticed, though effects on the relatively short-lived herbs, particularly those near the limits of their geographical range, may be more conspicuous.

Compared with other ecosystems, however, mature woodlands provide essentially stable habitats, saturated in the sense that all the niches that they contain are usually occupied. Here all the organisms present compete for survival with others that are also well suited to life in climax forest. Nevertheless, there are some places within the woodland mosaic where **open habitats** exist. Recently burnt or coppiced sites, and those where trees have been windthrown, are for a short period open to colonization by a wide variety of life forms, though within a year or two they will usually be occupied by a closed community. In the woodland as a whole, however, such transitory sites are virtually always available to '*opportunist*' or '*fugitive*' *species* such as *Epilobium angustifolium* (fireweed, rosebay willowherb) and various bryophytes, of which *Funaria hygrometrica* is prominent in the first and second seasons after burning. In the spruce-fir forest of the Rocky Mountains fireweed grows along streamsides, on land slides and in clearings, but after forest fires whole mountainsides become covered with fireweed whose seeds are rapidly dispersed by wind. After a few years the trees grow again and the fireweed gradually diminishes. In Britain this plant has spread widely in the present century and is now, at least in some areas, a troublesome weed. The average annual seed output per plant is 76 000,[205] but *E. angustifolium* also propagates rapidly by adventitious shoots which arise from the long spreading roots. A comparable insect opportunist is the plague caterpillar, *Tiracola plagiata,* which exploits ephemeral clearings in S.E. Asian rainforest.[67] The strong flying moths can lay more than 1000 eggs, which develop into adults in 30–40 days, so that populations of several million can build up to strip a wide range of plants, either in temporary habitats or in agricultural crops.

There is wide variation in the weights of individual propagules of plants within the various habitat groups,[205] but mean propagule weights increase in the sequence—open habitat:semi-closed or closed non-shady habitat:herbs of scrub and woodland margins:shade species:shrubs:trees. Of the herbaceous groups the shade species found in woodlands have the lowest seed output; their increased seed weight on the other hand enables the seedlings of many of them to reach a relatively large size before becoming entirely dependent on their own photosynthetic production. In shaded habitats some species circumvent the problem of producing seedlings large enough to survive independently by reproducing vegetatively. *Lamiastrum galeobdolon* (yellow archangel), for example, reproduces by seed when growing in warm, well-lit habitats and by long stolons in cool shaded places.

Population growth and the r–K continuum

In and around woodlands competition and selection have operated differently on various plants and animals; these differences often result from the nature of the particular habitat. Southwood[219, 220] has likened an organism's habitat to a templet (literally a 'mould') against which evolution has fashioned for the organism a specific *ecological 'strategy'* which maximizes its chances of survival. To understand these strategies, and their relevance to competition and stability, we must first consider the nature of population growth.

Under ideal environmental conditions, in the absence of predation, competition or other restraints, an animal population with overlapping generations will increase geometrically, i.e. at an exponential rate. Its *growth rate*, representing the difference between birth and death rates, is constant and independent of population density; this is the intrinsic or innate rate of increase of that species population under that particular set of conditions (r_m). Such unrestrained growth cannot be maintained for long, even in the laboratory. One way in which the growth rate can be diminished is by progressively reducing the rate of increase per individual, r, to zero as the *population density*, N, approaches the *carrying capacity*, K, which is the maximum number of that species sustainable by the habitat (see[239]).

Regular oscillations are characteristic of certain natural populations, such as lemmings. Generally, however, one finds either erratic fluctuations, as in many pest species, or relatively stable populations (see Figs 1.8 and 7.1). The components of the contrasting strategies which are presumably responsible for these differences can be considered in relation to heterogeneity in the basic habitat dimensions of space and time. For example, adaptations of organisms can be related to an *adversity axis*, as in Raunkiaer's[192] classification of life forms of plants, while the *r–K continuum* of MacArthur and Wilson,[151] currently much used by ecologists, is one of many relating species distribution to the durational stability of the habitat. Stability ranges from ephemeral to relatively permanent habitats, and in all

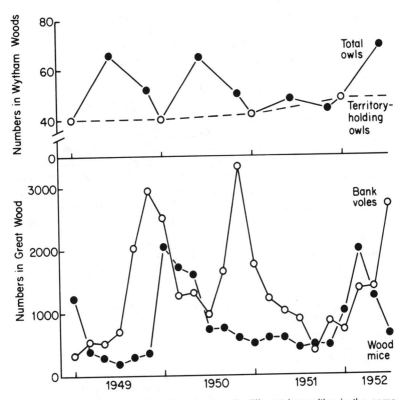

Fig. 1.8 Population fluctuations in animals with different longevities in the same locality: tawny owls (*Strix aluco*) in Wytham Woods (525 ha), near Oxford, and mark-and-recapture estimates of bank voles (*Clethrionomys glareolus*) and woodmice (*Apodemus sylvaticus*) in Great Wood, Wytham (95 ha). (Data from Southern;[217] redrawn from Southwood.[219])

cases the important relationship is between the generation time (t) of a species and the duration (H) for which a habitat remains suitable for breeding. The following summary describes some of the characteristics associated with the spectrum of strategies from r to K.

Extreme *K-species* (i.e. those which display K-strategies, evolved through K-selection) are adapted to living in basically stable, 'permanent' habitats, in which H/t is large, where they tend to maintain their relatively constant populations at or near the carrying capacity (K). Examples include certain long-lived species of vertebrates and trees. In contrast, *r-strategists*, such as the classic pest and weed species, are continually colonizing unpredictable or ephemeral habitats, for which H/t is small. Considerable investment in reproduction enables these species to exploit favourable conditions by rapid population growth (hence 'r'). This is followed by a marked decline (which may be partially related to intraspecific competition for food or space) as individuals die, form dormant propagules, or migrate. Since the next generation may arise elsewhere, overshooting the carrying capacity is not as detrimental as it sounds, and is in fact a common phenomenon. This is the 'boom and bust' strategy of the opportunist.

K-species, on the other hand, experience low mortality and recruitment rates, and have evolved high interspecific competitive ability, requisite for success in such 'desirable' habitats; considerable investment is made in defence, for example by plants against herbivores. Although fecundity is relatively low, much energy may be expended on each offspring, for instance by parental care. Some of the more obvious characteristics of species at the extremes of the r–K continuum are shown in Table 1.1. As climax forest is one of the most

Table 1.1 Features of extreme r- and K-strategists (modified from Southwood.[220])

r-species	K-species
Opportunistic, exploiting temporary habitats (H/t small)	Equilibrium-species, of stable habitats (H/t large)
Small sized and short-lived (relative to other members of the same taxon)	Large and long-lived
High fecundity	Low fecundity or iteroparous* (repeated breeding) with 'masting'
Rapid development (generation time, t, short)	Slow development (t long)
High capacity for increase (r_m)	r_m low
Low investment in 'defence'	High investment in 'defence'
Time efficient	Food and space resource efficient
Population density very variable—'boom and bust'	Population density relatively constant from generation to generation $\simeq$ K
High rate of dispersal (e.g. migration)	Low rate of dispersal

* Semelparous species, in contrast, have only one period—usually short—of sexual reproduction.

stable of ecosystems a preponderance of K-strategists is to be expected, with r-strategists occupying spatial (woodland rides and streamsides) and temporal (caused by fires or clear felling) gaps in the mature system.

Mature (but not senescent) individuals of large K-species such as bears, oaks and redwoods are seldom killed in nature by the attacks of other species, while r-species largely avoid predators by their higher rates of increase and their mobility (a 'hide and seek' strategy), rather than by chemical or physical defences. Most species lie between these two extremes and here natural enemies may play a role in establishing a stable equilibrium well below what would otherwise be the carrying capacity. As Conway[67] points out, biological control involving the use of predators, parasites or pathogens is likely to be most effective against intermediate pests.

High rates of increase enable r-species to recover quickly from unfavourable periods: their short response times cause the population to track environmental fluctuations much more closely than K-species, which have long response times for return to an equilibrium following disturbance. (Contrast the fluctuations of bank voles and wood mice with the relative stability of populations of tawny owls, whose main diet consists of these rodents—see Fig. 1.8.) Populations of K-strategists are not well fitted to recover from population densities substantially below their equilibrium level, and small populations of them are far more likely to die out than are those of r-selected species.

2

Primary Production: The Autotrophs

2.1 PLANT LIFE FORMS

Botanists have for centuries attempted to classify the life forms of green plants responsible for primary production in forest ecosystems, and the categories of woody and herbaceous plants have long been recognized. The most widely known scientific description and classification of life forms is that developed by Raunkiaer (1934)[192] who was the first to use life form to construct **biological spectra**. The main feature of his simple, but ecologically valuable, system is the position of the vegetative perennating buds or persistent stem apices in relation to ground level during the cold winter or dry summer which forms the unfavourable season of the year. Figure 2.1 illustrates the main life forms in a sequence which shows successively greater protection from desiccation, indicating the position of the vegetative buds when the plant is dormant.

Raunkiaer assumed that when the flowering plants evolved the climate was more uniformly hot and moist than it is now, and that the most primitive life form is that still dominating tropical vegetation. In such a climate large terrestrial plants (**phanerophytes**) can grow continually forming stems, often with naked buds, projecting high into the air. Other forms whose buds are protected from cold or desiccation by bud scales can be considered to be more highly evolved.

Tropical evergreens such as *Eucalyptus orientalis* are without the protective bud scales of evergreen phanerophytes of the temperate zone, for example, holly (*Ilex aquifolium*) and Scots pine (*Pinus*

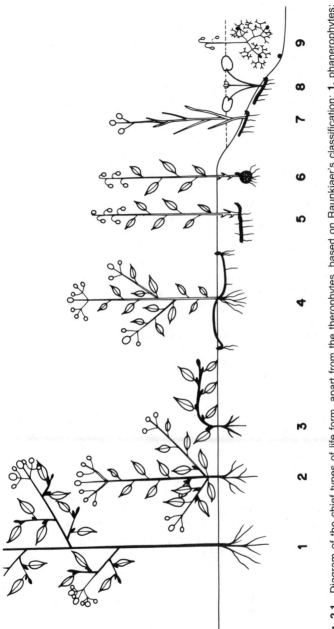

Fig. 2.1 Diagram of the chief types of life form, apart from the therophytes, based on Raunkiaer's classification: **1**, phanerophytes; **2–3**, chamaephytes; **4**, hemicryptophytes; **5–6**, geophytes; **7**, helophytes; **8–9**, hydrophytes. The parts of the plant which die in the unfavourable season are unshaded; the persistent axes and perennating buds are in black. The sequence shown represents increased protection of the surviving buds, which are most exposed in the phanerophytes. (From Raunkiaer,[192] courtesy of Clarendon Press, Oxford.)

sylvestris). Ash and larch belong to a third group formed by deciduous phanerophytes with bud scales. These large plants may be divided into four height classes: **nanophanerophytes**, woody plants with perennating buds between 0.25 and 2 m above the ground; **microphanerophytes**, between 2 and 8 m; **mesophanerophytes**, between 8 and 30 m; and **megaphanerophytes** of over 30 m. The two criteria of height and bud protection enabled Raunkiaer to divide the majority of phanerophytes into 12 groups, but he recognized others such as the epiphytic forms (including many aroids and orchids) which often grow on the trees of tropical and subtropical forests.

Woody climbers such as ivy (*Hedera helix*), honeysuckle (*Lonicera periclymenum*), Old Man's beard (*Clematis vitalba*) and the tropical lianas are specialized phanerophytes which profit from the stature of their neighbours. The more complex life form system of Ellenberg and Mueller-Dombois (see [164]) uses five main stem or trunk forms (normal woody, tuft trees, bottle trees, succulent and herbaceous-stem trees) in the subdivision of the phanerophytes.

Chamaephytes are woody or herbaceous low-growing plants whose perennating buds are on aerial branches not more than 25 cm above the soil, and frequently much lower, where the wind is not so strong and the air is damper. The perennating buds of **hemicryptophytes** are at the surface of the soil where they are even better protected, while those of **geophytes** are buried beneath the soil on rootstocks, rhizomes, corms, bulbs (Fig. 2.2) or tubers. Geophytes are particularly abundant in loose and soft soils, and form the largest group of **cryptophytes** (hidden plants) found in forests. **Therophytes** survive the unfavourable season as seeds, and are abundant in deserts and open habitats, in waste places and as weeds of cultivated land. Common in the early stages of the reversion of waste land to scrub, they become rarer as it progresses to mature woodland.

Life form is primarily determined by heredity and selection; it may be regarded as an adjustment of the vegetative plant body and life history to the habitat. Under some circumstances, however, the environment directly influences life form, for example stinging nettle (*Urtica dioica*) may overwinter as an herbaceous chamaephyte under favourable conditions, but is normally a hemicryptophyte. Conversely, severe weather conditions may kill the upper buds so that individual plants fall into the life form class below that normal to the species, as in the dwarfing of trees growing at high altitudes or subject to almost constant wind.

Raunkiaer employed six sizes of leaf in the finer details of his classification. **Leptophylls** each have an area of up to 25 mm², while the upper area limits of the next four members of the series (**nanophyll**, **microphyll**, **mesophyll**, **macrophyll**) increase by a factor of

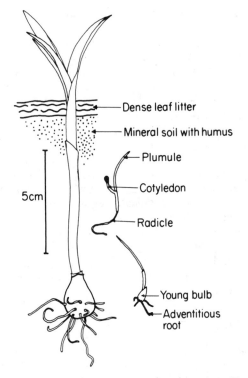

Fig. 2.2 Bluebell (*Endymion non-scriptus*), a bulbous geophyte. The pointed shoot, which can penetrate thick litter (see section 3.3), expands rapidly on reaching the light. The black seeds germinate at the surface; as the bulbs develop they form contractile roots which draw them downwards. The rarity of bluebell on the chalk scarps of S.E. England appears[49] to be due to the rapid drying out of the thin surface layer of soil and the physical barrier of the underlying chalk (which prevents the bulbs being drawn down into a deeper and moister zone), rather than to the high pH and calcium content of the soil.

nine in each instance, the largest leaves (*megaphylls*) exceeding a nominal value of 164 025 mm² in area. Leaves tend to be large in hot, wet regions (tropical rain forest), medium sized in temperate woodlands, and small in the cold or dry conditions of tundra and heaths. There is thus some justification for the use of the *leaf size spectrum*, based on the percentages of the different leaf sizes present, to characterize different vegetation types. However, light intensity and edaphic conditions, particularly soil nitrogen and phosphorus, are also important determinants of leaf size even within the same genotype.

Leaves may be needle-like, simple or compound. Those of the

tropical aroid genus *Monstera*, climbing shrubs which often mature as epiphytes with aerial roots reaching the soil, have rounded holes when mature. In tropical rain forests at least 80% of the species of trees present have leaves of the mesophyll size class (2025–18 225 mm^2): most are unlobed sclerophylls ('hard leaves') with a pronounced point known as a 'drip tip'. Microphylls predominate in montane rain forests where the climate is cooler.

Trees grade from *pachycaul* forms, such as tree ferns and palms, with thick, unbranched or little branched main stems bearing a terminal crown of large compound leaves, to 'twiggy' much branched *leptocaul* forms bearing smaller undivided leaves such as the elms. Common ash (*Fraxinus excelsior*), with its pinnate leaves and stubby twigs, has a tendency to the pachycaul habit, but no British tree has the massive frost sensitive apical meristem of a true pachycaul. Another method of biological classification is based on the principal agent of *seed dispersal*, usually wind, animals or water. Plants adapted to dispersal over long distances by wind are frequent in the taller strata. Herbs and trees, such as fireweed and birch, of pioneer communities usually spread more efficiently than species typical of climax vegetation.

2.2   BIOLOGICAL SPECTRA

A *biological* (or *life form*) *spectrum* for a particular area is constructed by expressing the numbers of the species in each life form class as percentages of all the species present. As a standard of comparison Raunkiaer used the *normal spectrum* derived from 1000 plants taken as a representative sample of the world flora. There is a strong correlation between the climate of an area and the life forms of the plants present: a *phytoclimate* is characterized by the life form which proportionately most greatly exceeds the percentage for its class in the normal spectrum. The phytoclimate of Raunkiaer's native Denmark is hemicryptophytic, like that of most of the cool temperate zone including Britain. In this system every species carries equal weight regardless of abundance or importance. Consequently, although the relatively few tree species native in Britain since the last glaciation were dominant almost everywhere until the advent of large scale agriculture, the phytoclimate is not classed as phanerophytic. The regions in which the four major world plant climates (*phanerophytic, therophytic, hemicryptophytic* and *chamaephytic*) occur, with their subdivisions, may be delimited by lines along which the biological spectra are similar.

The tropics are *phanerophytic* where rainfall is not deficient. Within this zone a greater proportion of the larger forms are found in the wetter areas. Subtropical desert areas are *therophytic* and spring to life after the very occasional periods of heavy rain. Geophytes are best represented in regions with a Mediterranean climate where the unfavourable season is the hot dry summer. Plants with this life form are at a disadvantage where the soil warms slowly in spring and the growing season is short. The resting buds of *hemicryptophytes* in the cool temperate zone are protected by snow in hard winters, but are warmed by the sun as soon as it melts. *Chamaephytes* characterize the cold zones near the poles where the cushion forms in particular derive protection from snow, but grow as soon as the spring melt commences.

Shimwell[216] presents data for eight temperate broadleaved woodlands in Britain and North America. Hemicryptophytes are abundant in all, but especially in the northern sites, while cryptophytes are more important in the southern and drier sites. The type of life form spectrum in which all species count equally can also be employed to contrast woodland floras in adjacent areas subject to different environmental influences, as for the neighbouring Nigerian forest and savanna woodland described by Hopkins,[113] where the latter, in which hemicryptophytes, geophytes and therophytes were prominent, was subject to repeated fire.

Figure 2.3, which gives the biological spectra and numbers of species present in three of the ten Polish forest associations shown in Fig. 2.4, indicates that the upland oak forest has much greater diversity than the bog pinewood or the fir forest. The mean biological spectrum for the forest area, which can be taken as an expression of its phytoclimate, was obtained by averaging the spectra for the ten forest associations, rather than using the total flora of the region. It consisted of phanerophytes 21%, chamaephytes 8%, bryophyte and lichen chamaephytes 13%, hemicryptophytes 47%, geophytes 8% and therophytes 3%. This spectrum is intermediate between a *mid-temperate mesophytic forest spectrum*, in which phanerophytes and hemicryptophytes are in nearly equal representation, and *far-northern spectra*, in which phanerophytes are rare but chamaephytes and bryophyte and lichen chamaephytes are very well represented. The preponderance of the two chamaephyte groups in the raised bog with scattered Scots pine and in the bog pinewood, where they total 57% and 53% respectively, reflects the arctic affinities of these two groups. The proportional representation of phanerophytes, hemicryptophytes, geophytes, and therophytes increases from the raised bog and bog pinewood communities to the various broadleaved forests shown in Fig. 2.4. Hemicryptophytes are at 44% in the 'hazelnut brush' (*Corylus avellana* scrub), and over 50% in the fir forest and the remaining broadleaved associations, reaching 64% in both the wet alder wood and the ash-alder carr.

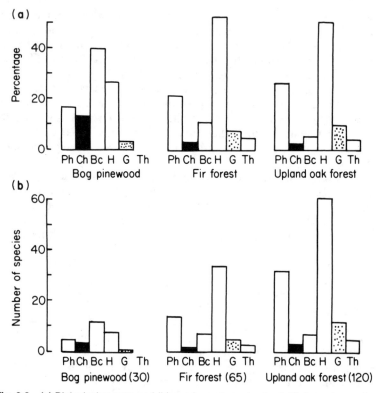

Fig. 2.3 (a) Biological spectra and (b) numbers of species in six life form classes for three Polish forest associations. Ph, phanerophytes; Ch, chamaephytes; Bc, bryophyte and lichen chamaephytes; H, hemicryptophytes; G, geophytes; and Th, therophytes. Figures in brackets indicate total numbers of species in the stands examined. (Drawn from the data of Frydman and Whittaker.[92]) See also Fig. 2.4.

Figure 2.4 is an arrangement of stands in a space defined by two axes which are *gradients of change in species composition*. A forest dominated by *Abies alba* (silver fir) occupies a central place in the ordination, being found on well drained, moderately acid soils of intermediate character and forming the most extensive vegetation type in the upland regions relatively undisturbed by man. Values for

Fig. 2.4 (a) An arrangement of ten Polish forest communities in relation to two axes by polar ordination. Each sample is an average of a number of field samples representing a community-type. (Data of Frydman and Whittaker.[92]) The raised bog and hazelnut brush served as end-point samples for the first, *x*, axis; pine-bilberry forest and ash-alder carr for the second, *y*, axis. Samples were located by relative similarity (coefficients of community) to these end-point samples. The dashed lines

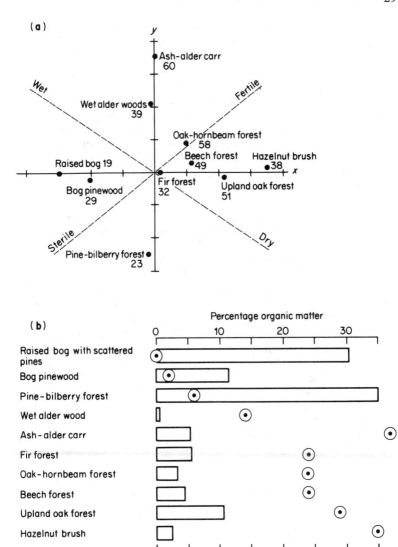

(a)

(b) Percentage organic matter

are gradients of soil characteristics that are oblique in relation to the axes; the figures are mean numbers of plant species in the field samples. (Diagram redrawn from Whittaker.[239] Copyright © 1975, Robert H. Whittaker.) **(b)** Mean values for percentage organic matter (bars) and pH (circles) for upper soil levels of the ten forest communities, arranged in the order in which they occur along the x axis of the ordination diagram. Drawn from the data of Frydman.[92]

the environmental variables of soil moisture and mineral nutrient concentration were superimposed for each community. When this was done it became apparent that soil moisture decreases from upper left to lower right while soil fertility increases from lower left to upper right. The pattern of the forest communities is thus related to the soil characteristics, which show wide variation. The soils of the raised bogs, for example, are of high organic content and C/N ratio (29.6), low pH and low exchangeable base content. At the other extreme the very shallow rendzina soils beneath the commonly south-facing hazel scrub are in the driest situations in the region and have a low C/N ratio (9.1). The alluvial mud occupied by the wet alder woods is different again, having moving ground water, very low organic content and low apparent nutrient availability.

In general, central European phytosociologists now use life form systems more complex[164] than those of Raunkiaer and also make full records of the bryophytes, lichens and fungi. Advances have also been made in incorporating *relative values for species* into biological spectra, rather than weighting each species equally. Such values can conveniently be based on cover-abundance ratings or on some quantitative measure such as cover, density or frequency. In their treatment of three forest areas near Hamburg, including two (oak-birch and spruce) on dry soils, Mueller-Dombois and Ellenberg[164] give separate biological spectra for vascular and non-vascular plants. Further ecological differences between the three forests are brought out by indicating the proportions of the plants which are either winter- or evergreen and those which are spring- or summergreen. Spring- and summergreen rhizome-geophytes are very common in beech forest on moraine. Evergreen vascular plants and thallophytes are far less common here than in the less shaded oak-birch forest. Given the same climate and tree cover, these plants usually become more abundant as the soil pH and nitrogen content decrease. They form the greater part of the ground vegetation in planted spruce forest whose evergreen foliage presents essentially the same shade throughout the year.

Life forms of terrestrial bryophytes

There is considerable scope for the use of life form analysis in future work on British woodland bryophytes. Five main types have been described—*cushions* (e.g. *Leucobryum glaucum*), *turfs* (e.g. *Dicranum majus* and *Polytrichum formosum*), *canopy formers* (*dendroid forms* such as *Climacium dendroides* and *Thamnium alopecurum*), *mats* and *wefts*.[96] Rough mats, smooth mats and dendroid forms are the commonest types on rocks but a wide variety grow on soil (see section 5.5).

2.3 PROCESSES OF PRIMARY PRODUCTION AND THE LIGHT CLIMATE

The life of all components of the food web is maintained by the latent chemical energy bound in organic compounds during photosynthesis. The overall course of the production of a hexose sugar by photosynthesis is represented by the equation

$$6CO_2 + 12H_2O \xrightarrow[\text{of chlorophyll}]{\text{Light in presence}} C_6H_{12}O_6 + 6H_2O + 6O_2$$

This process utilizes only a small proportion of the solar radiation impinging on the woodland as most of it is immediately transformed into heat, some of which drives the hydrologic cycle (Figs 1.2, 1.4). Some 40–45% of the energy of this radiation consists of wavelengths in the visible light range (380–740 nm), which corresponds to the band absorbed by the photosynthetic pigments, though photosynthetically active radiation (PhAR) is generally considered as extending from 400 to 700 nm. PhAR is bounded by ultraviolet radiation (UV) on the short wavelength side and by infrared radiation (IR) on the long wavelength side.

The proportions of the radiation striking a leaf which are reflected, absorbed, or transmitted through it vary according to wavelength, the angle at which light strikes the leaf, and the nature of the leaf itself. Transmission of visible light is greatest at wavelength ranges where reflection is also high.[163] Tree foliage is a selective filter; radiation which has passed through it on its way to the forest floor is rich in green light and in the near IR, but deficient in UV and also in the red and blue zones in which the chlorophylls absorb strongly. Leaves absorb the vast majority of the far infrared; the resulting heat load is dissipated by increased transpiration and by convection currents. A further change, in the ratio of red (R) to far red (FR) light, is of great importance in plant responses controlled by *phytochrome*. Physiologically active FR is proportionately far more abundant in light which has passed through tree leaves than in normal daylight, whereas the reverse is true of R. Light-requiring seeds are affected by the quality of the light to which they are exposed. In the open, the effects of R normally predominate, and such seeds (when imbibed) germinate if freely exposed to light, while in woodland FR tends to inhibit germination. If a gap arises in the leaf canopy, seeds of certain herbs often germinate in large numbers—the seeds can detect changes in *light quality* by means of phytochrome.

The *photosynthetic pigments* of the primary producers are frequently well suited to the spectral composition of the irradiation available to them. For example, the higher proportion of chlorophyll *b* relative to chlorophyll *a* found in some shade plants enhances light absorbing capacity in the blue-green wavelengths (between the main blue and red absorption bands of chlorophyll *a*), which are relatively abundant on the forest floor. The **light reactions** of photosynthesis involve the absorption of light by chlorophylls *a* and *b*, leading to the formation of $NADPH_2$ and of the energy-rich compound ATP, both of which are essential in carbon fixation during the ensuing dark (thermochemical) reactions. These, unlike the light reactions, are often limited by temperature under natural conditions. Respiratory rates are also influenced by temperature; Fig. 2.5 shows how greatly **net**

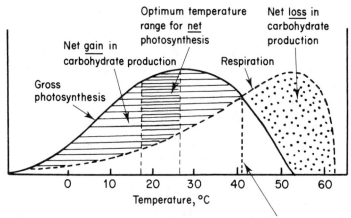

Fig. 2.5 Generalized relationship between photosynthesis and respiration with increasing temperature, under conditions in which photosynthesis is not limited by the amount of CO_2 or light available to the plant. Net photosynthesis (the difference between gross photosynthesis and respiration) is indicated by the hatched area. (Redrawn from Daniel, Helms and Baker.[4] Copyright © 1979, McGraw-Hill, Inc., used with the permission of McGraw-Hill Book Company.)

photosynthesis (gross photosynthesis − respiration) is dependent on it. Forest trees, and most of the smaller plants of temperate lands, fix carbon by the C_3 pathway; the C_4 pathway and crassulacean acid metabolism[245] are of negligible importance in the World's woodlands. The carotenoids, which are largely responsible for the yellowish colour common in the leaves of sun plants, seem relatively inefficient at light-gathering in photosynthesis; their main function may be to afford protection to chlorophylls from photo-oxidation.

Rates of photosynthesis are frequently limited by temperature, the amount of CO_2 available to the plant, or the available light. CO_2 concentrations are frequently lower in actively photosynthesizing tree canopies than near the forest floor, where decomposer organisms respire actively as they break down the litter. The proportion of the available light which a plant can use in photosynthesis is influenced by many factors including the nature and concentration of the pigments in its photosynthetic cells, the arrangement of the cells in the leaf, the surface texture of the leaf, the arrangement of leaves in space and the angles which they present to the direction of the light. Shading by the leaves of the same or of different plants is common, while variations in leaf size and shape, as well as the distances between any layers of leaves that may be present (see Section 5.3), can be crucial. Figure 2.6 shows the pattern of attenuation of

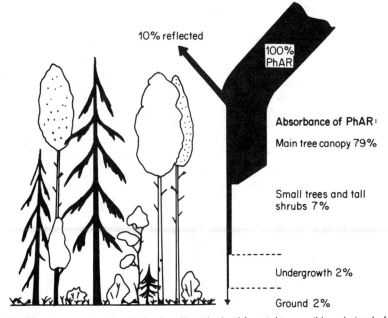

Fig. 2.6 Attenuation of radiation in a boreal mixed forest. In an unthinned stand of this structure only 2% or less of photosynthetically active radiation (PhAR) reaches the ground. (Drawn from the data of Kairiukštis, L. A. (1967); in *Svetovoi režim fotosintez i produktivnost lesa* (Celniker, Ju. L., Ed.), pp. 151–66. Nauka, Moskau.)

radiation in a boreal mixed forest in summer. On cloudy days most of the light incident upon the forest canopy is *diffuse* (skylight), while even on clear days the only *direct light* (sunlight) reaching the forest floor away from glades and trackways is in the form of *sunflecks* produced when the sun's rays pass through gaps in the leafy canopy. In some instances the radiation received is so intense as to cause damage through overheating; Rackham[191] quotes an example in which an area of *Mercurialis perennis* became scorched by the passage of a large sunfleck after rain. Most PhAR is absorbed in the crowns of trees and the amount reaching the ground can be very small indeed. This is important because at the low irradiance of most forest floors when the trees are in leaf the rate of photosynthesis is often limited by PhAR, whereas at higher irradiance the rate may be governed by the thermochemical or 'dark' reactions.

Seasonal variations in the light climate

Comparative studies of sun and shade plants, and of the phenology of the communities to which they belong, have gone hand in hand with investigations of the quantity and spectral composition of the radiation which they experience. Light conditions within a woodland vary in respect of intensity, and of directional and spectral composition, from hour to hour and year to year as well as from month to month. The problems of making meaningful light measurements[14] and of creating suitable experimental light regimes in shading experiments are too complex to discuss in detail here, but introductions to these important subjects are provided by Table 2.1, further reading[8,14] and the references.[37,38,42,48,89,246] There is now a great variety of light-measuring equipment; some modern meters have three separate heads giving direct read-outs of illuminance (in lux), total radiant energy (watts m^{-2}), or quantum fluxes of PhAR (μE cm^{-2} s^{-1}). Modern instruments can give a direct reading of PhAR below, or at a defined position within, a leaf canopy as a percentage of that above it. With different types of apparatus light measurements may be made at particular times or integrated over a period. Instruments vary in their spectral qualities and this must always be borne in mind when designing experiments or assessing their results.

As early as 1916 Salisbury[200] laid the foundations of the study of shade as an ecological factor, using the darkening of photo-sensitive paper when exposed to light to compare the amount of light in the open with that reaching the woodland floor. To present the results of shading as a percentage reduction of the light in the open, however, fails to take account of the great variation, in absolute terms, between sites in different climates and latitudes, and also between different occasions at the same site. This method of light measurement also ignores the quality of light penetrating the canopy. Young[246] illustrated the importance of this aspect of the light climate by growing plants of *Impatiens parviflora* at various R/FR ratios.

Table 2.1   Units involved in the measurement of light.

Unit of ENERGY	$1\,J = joule = 1\,N\,m = 1\,kg\,m^2\,s^{-2}$ (one newton, N, is the force needed to accelerate one kilogram at the rate of one metre per second per second) $kJ = 10^3\,J$ $MJ = 10^6\,J$ 1 cal (calorie) $= 4.18\,J$
Unit of POWER	$1\,W = watt = 1\,J\,s^{-1}$ $mW = 10^{-3}\,W$
Unit of ILLUMINANCE	lx (lux) $=$ lumens m^{-2} $klx = 10^3\,lx$
QUANTUM ENERGY	1 mE (millieinstein) $= 6.02 \times 10^{20}$ quanta 1 μE (microeinstein) $= 6.02 \times 10^{17}$ quanta

Light is measured in various ways for different purposes; in addition several systems of units have been used. In this book the units given for light values are those employed by the authors in their original measurements, i.e. milliwatt hours per square centimetre (as measured with electrolytic meters and an actinograph) in Fig. 2.7, kilolux in Fig. 2.11 and $kJm^{-2}d^{-1}$ in Section 5.3.

Complications arise in making photometric measures such as **illuminance**; the apparent colour of the test light source being measured should be the same as the standard;[14] also conversion of such units into energy terms usually presents difficulties. Most cheap and convenient light-measuring instruments are calibrated photometrically, being designed for use by lighting engineers. Photometric units, such as klx, are less appropriate in ecological work than the radiometric units mentioned below.

The recommended SI units for **irradiance**[8] are joules per square metre per second, which can be simplified to watts per square metre. Values of hundreds of $W\,m^{-2}$ are often encountered in the open; those in the shade are usually less than $100\,W\,m^{-2}$. When energy is integrated over time, the megajoule per square metre per day is a convenient unit, ranging at the latitude of Britain from the order of 2–5 in the open during winter to the order of 20–25 in summer (calories per square centimetre per day were commonly used before the adoption of SI units).

Of major physiological and ecological significance is the light which is important in plant growth; this **photosynthetically active radiation** (PhAR) is usually taken as being bounded by the wavelengths 400 nm and 700 nm. This radiation may appropriately be measured in terms of the **quantum fluxes** (in microeinsteins) at defined wavelengths.[14]

Though all plants received the same intensity of radiant energy, lowering the **R/FR ratio** caused an increase in specific leaf area (see Table 2.2) and in internode elongation. With modern techniques, radiation can be measured in absolute terms instrumentally as Anderson[37,38] did in her long-term studies (Fig. 2.7) in Madingley Wood, Cambridgeshire.

Hemispherical camera photographs such as that shown in Fig. 2.8 make it possible to estimate, with reasonable accuracy, the amounts

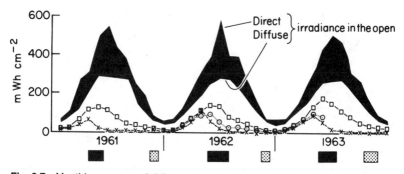

Fig. 2.7 Monthly averages of daily irradiance in the open at three sites in Madingley Wood, with the contribution of direct irradiance in the open shown in black. □, large clearing (some 20 m in diam.); ⊙, small clearing; ×, photosite. The 'photosite' was in the middle of a stand dominated by *Ulmus carpinifolia* with some *Quercus robur* and an understorey largely of hazel. The small clearing was only 5 m from the photosite and canopy conditions there were similar, apart from a small patch of open sky near the zenith. The horizontal bars at the bottom of the figure represent tree leaf expansion (black) and leaf fall (stippled). Measurements of the light conditions were made with integrating electrolytic photometers and bimetallic actinographs; gaps in the record were filled by photographic estimates of direct and diffuse light. The more strongly shaded the site the more is its annual peak of irradiance shifted away from mid-summer towards the spring. (From Anderson,[38] by courtesy of the *Journal of Ecology*.)

of light reaching particular woodland sites without the continuous use of recording instruments. Estimations of direct light are made using solar track diagrams, whereas diffuse light[37] is calculated using a grid which divides the photographs into a number of areas each of which, in the absence of interference by the tree canopy, would receive the same amount of skylight. Photographs taken in summer are used to estimate the proportion of skylight able to pass through the foliage.

In evergreen forests the shade offered by the tree canopy is much the same throughout the year, so the monthly light totals can be expected to show a symmetrical seasonal trend similar to that in the open. The situation is different in deciduous woodlands where Salisbury recognized a '*light phase*' in which the trees are bare of leaves, and a '*shade phase*' in which the tree canopy is present. In the English midlands the light phase, which Rackham[191] refers to as the '*bare half-year*', usually lasts at least five months. In open sites in Britain approximately half the total light energy is sunlight direct from the sun and the other half is skylight diffused from clouds or blue sky. During the bare half-year the spectral composition of light inside and outside the wood is very similar, although shading by trunks and branches reduces the amount of skylight received by most of the forest floor to between a quarter and a third of that in the

Table 2.2 Definitions used in growth analysis.

Relative growth rate (RGR) is the rate at which a plant increases its dry weight per unit dry weight. RGR can, at a particular instant, be resolved into three components:

1. Unit leaf rate (ULR) = $dW/dt \times 1/L_A$
2. Leaf weight ratio (LWR) = L_w/W
3. Specific leaf area (SLA) = L_A/L_w
    where L_A = total leaf area
        L_w = total leaf dry weight
        W = total plant dry weight
        dW/dt = rate of dry weight increase of the whole plant

RGR = ULR × LWR × SLA

Leaf area ratio (LAR) is a morphological index of plant form, the leaf area per unit dry weight of the whole plant.

4. Leaf area ratio (LAR) = L_A/W = LWR × SLA

In contrast, *unit leaf rate* (ULR), the rate of increase in dry weight of the whole plant per unit leaf area, is a physiological index closely connected with photosynthetic activity. A high LAR together with low ULR is characteristic of heavily shaded woodland herbs in temperate forests.

Relative leaf growth rate (RLGR) is analogous to RGR and is the rate of increase in leaf area per unit leaf area.

5. Leaf area index (LAI) = L_A/Ground area occupied by plant

Stomatal index = Number of stomata per unit area (Number of stomata per unit area + Number of epidermal cells per unit area)

open. In December sunlight rarely penetrates to the ground (except in large glades), but by April its amount is almost as much as that of skylight. The proportional increase in total light from the winter minimum to April is greater inside the wood than in the open.

In the shade phase ('*leafy half-year*') the light climate in different parts of the wood is much more variable. Even skylight can be reduced to a fraction of 1% (of that present in the open) under the densest shade, while the light is green, and hence less useful for photosynthesis, after transmission through the leaves of the trees. The more heavily shaded a woodland site is in summer, the greater is the proportion of the year's total light received in spring (Fig. 2.7). Variation in the time at which the tree canopy expands, which differs considerably from year to year, greatly affects the total light received by the ground vegetation in spring, while daily light totals have been shown to vary at least fivefold within a week at Madingley Wood.

Most trees flourish when light is abundant, being *sun plants* (heliophytes), while many of the smaller plants growing beneath them are *shade plants* (sciophytes). The aerial environments of these

38

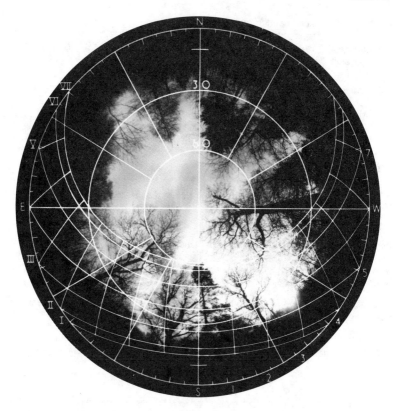

Fig. 2.8 Hemispherical photograph, with superimposed solar track diagram for 52°13′N, of the large clearing (Fig. 2.7) in Madingley Wood, Cambridgeshire. The fisheye lens has recorded a hemisphere on a single photograph, covering a vertical arc of 180°.

This photograph was taken at 1450 hours GMT on 2 March 1957 with a bright but hazy sky; the sun was mid-way between the solar tracks for 21 February (III) and 21 March (the equinox), and a little to the left of the 3 p.m. hour line. The spruce (*Picea*) a few degrees west of south, an ash (*Fraxinus*) 30° west of south, and an oak (*Quercus robur*) almost due west, were felled before the records shown in Fig. 2.7 were made,[38] but the basic pattern of the canopy was similar (cf. Anderson[37] Phot. 2, taken 10 January 1962).

The superimposed grid consists of concentric circles for 0°, 30° and 60° of altitude, together with radiating lines for each 30° of azimuth. 1–7 indicate hours from apparent noon. The seven solar tracks were computed by the method of Evans and Coombe[89] and apply to the following twelve days of the year, upon each of which the sun enters a sign of the zodiac.

I 22 Dec II 22 Jan / 21 Nov III 21 Feb / 22 Oct IV 21 Mar / 23 Sept V 22 Apr / 22 Aug VI 22 May / 22 July VII 22 June

Given the mean hourly irradiance data for the appropriate latitude and climate (see[37])

two groups differ, and the adaptations to these conditions involve major morphological and physiological differences considered in the next section.

2.4 SUN AND SHADE PLANTS

The most generally limiting factor for herbs, shrubs, and young trees in woodland situations is light and many of them show remarkable adaptations to different levels of PhAR. In deciduous woodlands, herbs such as *Anemone nemorosa*, *Endymion non-scriptus* and *Ranunculus ficaria* largely evade severe shading by having their main period of growth before the tree canopy expands—indeed *Endymion* is well known as a sun plant.[48,49] Others are truly **shade tolerant** (e.g. enchanter's nightshade, *Circaea lutetiana*), and in some the shade leaves are modified to such an extent—by increasing the light-catching area and chlorophyll content—that for the same expenditure of dry weight they achieve much the same rates of photosynthesis as sun leaves receiving considerably higher levels of radiation. Plants such as yellow archangel (*Lamiastrum galeobdolon*), which possesses great **phenotypic plasticity** and grows along hedgerows as well as in woodlands, show differences between their sun and shade leaves (Fig. 2.9) considerably greater than those demonstrated by Packham and Willis[177] in *Oxalis acetosella*, a plant well adapted to shade but not to sun. These and many other plants produce large, deep green, relatively thin, fragile leaves when under dense canopy; the **sun leaves** which develop under high light intensities are smaller, thicker and often yellowish-green. **Shade leaves** in many species commonly have a spongy mesophyll with very large air spaces and palisade cells, known as **funnel cells**, which taper downwards from the margin adjoining the upper epidermis. They also have a thinner cuticle, large epidermal cells and a lower vein density than do sun leaves.

---

such solar track diagrams can be used to estimate the percentage of direct light reaching the site where the photograph was taken at any time of day or period in the year. The longer the period taken the more accurate will be the estimate. Pope and Lloyd[188] deal with the special considerations that apply to sloping sites.

This photograph has been prepared by Dr D. E. Coombe from the original negative but with a more accurate orientation of the solar track than that shown in Phot. 6, Evans and Coombe.[89] (Coombe's 1957 photograph was taken at a point about 2 m N.W. of Anderson's 1962 photograph so that the orientations of the trees vary somewhat.)

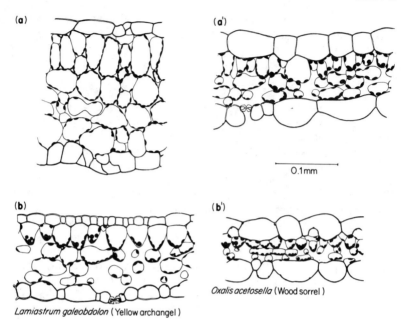

(a) (a')

0.1mm

(b) (b')

Oxalis acetosella (Wood sorrel)

Lamiastrum galeobdolon (Yellow archangel)

Fig. 2.9 T.S. leaves of *Lamiastrum galeobdolon* subsp. *montanum* (left) and of *Oxalis acetosella* (right). Both species are hypostomatous (stomata on the underside of the leaves only). **(a), (a')** Sun leaves; **(b), (b')** shade leaves, whose palisade mesophyll consists of funnel cells. **((a'), (b'))** From Packham and Willis,[177] by courtesy of *Journal of Ecology*.)

Adaptations to shading

Growth analysis techniques[87] are valuable when studying the ways in which plants react to changes in light level, humidity regime, temperature and other features of the environment which are altered by shading. Chlorophyll content per unit dry weight is usually considerably higher in shade leaves than in sun leaves, except where shading is so extreme as to result in the production of relatively small etiolated leaves. Differences in chlorophyll contents between sun and shade leaves appear much greater when expressed on a dry weight than a fresh weight basis, while chlorophyll values per unit area may actually be lower for shade leaves than sun leaves. Thin leaves are not always characteristic of shade plants;[50] many rainforest species such as *Cordyline rubra* and *Lomandra longifolia* have the thick leaves associated with a low specific leaf area (SLA). (This term is defined in Table 2.2, together with others used in growth analysis.) The latter leaves do possess high chlorophyll contents, however, and the unusually large chloroplasts are concentrated in the upper palisade.

Stomatal frequency and pore size vary amongst rainforest plants but differences between sun and shade species are not significant.

Besides the major morphological and physiological differences between woodland species and plants of other habitats, environmental and genetic factors result in variations within individual species, a point illustrated by Fig. 2.10 which shows the results of a shading

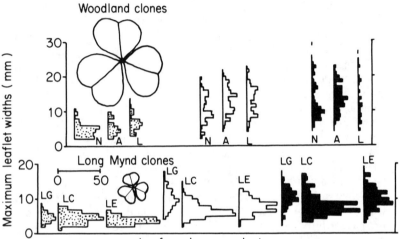

Fig. 2.10 Variation in leaflet widths of clones of *Oxalis acetosella* from two contrasting habitats in Shropshire. Clones N, A and L were from a woodland streamside near Telford; clones LG, LC and LE from beneath *Pteridium aquilinum* in a montane pasture on the Long Mynd. Clones were gathered from the wild in late March 1971 and grown in cold frames under three light regimes: under clear polythene only (stippled); in light further reduced by a muslin shade (white); and in light greatly reduced by a muslin shade (black). The plants were harvested in August 1972. While phenotypic plasticity is very important, genetic influences are also involved. Clones from both sites show greater leaflet widths as the light levels are reduced, while the leaflet width/leaf number relationships of the two populations differ, plants from the Long Mynd tending to have smaller leaflets but a greater number of leaves than those from the woodland. Individual clones from the site also differ in their behaviour, as seen in the contrast between clones LG and LC. (Redrawn from Packham and Willis,[177] courtesy of *Journal of Ecology*.)

experiment. Using artificial shading under controlled conditions, Hughes[118] showed that the meristematic activities of the sun and shade leaves of small balsam (*Impatiens parviflora*) are fundamentally similar, and that the difference in structure at maturity is caused by the greater expansion of the shade leaves which consequently have lower stomatal frequencies. This situation is common amongst temperate plants and explains why the stomatal frequency can vary according to shading regime while the *stomatal index** remains similar.

Young[246] found that though the *leaf weight ratio* (LWR)* of *I. parviflora* is markedly affected by the rooting medium, it is little altered by changes in total daily light. SLA varies with temperature, rooting medium, daylength, total daily light and the 'physiological age' of the leaf or plant. As SLA is, over a substantial range of daily light level, inversely proportional to total daily radiation received, while *unit leaf rate* (ULR)* is directly proportional to it, the net effect of these two relationships is that the *relative growth rate* (RGR) of *I. parviflora* remains approximately constant over the range concerned.

The proportion of total plant weight devoted to roots is commonly low in shade plants, although the *root/shoot ratio* appears to be related to soil moisture content as well as the intensity of radiation. Temperate shade species grown under lower PhAR tend to possess high fresh weight/dry weight ratios and SLAs, while RGR is low. The very low levels of radiation at which some shade plants occur in nature are often well below the optimum for the species. Heavy shading, however, has the effect of eliminating competition from sun species of much higher potential RGR.

Above quite low radiation levels shade plants are unable to make use of additional light, while in sun plants net photosynthesis increases until very much higher levels are reached. The higher capacity for CO_2 fixation per unit leaf area in sun plants appears to be directly related to the greater amounts of the carboxylating enzymes and to the greater volume of the leaf per unit leaf area. The proportion of chlorophyll *a* to chlorophyll *b* increases in plants grown at high light intensities; even fully grown leaves may partially adapt to a change in light level by a modification of their enzyme systems.

The phenotypic plasticity which enables a given genotype to adapt to various light levels is effected by a wide variety of morphological, physiological and biochemical mechanisms; these are reviewed by Boardman.[50] He concludes that the light levels to which a genotype can adjust reflect a genetic adaptation to the conditions of its native habitat. Moreover, adaptation for great photosynthetic efficiency in strong sunlight precludes high efficiency in dense shade.

Radiation profiles and photosynthetic activity of trees

The density of foliage and the shape of the crown cause great variations in the amount of light reaching individual leaves; every tree has a characteristic radiation profile. In cypress (*Cupressus*) the amount of light reaching the interior is about 0.5% of that present at

* See Table 2.2.

the surface of the crown and no leaves are present in this *dysphotic zone*. Leafy branches are present even in the innermost region of the more open crown of the olive (*Olea europaea*). The relative irradiance (mean value of radiation compared with that for an entirely open site) corresponding to the minimal requirements for shade leaves in trees with open crowns (*Betula, Larix, Pinus sylvestris*) is, according to Larcher,[142] between 10 and 20%, while in *Picea, Abies* and *Fagus* which have dense crowns it is 1–3% of the incident radiation. In parts of the crown where the average amount of PhAR is insufficient to meet the minimal needs of the shade leaves, existing side shoots frequently wither and no new leaves are formed. It is probable that the critical radiation level which prevents this *self pruning* process is that which just allows a branch to make a net gain in photosynthesis. Conversely epicormic shoots become prominent in certain trees, such as larch, if strong light is again allowed to reach trunks which have become bare as a result of severe shading.

In trees, differences occur in the intensity and seasonal duration of photosynthetic activity of sun and shade leaves borne on the same plant, as is illustrated by the investigations of Schulze[209] on a single tree of *Fagus sylvatica* from the Solling Mountains of Germany. The rate of CO_2 uptake in sun and shade leaves was about the same in relation to leaf dry weight, but on a leaf area basis assimilation in the shade leaves was approximately half that in the sun leaves. In relation to chlorophyll content the apparent assimilation of the shade leaves was only one-third of that of the sun leaves. By the time the shade leaves of *Fagus* reached maximal assimilation in August the photosynthetic activity of the sun leaves had already declined. Senescence of the sun leaves began much earlier than in shade leaves, as in cold frame experiments with the herb *Oxalis acetosella*.[177] In both instances differential senescence was probably caused by the higher temperatures and by accelerated photo-oxidation of photosynthetic pigments at greater light intensities.

Variation in light compensation point

Investigation of a number of herbs growing beneath *Fagus* on the Solling Mountains[210] demonstrated the ecological importance of some of their physiological and morphological differences. *Light compensation point*, at which the amount of CO_2 fixed in photosynthesis is equal to that released in respiration, lay between 300 and 500 lux for *Oxalis acetosella, Athyrium filix-femina* (lady fern), *Luzula luzuloides*, and young beech plants. Amongst these four plants *light saturation*, the light intensity at which further light does not increase net photosynthesis, is attained at the lowest levels by *Athyrium* (2000–3000 lux) and by *Oxalis* (5000–6000 lux); these two plants also had higher maximum rates of photosynthesis than the others. *Deschampsia flexuosa*, in contrast, acted more like a sun plant having a compensation point of 2000 lux and a net rate of photosynthesis which increased linearly up to 12 000 lux. As a consequence, the existence of this plant on the forest floor is far more dependent on the occurrence of **sun flecks** than is that of the other species (Fig. 2.11).

The **photosynthetic temperature optimum** of *Oxalis*, which is always low, was found to diminish from 13–18° C at 8000–12 000 lux to a range of even lower temperatures (9–12° C) at 1000 lux. This feature is of value in a wintergreen plant receiving little light and assists *Oxalis* to increase in weight longer into the autumn than most other species. Calculations of net photosynthetic gain are normally made with regard to the leaves rather than the whole plant. On this basis *Oxalis* has a higher net gain than *Luzula luzuloides* whether the reference system is unit dry weight, surface area or chlorophyll content. The greater competitive ability of the latter, at least in the Solling Forest, is partially explained by the different **life forms** of the two species. *L. luzuloides* is a **hemicryptophyte** and some 63% of its total dry weight increment is partitioned to its aerial parts as against only 42% in *Oxalis*, which behaves as a **rhizome geophyte** in this habitat, though it can also grow as a rosette hemicryptophyte or as a herbaceous chamaephyte.

Shade-tolerant plants characteristically possess low metabolic rates which lead to low compensation points, a feature which contributes to their success in poorly lit habitats. In contrast, shade-intolerant species have higher compensation points, despite the fact that their rates of photosynthesis may exceed those of some tolerant species even at low radiation levels. Grime[100] points out that the reserve of respirable materials, a good index of the ability to survive, is largely dependent upon conversion of photosynthate into plant structure. Intolerant species may fail to survive in shade because they quite quickly utilize a high proportion of the photosynthate produced during the period above the compensation point. Shade-tolerant

---

Fig. 2.11 Apparent photosynthesis in the grass *Deschampsia flexuosa* and in *Oxalis acetosella* (a shade species) measured under natural conditions in a montane beech forest in West Germany. CO_2 exchange during a summer day is shown in terms of leaf dry weight (d.w.), leaf area and chlorophyll (chl) content of the leaves. (N.B. CO_2 exchange for *Oxalis* is plotted on a smaller scale than that for *Deschampsia*.) In contrast to the low amount of light reaching the forest floor, the crown top of the beech (*Fagus sylvatica*) may receive more than 80 klx at midday in summer. The shade leaves of the tree receive less than 15% of this and are light saturated at 6–7 klx during the summer, while the sun leaves are light saturated at 30–40 klx. (Redrawn from Schulze.[210])

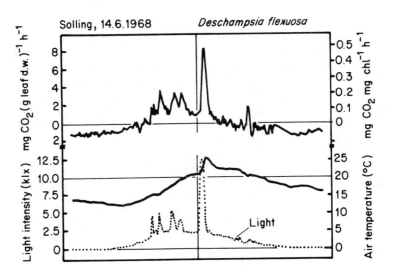

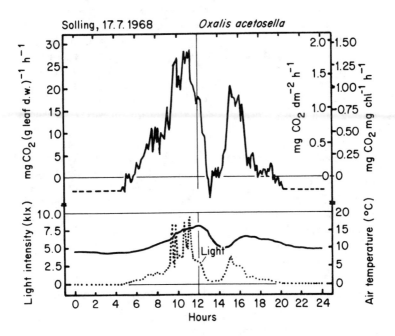

plants retain larger reserves that enable them to survive relatively long periods when PhAR is below the compensation point. Failure of seedlings in dense shade is often caused by fungal pathogens which are normally resisted if high sugar levels are maintained. Seedlings of common ash (*Fraxinus excelsior*) in woods with a well-developed herb layer often spend much of the year near the compensation point. Deaths usually occur in winter; after leaf fall new photosynthate is no longer produced and respiration soon depletes the small reserves of seedlings. Some disappear within a few days, while others first exhibit the 'wirestem' effect in which only the stele remains after the epidermis and cortex have been attacked by damping-off fungi. Only a few survive to grow above the herb layer. Rapid height increase does not enable herbs growing beneath forest trees to avoid shade, and stimulation of excessive extension growth at low PhAR, as often occurs in shade-intolerant species, is disadvantageous as energy resources are dissipated and the seedling predisposed to fungal attack.

Leaf arrangement and leaf area index (LAI)

When poorly lit, plants tend to produce fewer layers of leaves than when unshaded; the measure employed to quantify this aspect of plant form is *leaf area index*, the total area of the leaves growing above a given area of ground divided by the area of the ground itself. Horn[114] found that the ground beneath an oak-hickory forest in New Jersey was covered, on average, by 2.7 layers of leaves of the canopy trees, while the LAI values of the understorey trees, shrubs and ground cover, which of course received successively less light, were 1.4, 1.1 and 1.0 respectively. Shade leaves are usually held horizontally where they absorb the maximum amount of radiation. The *sun twigs* of *Abies*, *Sequoia* and *Sequoiadendron*, however, are held at angles which reduce the heat load caused by absorbing long-wave radiation in situations where PhAR is rarely limiting. The leaves of the seedlings and of the *shade twigs* of these three tree genera, on the other hand, are arranged horizontally and intercept the maximum amount of light. The pattern of *attenuation of radiation* passing through the forest is dependent on the cumulative LAI at a given level above the ground, the arrangement of leaves in *monolayers* or *multilayers* (see Section 5.3), and the angle at which the leaves are held to the horizontal. It is of great importance in influencing plant succession in forests, a subject considered in Chapter 5.

2.5 THE WATER RELATIONS OF FOREST PLANTS

The amount and seasonal pattern of precipitation are among the most important factors influencing the growth and natural distribution of trees; they must also be carefully considered when creating new plantations. The extremely tall coastal redwood (*Sequoia sempervirens*) grows along the Pacific coast of N. America in temperate rain forests which receive precipitation throughout the year. There is a cool maritime climate with abundant winter rain; in summer, clouds and fogs supply the tree foliage with water. In most of Britain this species grows less well than the big tree (*Sequoiadendron giganteum*), whose native habitat, at an altitude of 1200–2400 m in the Sierra Nevada, California, is much drier, and where most precipitation is as snow. Sitka spruce (*Picea sitchensis*), with a comparatively shallow root system, grows well when planted on the damp western side of Britain. In contrast, *Pinus sylvestris* and *P. nigra*, which have deep and effective root systems, grow well in Thetford Forest, East Anglia, which has an average annual rainfall of only 23 inches (584 mm) and experiences severe drought at times.

Temperature influences both the metabolic state of plants, which are unable to absorb much water during very cold winters, and the potential evapo-transpiration rate. Trees frequently avoid much water loss by shedding their leaves. This is seen in northern temperate forests where deciduous trees lose their leaves at the beginning of winter, and in savanna where many trees are leafless during the dry season.

Drainage and *soil type* are very important with regard to water relations; a very high water table severely limits the soil volume which can be exploited by most trees. Even minor alterations in the depth of the water table may affect trees adversely, though roots of lodgepole pine (*P. contorta*) can adapt to very damp conditions by forming air cavities in the stele. Root death in waterlogged soils is sometimes caused by the presence of ferrous ions, rather than by lack of oxygen (see Section 3.4). The *field capacity* of a soil, the amount of water which it contains (expressed as a percentage of the oven-dry weight of the soil) after it has been saturated by heavy rain and allowed to drain freely, is a most important character. Soils rich in clay and humus, colloids possessing a high affinity for water, have a high field capacity while that of soils containing a high proportion of the larger mineral particles, such as sands and gravels, is low.

The shoot systems of trees and other land plants normally replace the water which they lose to the atmosphere when the roots absorb more from the soil. Thus water uptake, the conduction of water from the roots to the transpiring surfaces and transpiration itself are closely linked aspects of the water balance of the plant. *Potential evaporation* is proportional to the vapour-pressure deficit of the air (the saturated vapour pressure minus the actual vapour pressure), and transpiration by the tree generally follows the same trend as evaporation from a physical system until regulated by stomatal closure or until water content becomes severely limiting.

Water in the soil-plant-atmosphere system tends to move along a **water potential gradient**, travelling from where it is more readily available to where it is less so. This movement is now usually described in thermodynamic terms;[142,160] the state of water in a plant cell or the soil is compared with that of pure water, the difference being expressed in terms of potential energy. **Water potential*** is an effective measure of the availability of water; the larger the negative value of Ψ the less available is the water. '*Readily available*' soil water can be easily absorbed by plants and represents the difference between the field capacity of the soil (where Ψ_{soil} is around -0.15 bar) and the **permanent wilting percentage** (PWP), which is the soil moisture content (% dry weight of soil) at which plants wilt and fail to recover overnight even when left beneath a bell jar to minimize transpiration. PWP varies with the species of plant, ranging from -6 bar for plants with a high moisture requirement to potentials of -30 bar in plants resistant to drought.

Plants can continue to absorb water from the soil as long as the water potential of their fine roots is more negative than that of the soil solution adjacent to them. The rate at which water is absorbed by roots is directly proportional to the active root area per volume of soil and the difference in water potential between the root and the soil. It is inversely proportional to the resistances to transport of water within the soil and from the soil to the plant. If the soil dries up in one place parts of the root system often desiccate and die, while in damper regions the roots may grow rapidly and produce an abundance of absorptive rootlets.

Water travels from the roots to the leaves along a water potential gradient which becomes more negative, owing mainly to an increase in solute concentrations from the root cortex to the leaf mesophyll, as the transpiring surfaces are approached. Water changes from the liquid to the gaseous phase as it moves from the mesophyll cells to the substomatal cavities, from which it is lost by diffusion. It thus moves through the plant in response to a vapour pressure gradient. The maximum velocity of the transpiration stream is greatest in plants possessing wide vessels offering little resistance to flow. All estimates available[4] can be considered only as approximations, but commonly quoted velocities (in m h^{-1}) are conifers 1–2; diffuse-porous hardwoods 1–6; and 4–44 in ring-porous hardwoods in which large and

---

* Water potential Ψ is equal to the difference in free energy per unit volume of matrically bound, pressurized or osmotically constrained water and that of pure water. Water potential is given in bar or erg cm^{-3}. 10^6 erg cm^{-3} = 1 bar.

conspicuous vessels are formed in spring. Velocities vary from 10 to 60 in herbs but reach 150 in certain lianas.[142]

The *water balance* of a plant reflects the difference between the amount of water which it absorbs and that lost in transpiration. In practice the water content of a plant varies constantly. Water balance becomes negative when transpiration exceeds absorption, often being restored, following a brief period when it is positive, after the reduction of transpiration accompanied by the continued absorption of water by the roots.

Alterations in the water balance are often observed by determining the *water saturation deficit* of the leaves. This is the percentage of water lacking from a tissue as compared with that present when it is 'fully saturated' i.e. turgid. As the water balance of plant leaves becomes more negative the osmotic pressure rises. Some species can withstand very considerable increases in osmotic pressure, whereas others are physiologically disturbed by much smaller increases. The ranges of osmotic pressure found in different groups of plants can be arranged in the form of an *osmotic spectrum* (Fig. 2.12). Osmotic pressures in herbs of moist woodlands are lower and cover a much smaller range than those of dry woodlands. Similarly maximum values for deciduous trees and shrubs are lower than those of conifers, and of woody plants growing in Mediterranean climates.

Figure 2.13 contrasts the *isohydric water balance mechanism*, in which stomatal regulation of transpiration prevents pronounced fluctuations in water content and osmotic pressure during the day, with the *anisohydric* type in which transpiration is not restricted until the water balance is strongly negative. The protoplasm of plants possessing the latter mechanism, many of which grow in sunny habitats, can tolerate extensive fluctuations in osmotic pressure, and hence in water potential, over short periods. Isohydric plants have stomata which respond rapidly to lack of water and their water balance during the day usually stays close to zero; they normally possess large and efficient root systems. Many, but not all, of these species are physiologically disturbed by relatively small increases in osmotic pressure.

Trees and shade herbs are usually isohydric, but the degree to which different species can reduce transpiration from the leaves by closing the stomata varies considerably. *Cuticular transpiration* of leaves, which continues after the stomata are closed, can be expressed as a percentage of total transpiration when they are open. This has been estimated[142] as 12% in *Betula pendula*, 21% in *Fagus sylvatica*, 12.5% in the herbaceous sciophyte *Oxalis acetosella*, and only 3% in *Picea abies* and 2.5% in *Pinus sylvestris*. Such values must vary with the seasons and within species, but the very low figures for the two conifers are noteworthy.

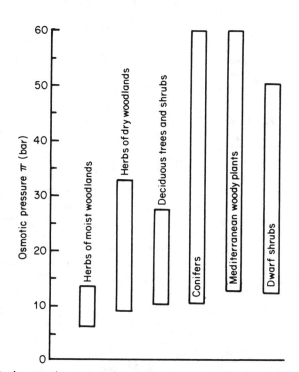

Fig. 2.12 An osmotic spectrum for woodland plants. Each column represents the difference between the lowest and the highest osmotic pressure found in the leaves of all the plants investigated in the ecological group concerned. (After Larcher;[142] after Walter (1960). *Einführung in die Phytologie*, Bd III/I. Standorts lehre, 2. Aufl. Stuttgart. E. Ulmer.)

The total areas of the transpiring surfaces of full grown trees are very large and distant from the roots. Even when there is abundant water in the soil, the rate at which water can be conducted up the trunk is insufficient to replace losses from the canopy in the absence of stomatal regulation at midday during clear sunny weather in summer. Even with regulation, the tensions resulting from rapid transpiration may be sufficient to cause cavitation in the xylem,[224] disrupting water movement between the roots and the leaves; water will usually continue to flow where cavitation has not occurred but the situation at the top of very tall trees seems likely to become critical during drought. In most trees the stomata are very sensitive to water deficit, reacting rapidly and preventing serious water loss; their closure causes the noon depression of transpiration characteristic of many trees on clear sunny days when the temperature, and consequently the vapour-pressure deficit, of the air are highest. ***Water***

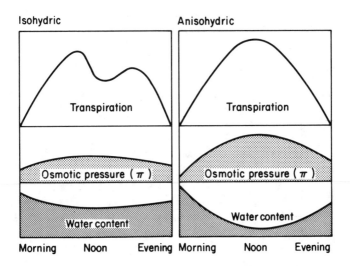

Fig. 2.13 The two main categories of water balance mechanism proposed by Berger-Landefeldt. In the isohydric type stomatal control prevents pronounced fluctuations in water content and osmotic pressure (π). This mechanism conserves water but results in reduction of photosynthesis on warm days. In the anisohydric type transpiration is not restricted until the leaf is very dry. Photosynthesis continues for extended periods during which the water balance is negative. (After Larcher;[142] from Stocker (1956), in *Handbuch der Pflanzenphysiologie*. Springer, Berlin-Gotlingen-Heidelberg.)

conservation in various parts of the canopy follows an orderly sequence (Fig. 2.14), occurring first in the shady parts of the crown. The leaves in sunny regions near the base of the canopy are the next to limit water loss, while those of the sunny top are the last. Water potential becomes more negative most rapidly at the top of the tree, so the leaves here are preferentially replenished with water. Daily variations in osmotic pressure in trees rarely exceed 3 bar so the protoplasm is not subject to great changes in water potential, though the forces drawing water upward in the early afternoon are much greater than in the morning and evening. Conifers, sciophytes and a number of heliophytic trees such as the oaks can control their water contents to a considerable extent, but others, including some species of ash, cannot and their leaves often wither in dry weather.

When the soil becomes depleted of water for considerable periods in summer the stomata of trees may be closed almost continuously. During summer drought in regions of periodic dryness this results in the leaves of well adapted trees and shrubs losing much less water per unit area than in the rainy season—a figure of 11% was estimated for

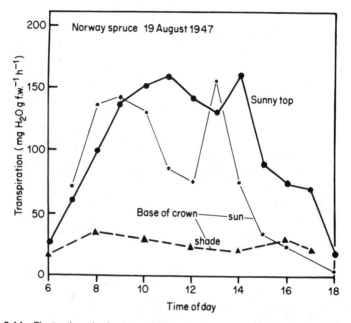

Fig. 2.14 Fluctuations in the transpiration of shoots of *Picea abies* at 820 m near Innsbruck, Austria, during a sunny August day preceded by dry weather. (Redrawn after Pisek, A. and Tranquillini, W. (1951). *Physiologia Plantarum*, **4**, 1–27.)

Quercus ilex in the Mediterranean maquis. Many species of dry habitats even shed a considerable proportion of their foliage.

Trees near alpine or polar timberlines often suffer severe damage when their water relations are disturbed by cold. Water in the conducting elements often freezes at $-2°$ C, while that in the surface soil remains frozen for months.[142] The most common damage occurring in isolated trees above the upper forest limit is caused by the slow desiccation of shoots projecting above the snow,[229] which lose water, often by direct evaporation, throughout the winter. This is a major influence in controlling tree growth near the timberline (see Section 3.3). In the European Alps the water content of *Rhododendron ferrugineum*, and of smaller individuals of Arolla pine (*Pinus cembra*), sometimes falls below the safety limit in early spring, when the sun warms the branches and transpiration increases before the ground has thawed. Larger trees are not so greatly endangered; their trunks contain sufficient water to tide them over until active absorption of water from the soil is resumed.

Climatic dieback of lodgepole pine (*Pinus contorta*) occurs in the Rocky Mountains of the U.S.A., where periods of relatively warm weather alternating with severe cold result in reddening of needles. Lodgepole pine planted at altitudes of 300 m or more in Scotland suffered similarly in 1979, again apparently as a result of excessive transpiration during a period when frozen ground prevented a compensating uptake of water. In Scotland, trees of coastal provenances (see Fig. 3.8) suffered more severely than those of inland origin, another example of the need to secure a satisfactory match between genotype and climate when planting exotic trees.

Prolonged drought is relatively uncommon in Britain but many trees, particularly of birch and beech, died after the very dry summer of 1976. Though some were post-mature individuals whose end was merely hastened by drought, many young saplings of a range of species were also lost. Trees on shallow soil in sites with sharp drainage were particularly susceptible; in the Wyre Forest, England, there were considerable losses of western hemlock (*Tsuga heterophylla*) on a sharply sloping site overlooking the Severn, whereas trees on the plateau above survived. Water relations inter-relate with other factors, for example, insect attack can increase water loss, while trees stressed by lopping are more susceptible to infestation by woodwasps (see Section 6.5). Alterations in the forest canopy influence air and soil temperatures, soil water content, and shading of the forest floor simultaneously. Forests are also important in buffering the effects of heavy precipitation, acting effectively as 'sponges' which gradually release water into rivers.

2.6 EVERGREEN AND DECIDUOUS 'STRATEGIES'

Though the photosynthetic capacity of their leaves is generally low, evergreen conifers frequently have high net production. This has often been attributed to the prolonged growth period; photosynthetic gains can be made in spring, autumn and parts of the winter when deciduous trees are bare of leaves. On the other hand, the turnover rate of leaves is also important; if these have to be replaced frequently the amount of photosynthate which can be partitioned into the formation of wood and bark is greatly reduced. Whereas cold deciduous trees such as beech replace their major photosynthetic systems annually, evergreen conifers retain most of their leaves which continue to contribute to net production for many years, though their photosynthetic capacity gradually falls (Fig. 2.15). Photosynthetic capacity and respiratory activity both tend, however, to be markedly higher in deciduous trees. When young leaves are forming they respire intensely, have a small surface area, and are usually low in chlorophyll. Consequently, they are, for a short time, a cause of overall carbon loss, though their photosynthetic capacity is at its peak within a few days of full expansion.

54

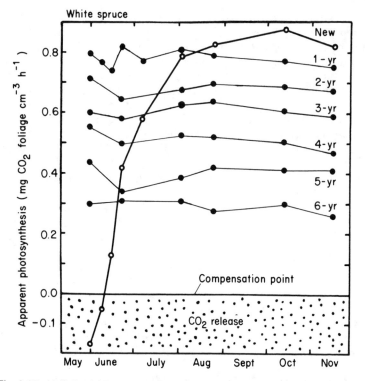

Fig. 2.15 Variation in photosynthetic capacity (per unit volume of foliage) of needles of white spruce (*Picea glauca*) with age. During the expansion phase the rate of photosynthesis is low and that of respiration high; as a result young needles give off CO_2 even in the light (stippled area). Though the photosynthetic capacity of current year needles increases until it exceeds that of 1-year-old needles in mid-summer, their total net CO_2 uptake during the complete growing season is less. (Redrawn after Clark,[63] with the permission of The State University of New York College of Environmental Science and Forestry.)

The International Biological Programme investigations into the growth of *Fagus sylvatica*[209] and of *Picea abies*[211,212] found within a kilometre of each other at 500 m on the Solling Plateau, Germany, afford an opportunity of comparing the production values of the conifer most commonly planted in German re-afforestation and the deciduous tree which dominates many natural forests in central Europe. For the complex measurements of photosynthetic capacity a typical tree of each species, a 27 m high 100-year-old beech and a 25.6 m high 89-year-old spruce, was examined in 1968 and 1972 respectively.

The deciduous beech and the evergreen spruce were found to differ in four major respects with regard to production. Both the sun and the shade leaves of *Fagus* had a much higher photosynthetic capacity per unit dry weight than even the 1-year-old needles of *Picea*. Beech had a shorter growing season than spruce; it showed positive CO_2 uptake during 176 days in the year as against 260. Beech had a higher annual production of leaves than spruce, but the latter had a much greater photosynthesizing biomass, because of the long life of its needles, some of which survived for as long as twelve years.

In the Solling it is the increased longevity of the foliage, rather than the longer growing season, which enables the primary production of spruce $(14.9 \text{ t C ha}^{-1} \text{ yr}^{-1})$ to be so much greater than that of beech $(8.6 \text{ t C ha}^{-1} \text{ yr}^{-1})$. Though the dry matter which spruce 'invests' in its leaves every year is less than that of beech, the long-term return is greater because the leaves continue to fix carbon so much longer, albeit at a slower rate.

This analysis helps to elucidate the basis of the high productivity of evergreen conifers such as *Picea abies* in central Europe, where *Fagus sylvatica* is frequently the dominant of many natural forests despite its much lower productivity. Beech is more shade tolerant, being able to germinate and grow where spruce cannot. It is also less affected by storm and snow and ice breakage; the deciduous habit entails a reduction of the surfaces on which ice can accumulate in winter. The surface rooting of *Picea* means that gales may topple it relatively easily and often its life is shorter than that of beech, a powerful competitor with other trees, which when growing actively suffers markedly lower mortality from fungal diseases than spruce.[212] Thus relative growth rate, though very important, is only one aspect of competitive advantage whose balance is often swayed by climatic factors.

Picea abies flourishes in the north of Scandinavia and of Russia, where *Fagus sylvatica* does not ripen seed and is unknown as a natural forest tree. The deciduous habit and the production of strongly constructed, even xeromorphic, needles are both quite well adapted to the water stresses of northern winters as the presence of *Populus tremulosa* and *Picea abies* in arctic Norway indicates. Rates of photosynthesis are still appreciable at low light intensities in stems of deciduous trees such as *Quercus petraea*, so stem photosynthesis must play some part in maintaining carbohydrate levels during the long leafless period. However, most boreal forests are dominated by evergreen conifers which clearly gain from the ability of their needles to photosynthesize for several years. In the very different climate of tropical rain forests, evergreen trees whose leaves have a low rate of CO_2 uptake can attain a high annual CO_2 gain because the active vegetative period is so long.

3

Soils, Climate and Zonation

3.1 SOILS AND TREES

The distinctive morphological characteristics of soils, with their often well-marked profiles (Fig. 3.1), result from the integrated effects of *five soil-forming factors*: climate, parent rock, vegetation and associated organisms, relief of the land, and time. These factors set the conditions under which the physical, chemical and biological processes operate to produce the horizons found in any profile. These processes[71] fall into four main groups: weathering, translocation, the organic cycle, and the influence of erosion or deposition which can nullify the effects of the first three.

Many rocks contain all the nutrients required by plants apart from nitrogen, which is generally in short supply. Though the combined nitrogen received in rain will gradually build up, it is significant that the first plants to establish, and thus commence the *organic cycle*, very frequently possess a nitrogen-fixing mechanism. When plants die and decompose they release nitrogen for their successors, and also leave humus in the soil which provides a reserve supply of nitrogen, forms part of a base exchange complex, and helps retain soil moisture. There is a major difference between grasslands and forests in respect of the distribution of organic matter added to the soil. The enormous masses of roots produced by grasses die after a relatively short time so that organic matter is added directly to the profile throughout a considerable depth. In trees a higher proportion of the organic matter contributed to the soil arises from the foliage and tends to accumulate at the surface. Trees are often responsible for transporting mineral nutrients from deep in the profile to the surface, where they become available to herbs.

Soil reaction is measured on the pH scale, pH 7 being neutral, and soils with higher values alkaline. The average pH value of northern English soils under natural vegetation is said to be about 5.[241] Such distinctly acidic soils often possess mull humus and may be quite rich in calcium ions adsorbed by colloids of the clay-humus complex, though lacking the calcium carbonate abundant in *rendzinas* (Fig. 3.1g), alkaline or nearly neutral soils in which an organic A horizon rests directly on calcareous parent rock. Soils with a pH as low as 4 are, however, markedly lacking in bases. Calcium is normally the dominant exchangeable cation in the soil. It causes clay particles to aggregate: Ca clays are flocculated, whereas Na clays, which are produced when the sea breaks through coastal defences, are highly dispersed and percolate down the profile in suspension. 'Clay shift' can occur under other conditions, especially in slightly acid or neutral soils. In more alkaline soils free bicarbonate ions inhibit movement; in more acid soils aluminium and dissociating ferric hydroxide have this effect.

Soil colloids, especially the clay minerals, are capable of ion exchange, absorbing cations of such bases as calcium, magnesium and potassium from solution and exchanging them for others. *Cation exchange capacity* or *base exchange capacity* is a measure of the extent to which soil cations can be exchanged in this way. *Base saturation* is a measure of the extent to which soil exchange sites are occupied by cations of bases rather than by hydrogen ions. In general broad-leaved deciduous trees require soils richer in bases than do conifers.

When substantial water is available for leaching, podzols develop relatively rapidly on sandstones, gravels and other permeable parent materials; they will also develop on boulder clay and other substrata under the appropriate climatic conditions. Soil solutions from the surface layer of mor humus (see Section 1.4) contain both carbonic acid and humic acids which leach bases from the eluvial Ea layer. The Ea layer often bleaches to an ashy grey colour, largely as a result of the downward translocation from it of iron and aluminium, probably in association with organic complexes. A siliceous residue of primary quartz grains remains: some secondary silica may also accumulate. Thus an increasing influence of mor humus will cause the Si/ (Al + Fe) ratio of the Ea horizon to rise as leaching becomes stronger. Humus and the sesquioxides are subsequently deposited in the Bh and Bfe horizons of humus-iron podzols. *Podzols* are base deficient, strongly acid and frequently support the growth of coniferous forest.

When waterlogged for long periods, soils become anaerobic and

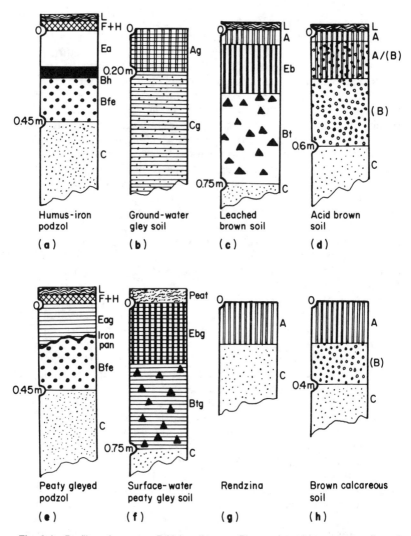

Fig. 3.1 Profiles of common British soil types. *Pinus sylvestris* grows naturally and well on podzolic soils **(a)**, but it is necessary to shatter the iron pan and improve the drainage of peaty gleyed podzols **(e)** when establishing new plantations of conifers. Beech (*Fagus sylvatica*) and oak (*Quercus* spp.) establish naturally on a wide range of soils, but are not grown commercially on, for example, podzols. Most broad-leaved British deciduous trees (e.g. *Fagus, Quercus, Ulmus, Tilia, Carpinus*) are more exacting than conifers in their requirements, growing well on brown earths **(c, d)**, especially those of higher pH. *Fraxinus excelsior* is widely established on brown earths and grows particularly well on rendzinas **(g)** and brown calcareous soils **(h)**; the latter will support a wide range of tree species. *Betula pubescens* often grows

lose the bright red and ochre colours associated with the presence of ferric iron. Bacterial and chemical action reduce iron and manganese to ferrous and manganous forms which are soluble and more mobile. Such *gleyed soils*, very common in valleys and low-lying areas, may undergo seasonal drying, in which case re-oxidation causes the deposition of yellow and rusty spots and streaks of ferric iron, and of black manganese concretions. Gley (g) horizons are often neutral or mildly acid; they are also usually deficient in phosphate. Peaty-gleyed podzols (Fig. 3.1e) are very common in upland Britain where

---

Soil horizon notation

Organic surface horizons
L   Plant litter, only slightly comminuted
F   Comminuted litter
H   Well decomposed humus with little mineral matter

Organo-mineral surface horizons
A   Dark brown, mainly mineral layer with humus admixture

Eluvial horizons that have lost clay and/or iron and aluminium
Ea   Bleached or pale horizon which has lost iron and/or aluminium
Eb   Relatively pale brown friable horizon which has lost some clay

Illuvial horizons enriched in clay or humus or iron and aluminium
Bt   Horizon enriched in clay
Bh   Dark brown or black horizon, enriched in humus
Bfe Orange or red-brown horizon, enriched in iron and/or aluminium

Other subsoil horizons
(B) Weathered subsoil material, not appreciably enriched in clay, humus or iron, distinguished from overlying and underlying horizons by colour or structure or both
C   Little-altered parent material

Notes
g   The addition of 'g' denotes mottling or greying thought to be caused by water-logging
A/(B)   Indicates transitional horizon

Mull is a characteristic A horizon, which may be covered by a thin L horizon, but F and H horizons are scanty or absent
Moder characteristically has an H horizon thicker than the L and F combined
Mor (raw humus) has thick L and F layers

---

amongst wet heath communities on surface-water gley soils, often with peat (**f**), but such soils need drainage, and often fertilization, to be of use in forestry. Ground-water gley soils with grey subsoils and rusty mottling near the surface are frequently wooded along minor streams. *Quercus robur* woodland with mull often occurs where water-logging is confined to the subsoil; in wetter sites *Q. robur* and *Alnus glutinosa* are often co-dominant and organic matter accumulates at the surface. *Salix* and *Alnus* are particularly common along river banks. (Redrawn from Burnham and Mackney;[61] by courtesy of the Field Studies Council.)

podzolization and gleying result in a thin dense iron pan and a surface layer of peat.

Burnham[60] found a strong correlation between the soil regions of Britain (Fig. 3.2) and five different climatic regimes (Table 3.1), as

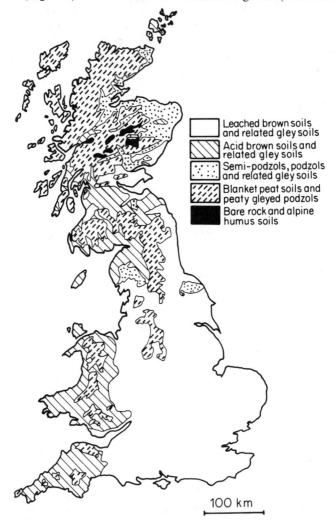

Leached brown soils and related gley soils

Acid brown soils and related gley soils

Semi-podzols, podzols and related gley soils

Blanket peat soils and peaty gleyed podzols

Bare rock and alpine humus soils

100 km

Fig. 3.2 Soil regions of Great Britain. The distribution shown is simplified and very generalized; there are large local variations and there may be two or three different soil types within a single field or wood. (Redrawn from Burnham.[60]) For a more detailed map and account of the soils of England and Wales, see *Field Studies*, **5**, 349–63.

Table 3.1 Correlation of climatic regimes and soil types in Britain (from Burnham[60]).

Climatic region	Mean annual temperature	Mean annual rainfall	Characteristic soils
1. Warm, dry	Over 8.3°C	Under 1000 mm	Leached brown soil
2. Cold, dry	4.0–8.3°C		Semipodzol/Podzol
3. Warm, wet	Over 8.3°C	Over 1000 mm	Acid brown soil
4. Cold, wet	4.0–8.3°C		Peaty gley podzol/Blanket peat
5. Very cold, wet	Under 4°C		Alpine humus soil

defined by mean annual precipitation (over or under 1000 mm) and mean annual temperature. Under the *warm, dry regime* the characteristic soil process is clay eluviation within the profile resulting in *leached brown earths* of such high value for agriculture that forestry, being less profitable, is relatively uncommon. In south and east England the soils often dry out in summer. Washing out (lixiviation) of the dry soil by the early winter rains brings clay particles near the surface of the profile into a suspension which passes into the subsoil, a process known as mechanical eluviation. Here the water is drawn into the dry lumps (*peds*) of soil leaving clay films on their external surfaces. Leached brown earths have been termed grey podzolic soils by some authors. Soils thus mapped in northern England and south-east Scotland do not show clear evidence of clay eluviation, but brown earths of high base status develop on parent material which would give rise to leached brown earths further south. Natural vegetation under this climate was almost everywhere broad-leaved deciduous forest, predominantly oakwood, though lime (*Tilia*) is now known to have been more abundant than orginally thought.

Parts of north and east Scotland, the North Yorks Moors and certain areas on the eastern slopes of the Pennines have a *cold, dry regime* in which both rainfall and potential evaporation are low. Parent materials of low base content prevail in the area and this, together with the considerable volume of water available for leaching, causes most soils to be acid. Podzolization is widespread. Oakwood was the natural climax vegetation on most of the lower ground where the humus form was mull or moder. Such sites are now occupied by intergrades (*semi-podzols* = brown podzolic soils) between brown earths and podzols. On higher ground pinewoods frequently grew on podzols, but climatic change and human interference have caused the development of heathlands in many places. Except in the far north, forestry is normally a possible land use though yields are low: *Pinus* is the characteristic timber tree, though few native woods of Scots pine now remain.[59]

Under the **warm, wet regime** of south-east England, most of Wales and coastal areas in north-west England and south-west Scotland subsoils are rarely dry and there is a high degree of leaching. Almost all sites bore deciduous woodland until cleared for cultivation and podzolization is weak, though it occurs in places. Forest yields on the **acid brown soils** are high and trees, especially *Picea sitchensis*, are quite extensively planted even on some of the better soils, modern plantations often employing very deep drainage ditches.

Much of the area having a **cold, wet regime** is too exposed for forestry. Use of other parts of the region for forestry often requires ploughing to break down the surface layers and improve surface drainage. Leaching is strong and weathering weak; recycling of nutrients is slow. Fertilization, particularly with phosphates, considerably improves the growth of trees. *Picea sitchensis*, sometimes planted with *Pinus contorta,* grows particularly well under damp conditions and is very successful in the less exposed parts of the region. On the other hand, British areas in which alpine humus soils have developed under **very cold, wet conditions** have never been forested.

The British Isles, being relatively small, do not show the diversity of climates which result in the even greater vegetational extremes found in other parts of the world, such as North America (see Fig. 3.8), in which variations in rainfall, potential evaporation, irradiation, temperature and length of growing season have major effects on both the soil type and the vegetation.

The above outline indicates the major features of soils and the way in which their regional distribution influences forestry in Britain. Some soils have been under woodland for very long periods, often for many hundreds of years; their characteristics are now considered.

Features of woodland soils

In Britain the most productive soils have normally been used for agriculture, so ancient woodlands[21] are usually on soils which would, in medieval times, have been regarded as having low quality. Such soils differ substantially from adjacent agricultural soils which have been limed, fertilized and drained, practices which have sometimes influenced the soils of modern plantations. Woodland soils, on the other hand, have been penetrated by tree roots which often grow to a depth of up to three metres.

The soils of the ancient woodlands of eastern England are frequently derived from **drift deposits**, from 1–70 m thick, of boulder clay, sands and gravels, laid down over bedrock in glacial times. Drift deposits are very variable; boulder clay is usually a heavy clay with lumps of chalk, yet woodland soils on it are often sandy or silty and include some of the most acid soils in Britain. In much of England the drift or solid geology is overlain by wind blown deposits, rarely as much as 1 m thick, of silt and fine sand. These are almost certainly *loess* deposits dating back to great dust storms in late glacial times. Such deposits have often been mixed into agricultural soils by the homogenizing action of ploughing. In other instances they have been removed; the downhill edge of an ancient woodland may be a low cliff formed through the removal of agricultural soil down the slope under the action of ploughing and sheet erosion.

The soils of ancient woods are more stratified than those used for agriculture. They may, nevertheless, be disturbed when old trees are blown over causing the root plate, sometimes with several tons of attached subsoil, to be pulled out of the ground. In other cases the trunks fall after major roots have decayed and the soil is not greatly disturbed. Many unfelled trees, however, merely rot above ground and fall to pieces leaving a stump. Superficial disturbance can be caused by rooting animals, particularly wild pigs. If grazing is heavy, or if many walkers use the area, the soil may become very compacted reducing pore space and increasing the likelihood of surface run-off. Earthworms, moles and other animals which live in the soil have the opposite effect, and also tend to mix the soil horizons.

The *humus type* found in woodlands is of great importance (Section 1.4). *Mull* has a higher pH and is more base-rich than the surface deposits of *mor*. Humus type is largely determined by the nature of plant litter; in some areas planting Scots pine will cause podzolization to begin and mor humus to be deposited, whereas adjacent birch-woods on the same parent material have mull.

In the damp British climate most soils are leached by rain, and in old woodlands surface soils very often have a lower pH and calcium carbonate content than does soil further down the profile. *Surface acidification* is especially obvious where the parent materials are uniform, as in Hayley Wood, Cambridgeshire, whose soils are derived from chalky boulder clay with a small admixture of loess. In this wood waterlogging on the central plateau is frequent and severe in spring, and relatively slight on the steeper slopes (which never exceed 4°). The dampest areas are in hollows on the plateau dominated by the large sedges *Carex acutiformis* and *C. riparia*, and the general pattern of zonation fits well with the resistance of the dominant species to ferrous iron (see Section 3.4). Soil pH profiles shown in Fig. 3.3 show that surface acidification is greater, and extends deeper, on the ill-drained plateau than on the slopes, where mixing by earthworms and moles, which are uncommon in waterlog-

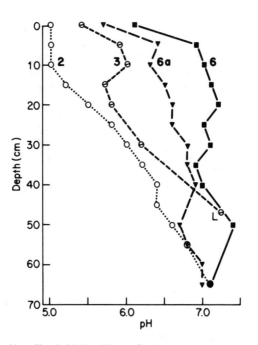

Fig. 3.3 Soil pH profiles in Hayley Wood, Cambridgeshire, from pits dug in ground vegetation zones **2** (plateau, dominated by varying proportions of *Filipendula ulmaria* and *Primula elatior*), **3** (slight slope, an open community with many species dominated by *Endymion non-scriptus* and *Primula elatior*), **6a** (greater slope), and **6** (greatest slope). Zone **6** is a closed community dominated by *Mercurialis perennis*. Soil pH measured *in situ* (except for the laboratory measurement L). (From Rackham.[191])

ged soils, helps to counteract the loss of calcium from the topsoil by leaching.

Trees vary in their influence on soil acidity. In Connecticut old fields topsoil beneath *Juniperus virginiana* has a raised pH while the pH of soil in the root zone is reduced; roots of this tree absorb considerable amounts of calcium and other bases which are returned in leaf litter. Foliage of *Juniperus communis*, which grows alongside, is of low base status and increases the acidity of the topsoil.[23] The mean pH of the surface soil (0–3 cm) of eighty Coal Measure woodland quadrats near Sheffield was higher than that at 9–12 cm in all six main polythetic groups, and in one group the difference was statistically significant ($P < 0.05$).[176] Again, bases contributed by tree litter are probably responsible for this effect.

Mycorrhizas are extremely important in forest soils; fungal associations with tree roots are almost universal amongst trees in woodlands of long standing. The fungi of ectotrophic mycorrhizas form a compact sheath of hyphae over the roots, which are stimulated to form numerous stubby branches of the kind commonly seen in beech, pine, oak and the Australian eucalypts. These fungi receive their carbon requirements from the trees as simple sugars, while mineral nutrients absorbed from the soil by the fungi are passed on to the trees. Growth of trees is often limited by the level of available phosphate (see Section 9.2), and much improved by the association with mycorrhizal fungi.

In some woodland areas a diversity of rock types outcrop very close to each other. This is true of the Ercall, near Telford, Shropshire (Fig. 3.4), where podzols occur above strongly acid, coarse-grained rocks, whether igneous (granophyre) or sedimentary (Cambrian quartzite), and acid brown soils on the more base-rich, finer-grained rocks. This is a fascinating area where variations in soil type, slope, and water regime result in a complex pattern of vegetation types. As calcareous soils occur in Limekiln Wood, just over a kilometre away, all the major soil groups of Shropshire are represented within two square kilometres.

Heathy oakwoods (*Quercus robur* and *Q. petraea* are both present), with a field layer in which *Calluna vulgaris, Deschampsia flexuosa* and *Vaccinium myrtillus* are prominent, occur on the north-west face of the Ercall. Oak grows in places on the southeast slope, but here birch is more common. Much of the birch was burnt in the early 1960s, but it soon regenerated from seed and by sprouting from the stumps. Surface soils on the Cambrian siltstones and glacial deposits are damper and more base-rich; the calcicole *Sanicula europaea* is present on the boulder clay. The vegetation of this lower area is more species rich and the alluvial deposits along the stream have a particularly diverse flora including *Athyrium filix-femina, Dryopteris dilatata, Caltha palustris, Carex remota, Filipendula ulmaria* and *Valeriana officinalis* as well as most of the species found in adjacent drier areas. A 5 m x 5 m quadrat beneath *Alnus glutinosa* here included 27 species of vascular plants and nine species of bryophytes, and there were many more growing under similar conditions within the immediate area. In this quadrat soil reaction varied greatly; five soil samples (0–5 cm depth), taken at the centre and near each of the corners, had pH values varying from 4.4 to 6.2 (mean value 5.7).

Various relationships between soil, climate and trees have been discussed above. The next section extends this theme to a consideration of the roles of root systems and the mineral nutrient requirements of various plants in competition.

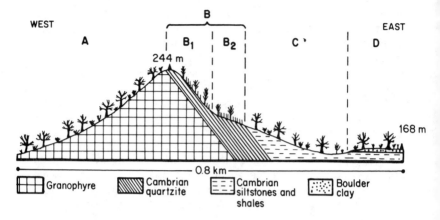

	Soils	Vegetation	pH	
			Topsoil	Subsoil
A	Podzols and podzolized acid brown soils	Oak-birch coppice; heather, bilberry, bracken or wavy hair grass locally dominant. The mosses *Leucobryum glaucum* and *Plagiothecium undulatum* are conspicuous	3.9	4.5
B₁	Humus-iron podzols and podzol rankers	Bracken, some birch scrub and heather	3.7	4.4
B₂	Gley podzols	Bracken, some birch and bluebell	3.8	4.6
C	Silty acid brown soils	Oak-birch coppice, with rowan and holly, very variable field layer including male fern, ivy, honeysuckle, bluebell, bramble, creeping soft-grass, wood sorrel, yellow archangel	4.1	4.3
D	Leached brown soils with gleying	Mixed deciduous woodland with ash, birch, elm (*Ulmus glabra*) and alder, with hazel, hawthorn (*Crataegus monogyna*), oak and ash regenerating; field layer includes dog's mercury, enchanter's nightshade, male fern, tufted hair grass, wood sanicle.	5.2	5.7

Fig. 3.5 Exposed roots of beech (*Fagus sylvatica*) growing on the Chalk Downs at Arundel, West Sussex, where its shallow root plates are sometimes pulled completely out of the ground in gales. (Photograph by J. R. Packham.)

3.2 ROOTS AND COMPETITION

Differences in the type and extent of plant root systems are largely peculiar to the species concerned, though often strongly influenced by external conditions. In plants such as the wild carrot the radicle develops into a dominant tap root, but in monocotyledons adventitious roots soon become more important, as in many dicotyledons. Roots may have other functions in addition to anchoring the stem and absorbing water and mineral salts: for example, aerial roots of epiphytic orchids may photosynthesize and breathing roots (pneumatophores) are common in mangroves and swamp cypresses (*Taxodium distichum*) growing in muddy swamps or damp soils. Beech trees on eroded banks are commonly held in place by massive exposed roots (Fig. 3.5) acting as buttresses while mangroves, many of whose seeds germinate viviparously, are supported over the oozing mud by aerial roots forming pillars and flying buttresses.

The root systems of three common European conifers show

Fig. 3.4 (*left*) Soil–vegetation relationships of the Ercall, Shropshire. Leaching has decreased the pH of the topsoils. (Redrawn from Burnham and Mackney;[61] by courtesy of the Field Studies Council.)

important differences. Of these three species, *Pinus sylvestris*, in its first year as a seedling, has the longest primary root, and much the largest number of secondary and tertiary roots. The many small roots help the tree to flourish in dry barren soils, while the plasticity of the main root system, whose tap root can penetrate very deeply in suitable soils, but in which the laterals usually dominate and are very widespread, enables the tree to succeed in diverse habitats. The primary root of Norway spruce (*Picea abies*) usually stops elongating after five years; as the mature root system is composed of shallow laterals the tree is commonly uprooted by wind. As a seedling, the roots of the silver fir (*Abies alba*) are the least branched, and the adult tree has a deep root system with a dominant tap which does not adapt easily to shallow soils, unlike that of *Pinus*.

Fraxinus excelsior has extensive, moderately branched lateral roots with long terminals which exploit a large volume of soil, while beech has shorter laterals with numerous short and extremely fine terminals which enable the tree to utilize a smaller volume of soil more intensively. Both systems function suitably under normal conditions but *Fagus sylvatica* suffers more than most trees in drought, having a limited ability to obtain water beyond its immediate vicinity. Though the root systems of broadleaved trees can be rather shallow they frequently spread horizontally for great distances: Seeger[213] records a radial spread of 18 m for 160-year-old *Quercus robur* growing on the alluvial gravels and loams of the Rhine plain.

The root systems of many tree species adapt very well to the soils on which they are growing.[23] Roots may even sometimes grow within old trees; in humid regions large internally decaying yellow birch (*Betula lutea*) trees may form roots that grow down through the decaying heartwood of the standing tree. Beech (*Fagus sylvatica*) can also form roots within its own damp, decayed and hollow trunks; a very large system of this type was revealed when a huge tree blew down in the Wyre Forest a few years ago. Many woody species have an **extensive root system**, the coarse roots of which extend great distances into a large volume of soil. Such a system is well suited to stony soils in which the water is not uniformly distributed, and also to winter-rain regions where the roots of the trees, unlike those of grasses, can draw water from great depths in the dry summers.

Just as trees and other plants show different tolerances of drought or water-logging, different tolerances are shown with respect to soil pH; when this is extreme, it may affect the viability of plants directly as well as influencing the nutrient supply (Fig. 3.6). Outside the range pH 3–9 the protoplasm of the roots of most tracheophytes is severely damaged.[142] Further, in very acid soils roots may be poisoned by increased concentrations of Al^{3+}, whereas borate poisoning is more

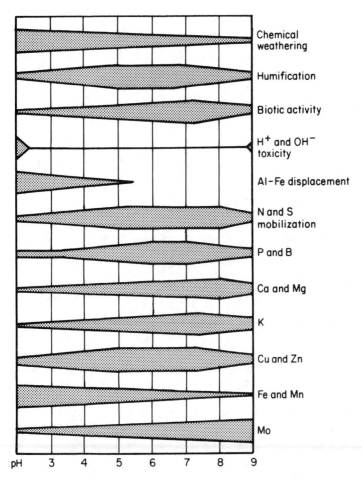

Chemical weathering

Humification

Biotic activity

H^+ and OH^- toxicity

Al–Fe displacement

N and S mobilization

P and B

Ca and Mg

K

Cu and Zn

Fe and Mn

Mo

pH   3   4   5   6   7   8   9

Fig. 3.6 Influence of soil pH on soil formation, mobilization and availability of mineral nutrients, and the conditions for life in the soil. The width of the bands indicates the intensity of the process or the availability of the nutrients. (Redrawn from Larcher;[142] after Schroeder (1969). *Bodenkunde in Stichworten*. F. Hirt, Kiel.)

likely at higher pH. The availability of iron and manganese is reduced in alkaline soils, sometimes to the point where they may limit the growth or performance of some species.

Most vascular plants can exist in single species cultures between soil pH 3.5 and 8.5, possessing a broad central optimum. Such *amphitolerant* species have an ecological distribution optimum corresponding to their physiological development optimum when they can compete successfully with others in the mid-range of the soil pH

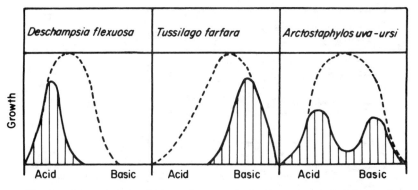

Fig. 3.7 Diagram of the pH-dependent growth of various plants in individual culture (*'physiological optimum curve'*, dashed line) and under conditions of natural competition (*'ecological optimum curve'*, continuous line enclosing hatched area). In the area between the two curves the various species can thrive only if they are cultivated in a stand of that single species and are not subjected to the pressure of competition by other, better adapted species. (Redrawn from Larcher;[142] after Ellenberg (1958). *Handbuch der Pflanzenphysiologie*, Bd IV (Ed. W. Ruhland), pp. 638–708. Springer, Berlin-Göttingen-Heidelberg; and Knapp (1967). *Experimentelle Soziologie und gegenseitige Beeinflussung der Pflanzen*. E. Ulmer, Stuttgart.)

which tracheophytes can tolerate. A number of plants are unable to do this and Fig. 3.7 shows three examples which in nature are often 'forced' into more extreme habitats. *Deschampsia flexuosa* resembles *Calluna vulgaris* in being **acidophilic-basitolerant**, while *Tussilago farfara*, a ruderal plant sometimes found along woodland rides, has an ecological optimum at the opposite end of the spectrum and is **basiphilic-acidotolerant**. The bearberry (*Arctostaphylos uva-ursi*), uncommon on soils of intermediate pH, competes best on acid and basic soils of moorlands, mountains and open woods.

Soil microorganisms are also strongly influenced by soil pH. Though soil bacteria commonly tolerate a range between pH 4 and 10, the optimum is slightly on the alkaline side of neutrality,[62] and some species have relatively narrow tolerance to soil reaction. Soil fungi are better adapted to distinctly acid soils than are bacteria. Even if fungi are restricted experimentally by the use of a fungicide, the low pH will itself prevent any vigorous colonization by bacteria of a strongly acid forest soil. As a result decay in acid soils is relatively slow and mineralization leads to an accumulation of ammonium rather than nitrate nitrogen.

So far this chapter has been largely concerned with soils, climate and competition. The wide variation in such environmental conditions within woodlands is of great importance to the mechanisms causing zonation and maintaining diversity, which are now discussed.

3.3   ZONATION: DISTRIBUTION IN SPACE

Zonation, the segregation of various species and communities in space, and *succession*, the changes which occur in communities with time (Chapter 5), are two of the great related themes of ecology. If climax vegetation is to develop, environmental conditions must remain stable for long periods, as they often did before human interference. The World now has only few areas of natural climax forest remaining; most forests have been planted, are still undergoing succession as a result of the influence of man, introduced pests or pathogens, or exist in a state of semi-equilibrium different from that formerly found in nature.

Vegetation maps of large areas are often primarily concerned with the plants which grew before the destructive influence of man (Fig. 3.8). Even now evergreen boreal coniferous forest (*taiga*) flourishes in the cold damp climates of northern Eurasia and America, eventually giving way to tundra. In temperate areas cold-deciduous trees become more important, while continental interiors often have too little rain for woodland and are occupied by steppe, grassland or even desert. The most luxuriant vegetation of all is *tropical rainforest* where growth is continuous and the number of animal species exceptionally large. The zonation of vegetation is clearly related to the available flora, the climate and the soil. In the great land masses *zonal soils* (in whose formation climate played the leading part), such as podzols, brown earths and chernozems, often extend in belts hundreds of kilometres wide. These were formerly, and to some extent still are, characterized by well marked vegetation types such as the *cold-deciduous forests* on the brown earths of Europe. Local factors such as parent material and topography dominate the formation of *intrazonal soils*. These too are often the habitats of particular tree species, such as pines on peats, and common ash on rendzinas.

Indices of similarity and gradient analysis

In some respects North America (Fig. 3.8) offers better examples of forest zonation than Europe, where the mountains are not so high, the climatic differences not so extreme, and man has changed the natural vegetation more extensively (Section 5.4). Although authorities often disagree as to exactly where boundaries should be drawn, there is widespread agreement as to the existence of *floristic provinces* separated by *tension zones* which coincide with the distributional limits of many species. The floras of stands near such a boundary, or within a single province, can be compared as follows, using species presence only to obtain an objective measure of similarity. Where the

Fig. 3.8 Zonation of the vegetation of North America showing the main forest and woodland types. Mangroves fringe the coast southwards from the Gulf of Mexico. The key shows a few of the important trees growing within the major temperate forest zones. ★ indicates North American species now widely planted in other parts of the world. **M**, Monterey; **NY**, New York; **P**, Panama; **QCI**, Queen Charlotte Islands; **SF**, San Francisco; **V**, Vancouver. *Pinus radiata*★ and *Cupressus macrocarpa* grow naturally on the Monterey peninsula. Zonal boundaries redrawn and simplified from Schmithüsen, J. (1976). *Atlas zur Biogeographie.* Geographisch-Kartographisches Institut Meyer, Mannheim.

TUNDRA AND ALPINE

 EVERGREEN BOREAL CONIFEROUS FOREST (TAIGA) AND OPEN CONIFEROUS WOODLAND. *Abies balsamea, Betula papyrifera, Larix laricina, Picea glauca, P. mariana, Populus tremuloides*

MONTANE CONIFEROUS FOREST. *Betula, Pinus contorta*, P. lambertiana, P. ponderosa, Pseudot- suga menziesii*, Sequoiadendron giganteum**

 COLD-DECIDUOUS BROADLEAVED FORESTS WITH CONIFERS. *Abies, Acer, Carya, Fagus grandifolia, Liquidambar, Magnolia, Picea, Pinus, Quercus*

 COLD-DECIDUOUS BROADLEAVED FOREST. *Acer saccharum, Carya, Castanea, Fagus, Juglans, Liriodendron tulipifera, Quercus, Sassafras, Tilia, Ulmus*

 TEMPERATE RAINFOREST. *Abies grandis*, Picea sitchensis*, Pinus contorta*, Pseudotsuga menziesii*, Sequoia sempervirens, Thuja plicata*, Tsuga heterophylla**

 SUB-TROPICAL SUMMERGREEN CONIFEROUS SWAMP FOREST. *Populus, Taxodium distichum*

 ATLANTIC PINE BARRENS AND EVERGLADES. *Pinus elliottii, P. palustris, P. taeda, Taxodium distichum*

 CONIFEROUS DRY WOODLAND AND XEROMORPHIC SCRUB

 SUMMERGREEN TREE STEPPE

 STEPPE AND GRASSLAND

SCLEROPHYLLOUS WOODLAND

THORNBUSH AND SUCCULENT VEGETATION

THORN SAVANNA

TROPICAL DRY WOODLAND

TROPICAL RAINFOREST

number of species found in one community is **a**, the other contains **b** species and the species common to both is **c**:

$$\text{Index of similarity} = \frac{2c}{a + b}$$

(The index of similarity is sometimes called the **coefficient of community** or the **Sørensen coefficient**.) The forests of Wisconsin, to the south of Lake Superior, afford an example of relatively rapid transition. The northern mesic forests contain 27 tree species and are dominated by sugar maple, eastern hemlock, beech, yellow birch, and basswood (*Tilia americana*). They have 17 species in common with the southern mesic forests which possess 26 tree species of which the most important are sugar maple, basswood, beech, and northern red oak (*Quercus borealis*). The index of similarity for the trees of these two areas is

$$\frac{2 \times 17}{26 + 27} = 0.64$$

The boreal forest, or taiga, of North America forms a broad crescent extending from Alaska to Newfoundland. In undisturbed sites it is usually dominated by three species, white spruce (*Picea glauca*), black spruce (*Picea mariana*), and balsam fir (*Abies balsamea*), which often occur together. La Roi[143] sampled 34 taiga sites,

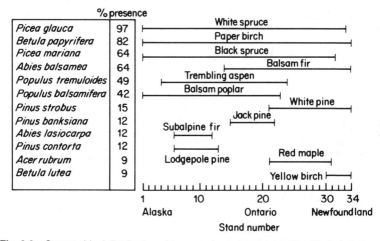

Fig. 3.9 Geographical distribution of tree species in 34 stands of the North American boreal forest. Horizontal bars show the range from the most easterly to the most westerly stands in which each species is present; percentage presence in the 34 stands is also given. (Redrawn from Krebs (1972),[140] data of La Roi.[143])

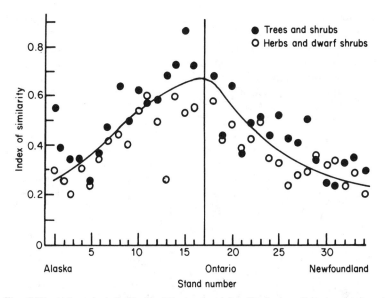

Fig. 3.10 Index of similarity for 34 stands of the North American boreal forest dominated by white spruce and/or balsam fir. Stand 17 in Manitoba was chosen as a central location and all stands were compared to it. Trend line fitted by eye. (Redrawn from Krebs (1972),[140] data of La Roi.[143])

all dominated by white spruce and/or balsam fir, arranged in an arc from near the arctic circle in Alaska, where balsam fir did not occur, to Newfoundland. While simple presence lines are sufficient to demonstrate differences in the distributions of the major tree species (Fig. 3.9), an index of similarity is a useful comparative measure when all the flowering plants are considered (Fig. 3.10).

The extent to which vegetation can be regarded as a complex *continuum* of populations which gradually blend with each other, rather than a series of integrated communities with discrete boundaries, has been much discussed. Brown and Curtis[57] support the continuum concept and use the statistical technique of *gradient analysis* to illustrate the gradual nature of the transitions between species populations in the upland conifer-hardwood forests of Northern Wisconsin.

However, some consider that if the hypothesis that discrete associations occur in nature is to be tested, the vegetation should be in equilibrium; a number of stands studied by Curtis and his co-workers had been clear-cut only 26 years before and others had been selectively logged. Daubenmire[74] also considers that the failure of gradient analysis to recognize that some species are *ecologically* dominant to others is a serious deficiency. He recognizes that there is a continuum in the distribution of coniferous trees with respect to altitude in the Rocky Mountains (Fig. 3.11), but takes this to be a *floristic* rather than an *ecological continuum*; the competitive dominance of one species of tree over the others present can, on such a view, be sufficient justification for recognizing discrete communities in an altitudinal transect.

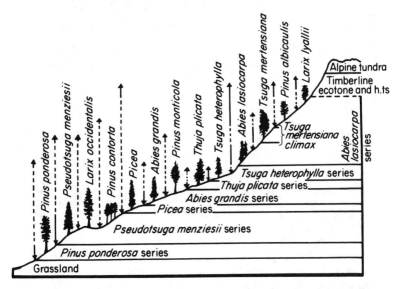

Fig. 3.11 Coniferous trees in the Rocky Mountains of northwestern Montana, arranged to show the usual order in which the species occur with increasing altitude. The relative altitudinal range of each species is shown by arrows. The dashed portion of each arrow shows where a species is seral (early successional) and the continuous portion where it is the potential climax dominant (late successional). The temperature–moisture climatic gradient runs from the lowlands where the conditions are warm and dry to the timberline where they are cold and wet. There are several timberline habitat types (h.ts): all have a timberline ecotone with krummholz above them. (After Pfister, Kovalchik, Arno and Presby.[183])

In detailed investigations of forest communities Daubenmire names the groups (*unions*) of overstorey and understorey species after the dominants. Different habitat types[73] are distinguished by specific combinations of these unions, for example, the *Thuja plicata/Pachistima myrsinites* association, so that the influence of both the subsoil and the topsoil is taken into account. Habitat-type classifications based on this approach are now widely used for commercial forestry in western U.S.A.[183] Late successional trees are used to define tree-species *series*. Within each of these there is one or more characteristic understorey plant union which, together with the tree overstorey, defines the *habitat type*, which is based on the potential climax vegetation. A third level (*phase*) is sometimes used to subdivide the habitat type.

Treelines and altitudinal zonation

Timberlines, and altitudinal zones in general, are usually at greater altitudes in regions of large mountain masses than on isolated mountains. It is possible that wind velocities are lower, or snowfall greater, in large mountainous areas such as the Rocky Mountains or the European Alps; either of these factors would result in more soil water being available for summer growth. Within the forest winter-desiccation is much less severe than on a deforested slope, but above the sharp timberline conditions rapidly deteriorate and trees of normal stature occur only on particularly favourable sites. Above the alpine timberline (or forest limit) is a timberline ecotone (*kampfzone*, struggle zone). An *ecotone* is a zone of transition between two ecosystems, in this case between forest and open mountainside. At the *krummholz* ('bentwood') limit, which marks the top of this ecotone, such trees as exist are very contorted, and often have such a low stature that they are almost completely covered and protected by snow in winter. Many species take a multistemmed low bush form in the kampfzone; these *elfinwoods* may well result from the conditions of growth though genetic factors may be involved. Trees such as *Picea abies* and *Larix decidua* may form adventitious roots on older branches weighed down by snow, and reproduce vegetatively by layering, often forming oval patches extending away from the prevailing wind. Islands of *Pinus cembra* in the kampfzone do not arise from layering but from the activities of the nutcracker, the corvid *Nucifraga caryocatactes*, which buries heaps of 10–30 seeds.

In some parts of the Austrian Tyrol[229] high altitude forests appear to have been felled during the Middle Ages to provide timber for mining. The forest zone has since gradually spread up the slopes, but the kampfzone is still unusually wide, whereas in undisturbed regions close by the transition at the upper forest limit is very abrupt.

Tree root systems at the timberline show intensive development of mycorrhizas. Almost all the short roots of *Pinus cembra* at central European alpine timberlines are mycorrhizal, and mycorrhizal fungi are known to have evolved high altitude strains adapted to low temperatures. Mycorrhizas must be present if such diverse species as *Nothofagus solandri*, *Eucalyptus pauciflora*, *Picea engelmannii*, *Pinus contorta*, *P. flexilis* and *P. hartwegii* are to establish near timberlines.

Treelines are usually sharp; these upper limits to distribution are set by temperature, moisture and wind conditions.[140] As a mountain is ascended conditions become, on average, windier, wetter and colder—but above all more variable. In exposed parts of the northern Rocky Mountains seedlings of *Picea glauca* are killed by exposure to a few hours of high temperature at ground level which causes stem girdling, though at night the temperature drops sharply. Partial shading prevents most heat deaths in this tree and drought is then the most likely cause of mortality, especially as growth at high altitudes is so slow that seedlings take several seasons to form tap roots long enough to enable them to survive a drought.

In New Zealand, evergreen *Nothofagus* forests end abruptly at between 1000 and 1500 metres above sea level. Near this treeline *Nothofagus* seldom has good seed years and the seed shows poor germination (0–3%). Such seedlings as develop often die, their tops drying out. When small seedlings were planted higher up the mountain, all those in the open died in the first year, but shaded seedlings survived and established 200 m above the treeline.

Figure 3.11 shows the order in which a number of conifer species are found with increasing altitude in a northwestern region of the U.S.A., where there is a well marked temperature-moisture gradient from the warm, dry lowlands to the cold, wet mountain peaks. The lower limit of distribution for these trees usually shows a gradual transition, which is apparently set by soil moisture levels. Ponderosa pine (*Pinus ponderosa*), Douglas fir (*Pseudotsuga menziesii*), Engelmann spruce (*Picea engelmannii*: not shown in Fig. 3.11) and alpine fir (*Abies lasiocarpa*) are encountered at successively greater altitudes and their roots will usually grow in successively moister soils. This tallies with their drought resistance, which is highest in Ponderosa pine and least in alpine fir. Temperature seems not to be the major factor; all the species can be grown at low altitude if watered, while dry atmospheres produce little effect as long as there is sufficient soil moisture.

Climate (especially the wind, water and temperature regimes), soil type, altitude, and biotic factors including the influence of man, are thus major influences that have caused the zonation of the World's forests and woodlands. These include the most diverse plant communities known; the mechanisms which maintain this diversity are now considered.

3.4 DIVERSITY IN COMMUNITIES OF WOODLAND PLANTS

Factors associated with the regeneration gap (Section 5.2) are of major importance in helping to maintain species diversity in woodlands, but other mechanisms[103] are also involved and are discussed here. One of the most important concerns the difference in *life forms*, whose complementarity is shown in a particularly marked way by woodland plants (Sections 1.2, 2.1). In a mature woodland the dominant trees do not utilize the resources of the area completely, indeed they often bear epiphytes themselves. One or more species of shade-tolerant shrubs or herbs (Section 2.4) can usually co-exist, often in places where the tree canopy is thin so that the shoots of smaller plants receive sufficient light to persist or even flourish. Trees, shrubs and herbs frequently compete for water and mineral nutrients, but the different sizes of these plants helps the various species to fit together in a diverse mosaic which allows the minimum needs of them all to be satisfied. Heterogeneity is further enhanced by *dependence-relationships* between trees and their epiphytes, parasites, hemi-parasites and the saprophytes which can grow on their dead products in very dense shade.

Differences in phenology are of great importance in enabling several species to grow vigorously in the same place but at different times of year. The phenology of the herb sequences of north temperate deciduous woodland (Section 4.4) has been extensively investigated with regard to changing light and temperature conditions; its importance with regard to the transmission of mineral nutrients is also becoming apparent (Section 9.5). Equally interesting is the non-coincidence of flowering, fruiting and flushing periods found in trees of at least some tropical forests.

Temporal fluctuations in the environment, such as winters in which minimum temperatures are exceptionally low, may have important effects—in this instance favouring species whose distributions are predominantly in higher latitudes. Such fluctuations may involve biotic factors. *Host-specific parasites* and *herbivores* may play an important role in maintaining species-richness. When their activities are concentrated on adult plants they may inflict particularly high mortality on offspring near the parents. When pairs of species of the same age are grown together one will usually gradually oust the other, but the two species may sometimes move towards a position of balance which, once achieved at a given density and under particular environmental conditions, can persist indefinitely. *Balanced mixtures* may result when two species are limited by different factors, so that the balance of competitive advantage can change, as when mineral nutrient concentrations or soil pore-size vary locally. They may alternatively represent a balance of intraspecific versus interspecific competition—a possible cause of this is the production of autotoxins, substances more toxic to the species producing them than to others.

Many natural and semi-natural woodlands are of *uneven age*, which can result in the developmental (pioneer) phase of one species being pitted against the pioneer, building, mature or degenerate phase of another (Section 5.1), with various results. Plants of different physiological age have very different competitive abilities, so it is possible for two species to persist in mixture indefinitely when the plants are of various ages.

Soil type may substantially affect species diversity in grasslands and woodlands. In N.W. Europe grasslands on shallow calcareous soils, which are short of nitrogen, phosphorus and other mineral nutrients, have far more species than grasslands on deeper soils of pH 5–6 with a better supply of nitrogen and phosphorus, which are dominated by relatively few species of high RGR. If species-rich, nutrient-poor grasslands are fertilized, standing crop is increased and diversity decreased because many of the species with low RGR, formerly favoured by their diverse regeneration requirements, are suppressed by the vigorous growth of their taller competitors in the mature phase. In contrast with natural grasslands in the same regions the field layers of beechwoods in central and northern Europe on deep, fertile soils of pH 5–6 (Asperulo-Fagion) are generally more species-rich than those on shallow calcareous soils (Cephalanthero-Fagion). Several factors are involved here. Heavy shade prevents rapid growth of shrubs and herbs of potentially high RGR even on fertile soils, while relatively few strict calcicoles grow in woodlands, though many do in grasslands. It is also significant that many species common on soils with a pH of less than 5 can grow at pH 5–6, but do not occur on highly calcareous soils.

Effects of tree litter upon plant diversity

Tree litter is an important constituent of all woodland ecosystems; information on its rate of decomposition is needed in attempts to understand more fully the processes of mineral nutrient cycling and energy flow. The litter on the forest floor affects the humus type and mineral nutrient status of the soil, while its physical presence often influences species differentially.

The direct effects of litter upon vegetation are particularly marked in many temperate and boreal forests, where tree litter often accumulates in large quantities on the woodland floor and individual leaves persist for years. In contrast, leaves are known to disappear completely in 2–7 months under the warm moist conditions of tropical forest. Persistent tree litter is often distributed very unevenly within woodlands, the highest densities occurring in hollows, which may be devoid of herbaceous plants. Litter is also trapped by robust ground-flora species including *Rubus fruticosus* agg. (bramble), *Pteridium aquilinum* (bracken), and *Vaccinium myrtillus* (bilberry).

Investigations of woodland floors beneath canopies of sycamore and oak near Sheffield[227] showed that the main ground flora constituents could be arranged in the series *Galeobdolon luteum**, *Endymion non-scriptus*, *Anemone nemorosa* > *Milium effusum*, *Holcus mollis*, *Poa trivialis* > *Mnium hornum* in terms of their tendency to occur in areas with a high density of litter. The emergence of aerial organs is a critical phase in the lives of woodland herbs;[201] species most frequently associated with persistent tree litter have shoots which can penetrate it effectively. This is well seen in bluebell (*Endymion non-scriptus*), whose spear-shoots can puncture the tough leaves of oak and force their way through the coherent heavy litter commonly present in early spring during wet weather. The evergreen overwintering shoots of *Galeobdolon luteum* connect to rather wiry stems ramifying through the litter which produce new shoots in early spring. The young shoots are robust, erect and with rather narrow apices well adapted to penetrate weak points in the litter, and this plant often flourishes on woodland floors in which much litter is trapped by a low growth of bramble. *Anemone nemorosa* has its young stems folded in the 'penknife' mode and these also can push through weak areas of the litter. Because of their small size, *Mnium hornum* and other mosses have poor powers of emergence through litter. Similarly many woodland grasses, particularly *Poa trivialis*, are not suited to resist burial by litter, having weak leaves and low growth forms when vegetative.

On the other hand, in the woodlands mentioned above, young seedlings of *Fraxinus excelsior* were most abundant where deep litter was present; perhaps fruits dispersed in litter are less conspicuous to predators. In the same region, slower rates of predation and smaller losses in viability have been observed where acorns were immersed in tree litter. Again *Oxalis acetosella* grows very much better where there is an abundance of broadleaved leaf litter in which its roots and rhizomes often run; it was found[235] to disappear gradually from plots beneath *Fagus sylvatica* into which the continued fall of leaf litter was prevented.

Soil conditions and vegetational mosaics

Local variations in edaphic conditions involving features such as soil depth, soil reaction and exchangeable calcium levels, strongly influence the distributions of many woodland species and frequently result in the development of vegetational mosaics. *Fagus sylvatica*, *Daphne laureola* (spurge laurel) and *Allium ursinum* (ramsons), for example, all grow well in soils rich in exchangeable calcium, whereas

*syn. *Lamiastrum galeobdolon* (yellow archangel)

Vaccinium myrtillus (bilberry) is a strong **calcifuge** in all respects, growing in distinctly acid soils in which calcium carbonate is absent and exchangeable calcium low. *Calluna vulgaris* (ling, see Section 3.2), normally grows in soil devoid of calcium carbonate and its seedlings are markedly calcifuge. Species which in nature usually behave as **calcicoles**, such as *Sanicula europaea* (wood sanicle), or **calcifuges**, such as ling and bilberry, tend to have much narrower ranges in respect of soil reaction and exchangeable calcium than do, for example, *Pteridium aquilinum* (bracken), *Mercurialis perennis* (dog's mercury) and *Teucrium scorodonia* (wood sage).

Mercurialis perennis, *Brachypodium sylvaticum* (slender false-brome) and *Deschampsia cespitosa* (tufted hairgrass) grow well on many woodland soils (mulls and rendzinas) containing quite moderate amounts of phosphorus. In some instances where *Urtica dioica* (stinging nettle) grows in the vicinity it has been found that its seedlings cease growth at an early stage if transferred to the *Mercurialis* soils. *Urtica* grows vigorously on these soils if phosphate is supplied, but in its absence the addition of other nutrients, including nitrogen, has little effect.[187] The seedlings of *Mercurialis perennis*, *Brachypodium sylvaticum* and *Deschampsia cespitosa*, however, scarcely respond to additional phosphate and grow successfully on the natural soils. *Epilobium angustifolium* and *Sambucus nigra* (elder) respond very positively to additions of phosphate, but *Galium aparine* (cleavers), a large fruited annual herb, was found to be checked at an early stage when grown on soil from beneath *Mercurialis* in Buff Wood, Cambridgeshire, and resumed vigorous growth only when phosphate and nitrogen were added together; either alone produced little response.

On the chalky boulder clay of Cambridgeshire woodlands, such as Buff Wood and Hayley Wood, *M. perennis* is confined to the well drained and better aerated soils, whereas *Primula elatior* (oxlip) grows on soils with poor drainage which become surface waterlogged during the spring months of most years. In pot experiments *Mercurialis* grew as well, and sometimes better, on soil from the *Primula elatior* areas (mean pH 5.86) of Buff Wood as in soil from the *Mercurialis* areas (mean pH 7.17), thus eliminating soil acidity and mineral nutrients as the direct causes of the distributional pattern shown here by *M. perennis*.

Though *M. perennis* is confined to areas where soil oxygen diffusion rates are generally high, Martin[157] has shown that it is the presence of ferrous ions (Fe^{++}) in damp soils which causes root death in this species. Sand culture experiments in which waterlogging occurred in the absence of ferrous ions did not cause injury. There is a clear correlation between the extent of intercellular airspaces in the roots and the ability of species to grow in parts of these Cambridgeshire woodlands that are waterlogged in spring. *M. perennis* has small intercellular airspaces at the angles of the cortical cells and does not form enlarged airspaces in response to poorly aerated root environments. In contrast, *Primula elatior* has larger airspaces and occasional small lacunae, *Filipendula ulmaria* (meadowsweet) has a spongy root cortex of small, loosely packed cells, while in *Deschampsia cespitosa* well developed aerenchyma forms a lacunar system round the central stele. By measuring rates of oxygen diffusion from the roots of *Deschampsia cespitosa* and *Mercurialis perennis* in deoxygenated water, Martin[157] showed that the former had by far the greater power to oxidize the surrounding root medium, a characteristic of plants which grow successfully in bogs. When *M. perennis* survives on soils liable to poor aeration in the wet season, it does so by producing an entirely superficial root system absent from regions of the soil profile in which reducing conditions occur. Plants with such a growth form are very susceptible to summer drought.

Martin[157] showed an increasing tolerance to ferrous ions in the series *Mercurialis perennis, Endymion non-scriptus, Brachypodium sylvaticum, Geum urbanum, Circaea lutetiana, Primula vulgaris, P. elatior, Carex sylvatica, Deschampsia cespitosa* when species were grown in well aerated water cultures. The main symptom of ferrous ion toxicity was root death and the order given above corresponded with the ecological behaviour of these species towards waterlogging, with *D. cespitosa* being tolerant of both waterlogging and ferrous ions, while *Mercurialis perennis* is very sensitive to both. Ferrous ion solubility is mainly determined by **redox potential** and pH, being greater in more acid soils. (Redox potential is a quantitative measure of ability to gain or lose electrons, and hence, respectively, to be reduced or oxidized.)

Distribution and performance of *Mercurialis perennis*

Dog's mercury grows as a woodland herb in many parts of Europe, where, as indicated above, its success in a variety of habitats is influenced substantially by several environmental factors, especially light, calcium levels, the nutrient status of the soil, and soil waterlogging. It is a hairy perennial hemicryptophyte with erect stems and long creeping rhizomes which bear roots whose 'working depth' varies according to soil type. In soils in which water and humus contents are both high the roots branch profusely, but are mainly confined to the upper 10 cm of soil. Root growth is poor in sandy soils and even poorer in peat. In calcareous clays the greatest development is at 15–20 cm and the plant grows well on this soil type.[165]

Plants associated with vegetation types that are seldom disturbed and of moderate productivity usually have characteristics intermediate between those of competitors and stress-tolerators. *Mercurialis perennis*, which has a marked capacity for local vegetative spread, is a woodland, and hedgerow, example of such a **stress-tolerant competitor**,[101] with a pronounced ability to endure low light levels while itself, particularly the female colonies, casting a dense shade. Although shade-loving, it can also tolerate high light levels, i.e. it is a **sciophyte** capable of growing as a **facultative semi-heliophyte**. There are a number of habitat forms,[165] but the leaves tend to be larger, thinner, relatively wider, less hairy and a deeper green when the plants are in shade. Female plants grow in shady habitats; the development of male colonies is favoured by higher light intensities. The leaf canopy of dense stands of female plants in many woods where light levels are low is very complete, a major factor in the ability of this plant to suppress competitors (see Fig. 3.12). Tree

Fig. 3.12 Leaf mosaic of female colony of dog's mercury (*Mercurialis perennis*) in Cantreyn Wood, Bridgnorth, Shropshire. (Photograph by John R. Packham.)

seedlings, including those of common ash, are frequently shaded out or held in check until their shoots rise above the canopy of *M. perennis*. Light levels and water regimes influence the distribution of dog's mercury in non-woodland situations also; in the grasslands of the Sheffield area Grime and Lloyd[102] found it, together with *Anemone nemorosa* and *Oxalis acetosella*, amongst the familiar woodland plants restricted to, or concentrated upon, the comparatively cool and moist north-facing slopes. The distribution of *O. acetosella* within the heathland, grassland and flush communities of the Long Mynd, Shropshire, appears to be largely controlled by the water regimes of the various microhabitats.[174, 175]

Salisbury,[202] in early studies of the calcicole/calcifuge problem, noted that 'in woods on acid soils the calcicolous *Mercurialis perennis* occurs either in dry areas with a high calcium content (or low acidity) or in damp areas where the lime requirement is high (considered in terms of unit weight of dry soil) but is apparently ameliorated as a consequence of the high water content.' *Mercurialis* is known to grow in soil with pH values from 4.5 to 8.2, but its main roots are seldom in the more acid regions of soil profiles. When grown in a number of acid boulder clay soils with initial pH values varying from 5.7–6.7 there was a positive correlation between exchangeable calcium in the soil and dry weight accretion, although the most alkaline soil did not have the most exchangeable calcium.[76]

Hutchings and Barkham[120] studied clonal colonies of *Mercurialis* in Foxley Wood, Norfolk, in attempts to determine the extent to which its shoots were comparable to discrete units in populations. Their results suggested that the connected shoots of *M. perennis* are part of an integrated system, being mutually dependent rather than competitive in many activities. Rhizomatous perennials such as bracken and dog's mercury probably persist in pure stands because their dense shoot, rhizome and root systems exploit the resources of the habitat thoroughly and efficiently, preventing the entry of competitors, while not developing intense competition between individual shoots and other organs of the same plant.

4

Reproductive Strategies of Woodland Plants

4.1 REPRODUCTION AND FRUITING

In mature woodland most flowering plants are perennial, many being long-lived forms able to persist and propagate themselves vegetatively under conditions unfavourable to reproduction by seed. The formation of propagules—spores or seeds—which can be distributed by wind, water, animals, or explosive mechanisms, facilitates the invasion of habitats at appreciable distances from the parent plants. Three main *patterns of seed production* have been recognized[103] in forest communities: (a) moderate production in most years; (b) fruiting rather irregular; and (c) abundant fruiting strongly periodic. Different species in group (b) will be favoured in different years. Three corresponding patterns of flowering seem also to occur, though unfavourable weather conditions may prevent a heavy seed set resulting from extensive flower production. High winds or rain may prevent pollination in woodland species; periods of drought and high temperature must also affect seed set. These variations are important because the distribution of viable seeds, in both space and time, greatly influences the developmental patterns of woodlands.

The effective sexual reproduction of tracheophytes in forests often demands very special conditions if young plants are to become established. The habitat must be open enough for seeds to be able to develop into mature plants without succumbing to competition, and sufficient seed must be produced to allow for loss resulting from plant pathogens and herbivorous animals, a situation which leads to the concept of *predator satiation* by masting (Section 4.3). These constraints mean that in natural woodlands decades, or even centuries, may elapse between periods when substantial numbers of tree seedlings develop to maturity. *Mast years*, in which seed production is exceptionally high, are typically several years apart. Seedlings usually develop in large numbers after these, but are then often suppressed by competition for light, water and nutrients for many years and most of them die. Only if storm damage, felling or the death of a tree causes a gap in the forest canopy will some be able to mature.

Pollination mechanisms

Pollination of forest trees, notably of conifers, in temperate regions is mainly by wind (*anemophilous*), but towards the tropics many more tree species are pollinated by animals (see Section 4.3). *Entomophilous* (insect pollinated) flowers, whose features make them attractive to insects, often have bright colours, nectar and scent. The mechanisms may be very specific, as in a number of orchids in which pollination occurs after pseudo-copulation by male wasps, or the odour emitted by the cuckoo-pint (*Arum maculatum*) which attracts large numbers of small *Psychoda* flies. The pollen of insect-pollinated flowers is usually sticky, while that of anemophilous flowers is dry and produced in the enormous quantities necessary to the success of such a random method of distribution. Wind-pollinated flowers are usually well above the ground, the stamens are exserted and often with versatile anthers so that pollen is effectively distributed. Male flowers are often in catkins as in alder, birch and hazel. Flowers or plants of *separate sexes*, strongly marked *dichogamy* in which the stamens and stigmas mature at different times, and *self-sterility* are common in *wind-pollinated plants*, helping to ensure effective gene-flow and the production of new genotypes which, together with phenotypic plasticity, are important if the population is to remain capable of making major adaptations to changing conditions.

Although many species show quite extreme adaptation to pollination by wind, animals or water, there is a balance between anemophily and entomophily in such trees as lime (*Tilia*), willows (*Salix*) and sweet chestnut (*Castanea sativa*), all of which are visited by numerous insects, but possess flowers showing some indications of the '*syndrome of anemophily*'. Marked disparity in the effectiveness of two pollinating agencies in a particular species will influence the subsequent evolution of the floral mechanism. Most members of the olive family (*Oleaceae*) are entomophilous; indeed the mediterranean 'manna ash' (*Fraxinus ornus*) possesses a white corolla and its fragrant flowers are pollinated by insects.[189] Common ash, however, is anemophilous. Its flowers are simple and often bisexual (Fig. 4.1), having two stamens and a long ovary (which later develops into a flat

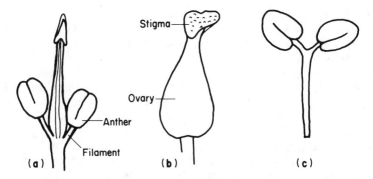

Fig. 4.1 Common ash (*Fraxinus excelsior*). **(a)** Single hermaphrodite flower, **(b)** female flower, and **(c)** male flower. Some trees of this protandrous wind-pollinated species function exclusively as males, some as hermaphrodites and yet others as females. Stem diameter, height, and volume of female ash were found by Rohmeder[197] to be considerably less than those of male trees, possibly because of the allocation of resources to seed production.

one-seeded 'ash key'), lack a corolla, and are borne in dark greenish masses on the naked twigs in March and April. Among the maples introduced to Britain, both sycamore (*Acer pseudoplatanus*) and Norway maple (*A. platanoides*) are pollinated mainly by bees. Temperate species of the Fagaceae such as *Fagus sylvatica*, *Quercus petraea* and *Q. robur* are predominantly wind-pollinated, while a number of subtropical oaks are entomophilous.

Similar examples of families possessing both wind- and insect-pollinated species can be found amongst the herbs: *Mercurialis perennis* (Euphorbiaceae) is an anemophilous member of a mainly insect-pollinated family. It is interesting that while the combination of features associated with anemophily has appeared independently in flowers with very varied basic structures, specialization to particular agents of pollination has often occurred within the evolutionarily recent past.

Most wind-pollinated deciduous forest trees flower while bare of leaves, when the numbers of active insects are low. The flowers are freely exposed to disperse and receive pollen[189] and the surrounding surfaces available to 'compete' with the stigmas for pollen are minimal. In the temperate zone most of the species which are dominant over large areas are wind-pollinated. Anemophilous plants tend to produce small numbers of ovules—grasses, sedges, *Corylus* and *Quercus* produce only one seed per flower—a distinct advantage in closed communities where the possession of large seeds confers higher competitive power.

Germination requirements

Dormancy and germination in seeds and bud dormancy and development are largely controlled by balances of the same growth promoters and growth inhibitors (see Section 4.4). Thiourea can be substituted for the natural germination stimulator which develops in *Fraxinus* seeds during chilling; it can also be used in place of cold temperature treatment in *Quercus, Larix, Picea* and other trees. The seeds of woodland species vary greatly in their germination requirements. The germination of fully imbibed seeds of ivy (*Hedera helix*) is inhibited by light, which acts as a dormancy-breaking agent in beech. Germination in *Anemone nemorosa* and *Theobroma cacao* is light-indifferent. Some seeds are affected not by short illumination, but by alternations between dark and light (photoperiod). Photoperiodic requirements may be altered by changes in other environmental conditions. *Betula* seeds at 15°C germinate only under long day conditions, requiring eight LD cycles to do so. If the temperature is raised to 20–25°C, a single exposure to light of 8–12 hours is sufficient to cause germination.

The seeds of *Quercus* and *Viburnum* germinate in the autumn at which time the radicle elongates. Both show 'epicotyl dormancy', however, as the epicotyl will not develop until the seed is chilled during the ensuing winter. Like many seeds, those of the herbs *Convallaria* and *Polygonatum* require a winter's chilling if the radicle is to grow; they are exceptional in that the epicotyl needs a further cold winter before it develops.

The seed is normally the first stage at which new genotypes are exposed to the processes of selection. Seeds also enable plants to perennate, multiply, and disperse, but they may serve a useful function by remaining dormant. *Digitalis purpurea* seeds can remain viable in brown earth soils for many years; they have a light requirement and so do not germinate while buried. When conifer plantations are felled the open conditions and freshly bared soil allow large populations of foxgloves to develop from seeds already in the soil. Populations of *Epilobium angustifolium* also build up quickly, but the seeds of this species are blown in by wind so the survival strategies of these two species, both of which have quite light seeds and flourish in well-lit sites, are different.

Seed size and distribution mechanisms

Species unadapted to vegetative existence in climax vegetation, such as mature woodland, are doomed to local extinction and are in this sense fugitive. The more frequently such a species undergoes the cycle *invasion-colonization-suppression-extinction*, the greater is the importance of a high intrinsic rate of natural increase and of dispersal as a means of escape to a more open habitat. Large seed number, small seed size, high powers of dispersal and a high proportion of net production partitioned to propagule production—all characteristics of r-species—can be expected in such plants.

The tendency for propagule weights to increase as the habitat becomes increasingly closed has already been referred to in Section 1.5. Seed weight varies among species over a range of ten orders of magnitude.[109] At one extreme are the dust seeds of the orchids, for example, *Goodyera repens* (0.000002 g), while at the other are the huge 'seeds' of the double coconut palm (*Lodoicea maldivica*) which weigh 14 000–23 000 g. Angiosperms with really large seeds are restricted to the Tropics or Sub-Tropics. The smallest known seeds are of plants with anomalous nutrition. Orchid seeds often lack any nutrient tissue and in nature the developing embryos are associated with mycorrhizal fungi. Total parasites frequently depend on host plants for early growth. Broomrapes (*Orobanche* spp.), of which *O. hederae* attacks ivy, are obligate parasites whose seeds require stimulus by a host root exudate if germination is to occur.

Seed dispersal mechanisms can be ecologically classified according to habitat: the mechanisms[109] associated with the various forest strata frequently differ. In north temperate woodlands, for example, herbs very commonly produce hairy or hooked animal-dispersed propagules (*Arctium, Circaea, Galium, Geum, Mercurialis*), while shrub layer species commonly bear fleshy fruits (*Crataegus, Cornus, Hedera, Prunus, Rhamnus* and *Sambucus*). Similarly *Taxus* seeds, which are poisonous to mammals, are surrounded by brightly coloured, sweet-tasting, fleshy arils that are very attractive to birds—a fact which may explain, at least partially, the wide geographical range of this genus of nine species which occurs in North America, Europe and Asia, extending into Malaysia. Pioneer species of the tree layer commonly possess wind-dispersed propagules (*Betula, Fraxinus, Pinus*), while later successional and climax woodland species often bear heavy seeds, dependent on the specialized collecting habits of mammals or birds, as in *Fagus* or *Quercus*. However, there are exceptions; *Sequoia* and *Sequoiadendron* form climax forests of great antiquity yet have small winged seeds which grow well on seed beds left by fire, to which the mature trees are resistant. Certain species with heavy seeds, such as *Quercus robur*, do well as pioneer trees if their seeds reach relatively open habitats, as can occur when acorns roll downhill or are transported by squirrels, pigeons or jays.

Mellanby[161] points out that birds in particular carry many acorns away from seed-bearing trees and drop them in the open where up to 5000 seedlings ha^{-1} (Fig. 4.2) may be found, far more than occur beneath oak woods. Though many of the vast surplus of acorns

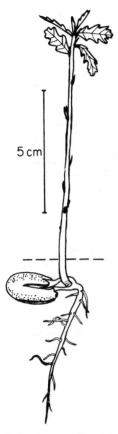

5 cm

Fig. 4.2 Seedling of English oak (*Quercus robur*). Germination is hypogeal and the cotyledons are largely concealed within the remains of the acorn.

removed by animals are consumed, the germination of those which they bury in the ground and subsequently neglect may be an important factor in regeneration.

4.2 MASTING

Since growth and behaviour vary considerably with environment and there are substantial genetic differences within species, studies of the flowering, fruiting, seed losses and germination of tree species in particular sites are of especial value. Gardner,[93] who made studies of this type on *Fraxinus excelsior* in a Derbyshire ashwood, found that fruit fall is evenly distributed throughout the wood, and continues from September to August. As Fig. 4.3 shows, the amount of fruit produced varies greatly from year to year and many of the seeds

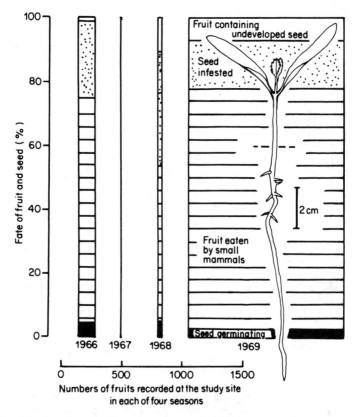

Fig. 4.3 A young seedling of common ash (*Fraxinus excelsior*) and diagrams showing fates of ash fruit and seed up to the time of germination (numbers per m^2) in Meadow Place Wood, Lathkilldale, Derbyshire, for the crops of 1966 to 1969. Most of the infested seed was spoilt by caterpillars of the moth *Pseudargyrotoza conwagana*. The largest seed loss was due to small mammals, notably wood mice (*Apodemus sylvaticus*) and bank voles (*Clethrionomys glareolus*). A very small crop was produced in the summer of 1967, of which no seedlings survived, and frosting diminished the crop of 1968. Following these two poor years, the crop of 1969 was very large. Seeds usually germinated in April or early May, about 20 months after falling in autumn. The values for seeds germinating are therefore based on the seedlings present in quadrats two years after flowering. See also Fig. 4.4 (d) which shows annual production of seed in the same wood for the period 1966–76. (Drawn from the data of Gardner.[93])

are destroyed; only a very small percentage of the seed finally germinates. Each ovary contains four ovules of which one usually develops, though some fruits contain no seed. 1.1% of the ash fruits were found to contain two seeds, however, and in one example all four ovules developed.

A tree of common ash may produce 10 kg of winged fruits, containing over 100 000 seeds, every second year, and seedlings of this pioneer species have been recorded 125 m distant from the parent tree. Observations (Fig. 4.4d) show a basic alternation of good and bad years, supporting the view that fruiting in common ash is biennial. As *F. excelsior* flowers on the wood of the previous year, a lack of carbohydrate or other nutrient reserve during that previous year could prevent the production of flower initials. A good fruiting year was expected in 1968 but the flowers of some of the trees were destroyed by frost; fruit production was intermediate rather than good and the drain of the carbohydrate reserves was low. The following year differed from the expected pattern in being an exceptionally good fruiting year, presumably because the photo-synthate for 1969 was supplemented with reserves saved from 1967 and 1968 by the loss of flowers in spring 1968. Ash fruit which falls in autumn is incapable of germinating immediately. A period of growth is required, during which the length of the embryo almost doubles. Embryo growth in ash ideally requires a temperature of 18–20° C and only after it takes place can prolonged *stratification* (exposure to low temperature), at about 5° C, overcome dormancy. Because of this, ash seeds usually germinate in April or early May two years after the flowering season in which they were formed, although a very small proportion germinate after the first winter. (When foresters wish ash to germinate quickly they pick the seeds green in August and sow them immediately.)

In north temperate regions periodic masting of *Tilia* and *Carpinus*, where photosynthetic appendages are associated with the flowers, is less conspicuous than in certain oaks, beeches and conifers, which lack such structures.[108] Examples of observations of *masting* amongst the latter group are shown in Fig. 4.4; it should be noted that the periodicity of each of these species is much more irregular than in the biennially fruiting common ash. For example, Jones[131] found that the interval between uniformly heavy crops of acorns of *Quercus robur* and *Q. petraea* over considerable areas of southern England was at least 6–7 years. In some parts of France the interval is 3–4 years while in others it is 8–10 years, and in many continental districts of Europe 20–25 years may pass without appreciable production of acorns, though a few trees may fruit heavily.

Masting in conifers is well seen in species of *Pinus*, *Pseudotsuga*, *Picea* and *Abies*. In Sweden the seeding of *Pinus sylvestris* is more irregular in the north than the south, where mast years are hardly discernible, whereas *Picea abies* is a much more erratic cone producer.[108]

Many species of tropical Asian bamboos are *monocarpic* (cf.

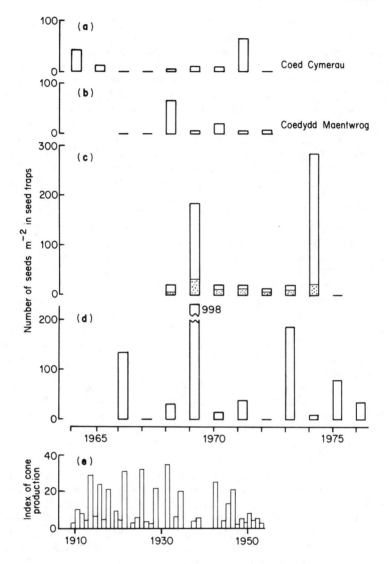

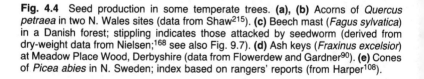

Fig. 4.4 Seed production in some temperate trees. **(a), (b)** Acorns of *Quercus petraea* in two N. Wales sites (data from Shaw[215]). **(c)** Beech mast (*Fagus sylvatica*) in a Danish forest; stippling indicates those attacked by seedworm (derived from dry-weight data from Nielsen;[168] see also Fig. 9.7). **(d)** Ash keys (*Fraxinus excelsior*) at Meadow Place Wood, Derbyshire (data from Flowerdew and Gardner[90]). **(e)** Cones of *Picea abies* in N. Sweden; index based on rangers' reports (from Harper[108]).

semelparous, see Table 1.1) flowering and fruiting only once and then dying. The length of time between germination and flowering ranges from 3–120 years, according to species, so that synchronized flowering is observed not only in local populations but also in widely transplanted individuals of the same genetic stock.

Different species of trees in temperate woodlands may display masting at the same time, but mast fruiting at the community level is particularly spectacular in certain evergreen rainforests on nutrient-poor white sand soils in Borneo and Malaysia. Here it is especially the various species of dipterocarp which fruit synchronously over areas of several square kilometres at intervals of 5–13 years.[123]

Janzen[125] suggests that the length of the inter-mast period is a genetic trait in 'semelparous' bamboos, whereas in masting trees this period seems to be determined by the environment. Many tree species, such as *Fagus sylvatica*, flower abundantly after a hot, sunny summer in which abundant carbohydrate reserves can accumulate. However, adverse weather at the time of fertilization or seed development, or the depredations of herbivores, can easily upset correlations which have been sought between weather and masting, especially in those conifers which have a long period of cone development. On the other hand vegetative growth is usually reduced in and immediately after mast years, so that, for example in *Fagus sylvatica*, annual ring increments may be half those of non-masting years.

Asian dipterocarps in sites of low primary productivity require a period of several years to build up sufficient photosynthate to produce a glut of fruit, and only then are they presumed to be sensitive to the environmental cue of several weeks without rain, as a break in an otherwise uniform climate. While Janzen[122,123] stresses that the significance of masting lies in the satiation of seed predators (see Section 4.3), Harper[108] suggests that reproductive advantage may also be gained by species typical of the later stages of succession producing large numbers of offspring as potential replacements should an aged parent die leaving a gap in which regeneration could occur.

4.3   INFLUENCE OF ANIMALS

In temperate woodlands various herbs and shrubs, but very few trees, are pollinated by insects.[189] Pollination by members of a wide range of animal groups becomes increasingly important towards the tropics, where the wide separation of individual trees of the same species (***conspecifics***) by other species would render wind pollination inefficient. Among insects an example of extreme specificity is shown by the various species of fig-wasp (*Blastophaga*), each mutualistically developing within the flowers of a separate species of fig; this relationship depends on asynchronous flowering within a fig population.[126] Males of the oriental fruitfly (*Dacus dorsalis*) are attracted to their specific sex **pheromones** ('external hormones' concerned with coordination between individuals) which are also produced by flowers of *Cassia* trees; similar chemical lures are produced by certain orchids pollinated by neotropical bees, where active searching over long distances enables pollen to be transferred between sparsely distributed plants. Many bees in evergreen tropical rainforests are social, the colonies requiring large amounts of food throughout the year; these bees tend to be pollen and nectar scavengers and robbers, rather than pollinators.

Vertebrates are the primary pollinators of 20% or so of tropical species, their year-round food requirements precluding the one-to-one specificity seen in insects such as fig-wasps. Hummingbirds are the sole pollinators of thousands of New World tropical species, being attracted to odourless but brightly coloured flowers, often red or orange; honeyeaters are a comparable Old World example. Trees pollinated by bats include baobab, kapok and balsa; they tend to have large, dull coloured flowers which open at night, producing copious nectar and a sour smell reminiscent of bats.

Contrasting **pollinator strategies**, observed by Janzen in two groups of Hymenoptera, also seem to occur within hawkmoths and hummingbirds, and can be exemplified by bats.[43] 'Opportunistic' species concentrate on plants which display synchronized mass-flowering over short periods; Old World bats of the sub-order Megachiroptera may migrate as flocks, following the sequential flowering of different species such as *Parkia clappertoniana*, each inflorescence of which yields up to 5 ml of nectar. 'Trap-liners', on the other hand, include certain American Microchiroptera which pay fleeting visits to plants which may open only one or a very few small flowers per day over an extended period. Each flower yields very little nectar or pollen, but presumably sufficient to justify the expenditure of energy on complex feeding routes of up to 20 km or more.

Fruits and seeds may be sought as food by animals, some of which void or spit out viable seeds (e.g. mistletoe by birds) while others, such as agoutis and squirrels, practise scatter-hoarding, the successful germination of the seeds depending on the animal's forgetfulness. In extreme cases, partial abrasion of the endocarp in a bird's gizzard is a pre-requisite for germination; it has been suggested that the demise of the dodo (*Raphus cucullatus*) has left *Calvaria major* trees on Mauritius without a vital aid to regeneration for the past 300 years.

During its life time a tree produces immense numbers of seeds, of which only one is required to replace it. The dangers faced by individual seeds and seedlings are, however, very great, and a successful species requires a reproductive capacity sufficient to allow it to invade new habitats. Janzen recognizes three basic strategies shown by plants which achieve dispersal despite seed predation. Some produce extremely small seeds, others satiate predators with an over-abundance of seeds, while others utilize chemical defences. Among Central American woody legumes, one species of *Indigofera* produces seeds weighing 3 mg, too small for the development of beetle larvae. Thirteen other species of legume average over 1000 seeds per m^3 of canopy, each of mean weight 260 mg, and even if all of an individual tree's crop is destroyed by larvae of bruchids ('pea-weevils'), predator satiation will be effective for the local population so long as a few seeds escape consumption. The remaining 23 species produce on average 14 large seeds per m^3, with a mean weight of 3 g, and these are completely protected from bruchids by toxic alkaloids. As an example of adaptations to defensive chemicals, 102 out of 111 species of bruchids developing within seeds of deciduous forest trees in Costa Rica are apparently single-host-specific, other potential predators being excluded.[124] The presence of up to 8% of L-dopa, a poisonous compound of great value in treating Parkinson's disease, protects the seeds of the leguminous 'vine' *Mucuna* from all insects, but certain rodents can include small amounts in a mixed diet.

Unlike plants which partition resources into chemical defence, masting species periodically produce an over-abundance of seeds which a wide range of predators finds highly edible. The essential characteristic of **satiation of seed predators**[122] is that at least some seeds escape discovery (or recovery, if hoarded) and so retain the ability to develop. Over-abundance and satiation imply that the predator population cannot cope with the glut. In temperate forests, unfavourable weather and shortage of seed may reduce predator numbers between mast years. In the lowland tropical forests of Africa and Central America, with their great diversity of plants and animals, no examples are known of mast fruiting at the population or community level. However, the local animal communities in S.E. Asian dipterocarp forests are low in numbers and species, and even when reinforced by migrant species of deer, ox, pigs and pigeons could be satiated by community masting of dipterocarps.[123] There may be a similar explanation for synchronized fruiting in bamboos.

The influence of man on the distribution and abundance of these vertebrate predators makes these hypotheses untestable, while it is no longer possible to assess the role of passenger pigeons, which apparently were the chief seed predators of species of Fagaceae in N.

America. Beech mast (*Fagus sylvatica*) is totally lacking in toxins[122] and Nielsen[168] found that on average 36% of the annual endosperm production was destroyed by seed worms (*Cydia fagiglandana*, Lepidoptera). The data in Fig. 4.4c demonstrate the occurrence of satiation of this species in mast years, while Fig. 4.3 possibly illustrates a similar situation for caterpillars attacking seeds of *Fraxinus excelsior*. Gardner[93] found that small mammals (*Apodemus sylvaticus* and *Clethrionomys glareolus*) were responsible for seed losses of up to 75%, removing them after seed-fall but before germination. Watt[233,234] strongly implicated small mammals in similarly removing acorns and beech mast, and also in severing emerging radicles. Mice, rabbits, slugs, wireworms and fungi were shown to attack seedlings, whose photosynthetic efficiency was decreased by sap-sucking bugs especially in shade. Watt suggested that percentage mortality of beech seeds and seedlings was lowest in good mast years and that potential regeneration was virtually restricted to those years, supporting Janzen's ideas on predator satiation by masting.

It is frequently stated that, largely because so many acorns and seedlings are eaten by birds and mammals, the oak does not regenerate sufficiently to maintain satisfactory stands in British oakwoods. Shaw[215] concluded that small mammals were the main predators of acorns, but when the crop is heavy[228] mice and voles consume only a small fraction of it, whereas squirrels and pigeons remove most of the seeds, a few of which germinate after being dropped or buried. Defoliation of seedlings by caterpillars, which drop on to them from mature trees, may be as important as the influence of light in determining the survival of young oaks.[215]

Environmental opposition may be so severe that regeneration occurs only under exceptional conditions. The lofty giant gum (*Eucalyptus regnans*) in S.E. Australia typically produces 7.5×10^6 seeds ha^{-1} yr^{-1}, but largely because of low germination and the deep burial of seeds by ants the seedling density is only *c*. 1500 ha^{-1}. Overheating of the surface soil, desiccation, attack by two species of litter fungi, and grazing by wallabies, together with their own poor competitive abilities, usually result in the death of all of the seedlings; consequently saplings are conspicuously absent from the mature groves, which are characteristically of even age. When summers are dry enough, however, these groves may be swept by fire as some were in 1939. A profusion of *Eucalyptus* seedlings then develops, which are able to grow before enemies have recouped their losses.[88] Though *E. regnans* reaches heights of well over 100 metres, it is a relatively short-lived pioneer species whose forests are **perpetuated by fire**. With its flaky bark and characteristic leaf oils it burns readily during summer hot spells. In the rare cases where swamps, cliffs, or other barriers prevent the spread of fire for a century or more, these short-lived eucalypts tend to disappear[23] and an understorey develops in which *Nothofagus, Atherosperma* and the tree fern *Dicksonia* are common. In the continued absence of fire these understorey trees gradually rise to dominance and a late successional southern hemisphere rain forest evolves.

4.4   SEASONAL CHANGES AND ASPECT SOCIETIES

Amongst the most significant environmental features of the temperate regions are the seasonal variations in temperature, light intensity, and often rainfall. This regular alternation of seasons favourable and unfavourable to growth is closely linked to the hormonally influenced **annual rhythms** of leaf production, dormancy, expansion and fall in deciduous forests. Many aspects of the control of growth and differentiation in plants, including the germination of seeds, and the production of flowers, fruit and storage organs, have been investigated in recent years;[232,206] some of their ecological implications are discussed in this section.

Importance of the cold season

The effects of low temperature upon plants are profound; this environmental factor probably limits plant distribution more than any other, although the availability of water is the factor which seems to limit most greatly the productivity of world ecosystems. Even a sudden fall in temperature in which freezing is not involved can cause **chilling injury**; a number of tropical species are killed when cooled to between $0°$ and $+5°$ C.

In winter deciduous trees lose their leaves and, like the evergreens, undergo a period of dormancy in which there is a relative suspension of the overall metabolism. Even in regions with mild winters photosynthesis is distinctly depressed, and in *Picea abies* photosynthesis ceases entirely when temperature maxima fall below $0°$ C. Perennial plants growing in northern climates often have little tolerance of frost during the growing season; indeed one of the causes of canker and dieback in *Larix* is late frost after the trees have resumed active growth in spring (another major cause is infection by the ascomycete *Dasyscypha willkommii*). Once the growing season is over the plant undergoes a series of phases during which exposure to successively lower temperatures makes it increasingly tolerant or **frost-hard**. The buds of most dormant trees are covered by bud scales, which reduce water loss rather than protect against frost. If the water in active plant cells freezes intracellularly, mechanical damage from ice crystals often causes death of the cells. During frost-hardening there is usually an accumulation of sugars and other substances which depress the freezing point of the cell sap. Changes in the cell membranes, however, appear to be of major importance in frost-hardening.

Dormancy

Some seeds are unable to germinate because their coats are impermeable, but others remain dormant because they have a *chilling or light requirement* similar to that of buds or other organs. In *Betula pubescens* dormancy of both seeds and buds is removed by the growth stimulator gibberellic acid, by chilling at 0–5° C, or by exposure to long days. Growth inhibiting hormones occur in both dormant buds and seeds; some seeds which fail to germinate if merely imbibed with water are capable of doing so if sufficient water is supplied to leach out the inhibitor.

In woody plants there is considerable variation in the time elapsing between the initiation of the flower and its complete development. The flower initials develop directly into mature flowers, as in herbs, in some late summer flowering trees (*Castanea*) and shrubs (*Hypericum*) where the flowers are formed on the current year's shoots. In black currants (*Ribes nigrum*), gooseberries (*Ribes uva-crispa*), and many other European genera including *Quercus, Fraxinus, Acer, Ulmus*, and *Pinus*, however, there is a suspension of the development of the flower (or cone) initials, which are formed during the summer in resting buds produced earlier in the same year. Buds containing the flower primordia become dormant in late summer or autumn with the onset of short days (SD). Dormancy is broken by winter chilling and the buds become capable of opening as soon as the temperature rises. In several species buds containing flowers can grow at lower temperatures than vegetative buds. As a result the flowers of such plants as hazel, willow, ash, elm, and oak are functional before the leaves expand, an advantage in wind-pollination.

In most of the north temperate woody species which have been investigated, chilling is necessary to break bud dormancy when it has been fully induced by SD. Even so there are a few species which can be induced to resume growth under long days (LD) or continuous light. Buds of leafless seedlings of *Larix decidua, Betula* spp. and *Fagus sylvatica* placed under continuous illumination during the autumn will soon expand. There is also evidence that bud-break in *F. sylvatica* and *Rhododendron* may be dependent on increasing day-length in the spring. The hormonal control of seed and bud dormancy is unlikely to be the same in all species. Plant tissues contain both growth promoters (gibberellins, cytokinins) and growth inhibitors such as the sesquiterpenoid abscisic acid (ABA). The control of bud dormancy appears to involve complex interactions between components of these two groups.

Annual rhythms

Phenology is concerned with the onset and duration of the activity phases of animals and plants throughout the year. As these are largely synchronized to long-term changes in the weather the dates on which they occur differ from year to year, although the order in which the various plant species unfold their buds, flower, fruit and senesce is much the same.

One of the best known phenological diagrams showing the periods of active vegetative growth and of flowering is that for an oak-hornbeam wood in Hertfordshire (Fig. 1.3). This shows three species with pre-vernal flowering which is almost completed before the leaves of *Carpinus betulus* (hornbeam) are fully expanded in mid-May. The aerial parts of *Ranunculus ficaria* and *Anemone nemorosa* completely die down by the end of June, but *Mercurialis perennis* remains active throughout the summer and shoots are still present during the winter in some sheltered British woodlands. *Endymion non-scriptus* continues to flower until mid-June (vernal flowering), but then dies down very abruptly, though its capsules are held high above the ground until early autumn. *Conopodium majus* commences vegetative growth at the beginning of March, has aestival (summer) flowering starting in May, and continues active growth throughout the summer. The actual times at which the various seasonal aspects occur alter with climate. This is reflected in the dates at which particular species begin flowering in various parts of their range. For *Ranunculus ficaria* this is usually late February in Hertfordshire, early April in Germany, and late April in the Ukraine where the climate is continental.

Figure 4.5 divides the species into broad *phenological groups*; it is based on central European woodlands, but the flowering sequence is similar to that in Britain. This diagram deals with far fewer species than the original version,[83] which shows a number of plants not native to the U.K. Hollow corydalis (*Corydalis cava*), for example, is common in beech forests on good soil in southern Sweden and central Europe but is not found in Britain, where bluebell replaces it. *C. cava* flowers at the same time as lesser celandine, but its foliage, though produced later, dies back slightly earlier. The conspicuous *chasmogamous* ('opening') flowers of *Viola* and *Oxalis acetosella*, which can be visited by insects, are developed in spring. Later in the year these plants form *cleistogamous* flowers which are closed, much reduced and self-pollinated. Those of *O. acetosella* have hooked peduncles and are often buried in the plant litter; most seeds of wood sorrel are

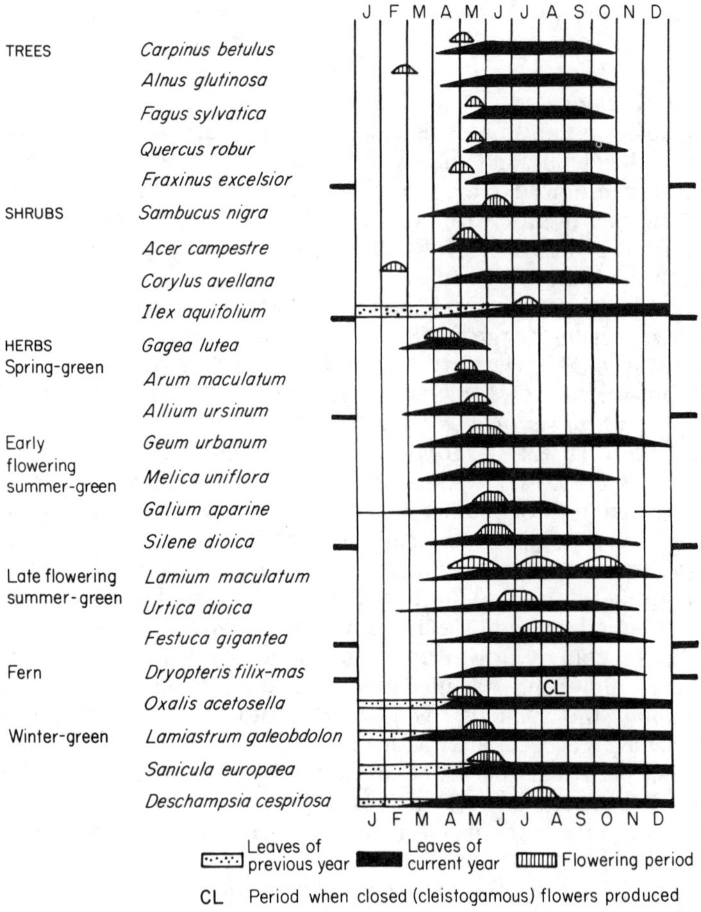

Fig. 4.5 Phenological development of different species in the tree, shrub and herb layers of central European damp oak-beech (*Quercus–Fagus*) forests. (After Ellenberg.[83])

produced by this type of flower. Cleistogamy is an efficient means of reproduction but its adoption reduces gene flow.

Recent studies of the phenology of such species as *Allium ursinum*[86] and *Endymion non-scriptus* (Fig. 4.6) have investigated percentage dry matter allocation to the organs of plants growing in their native woodland habitats; this contrasts with studies of plants grown in cultivation.[177] In both these geophytes the bulb is renewed annually, and there is considerable activity during the period spent

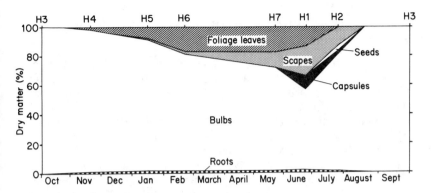

Fig. 4.6 Percentage dry matter allocation to plant organs in *Endymion non-scriptus* (bluebell) growing amongst *Pteridium aquilinum* (bracken) on an acidic sandy brown earth in an open region of Himley Wood, near Dudley, West Midlands. Note the high allocation to bulb weight. Each of the seven harvests (H1–H7) is based on the plants within a 0.1 m² area. Samples included plants of all the age classes present, but in this site there was a preponderance of mature bulbs, over 90% of bulb biomass occurring at a depth of 20 cm or more. (Unpublished data, by courtesy of P. W. Grabham.)

underground. At the beginning of October bluebell bulbs are hidden well below the surface of the soil, and have sloughed off the roots which were active in the previous summer. The roots beginning to emerge through the sides of each bulb are new; they arise from the base of a newly initated 'daughter' plant in the centre of the bulb. These roots make their way by enzyme action through the leaf and bud scales of the 'parent' bulb. By late autumn the bulb scales, specialized tubular scale leaves, foliage leaves, scape and flowers of the new plant are clearly differentiated. They increase in size as the old bulb withers; by mid February the shoot will often have emerged from the soil and begun to exploit the relatively high light intensities available on the forest floor before the tree canopy expands. The plant rapidly accumulates the food reserves needed for flowering and the formation of a new, and usually larger, bulb. In June flowering ends, capsules form, and the now flaccid leaves—which will soon decompose—come to rest on the soil surface. By autumn the cycle is complete and the seeds have been discharged from the capsules.

In *Endymion non-scriptus*, as in *Allium ursinum*, there is a high rate of seed output and seedling establishment per unit area of stand; vegetative propagation is relatively infrequent in both species. The reverse of this situation is seen in wild daffodil (*Narcissus pseudonarcissus*) where establishment by daughter bulbs is high in comparison to that by seedlings.

4.5   SILVICULTURE AND THE REPLACEMENT OF TREES

In natural forests most trees are maidens which have grown directly from seed, but in the past many managed woods were *coppiced*, the trunks being cut off near the ground so that fresh shoots grew from the stools every time a crop of poles was taken. Many species respond favourably to this treatment (Fig. 4.7) and are effectively rejuvenated by it; a hollow stool of *Fraxinus excelsior* on a rather damp site in west Suffolk is at least a thousand years old and has a diameter of 5.6 m (18½ft). Maple (*Acer*), wych elm (*Ulmus glabra*), oak, sweet chestnut, hazel, ash, alder, bass and lime (*Tilia* spp.), and the tulip tree (*Liriodendron tulipifera*) are amongst the species coppiced in various parts of the world, and some tropical trees such as teak (*Tectona grandis*) and *Eucalyptus* also shoot from the base after cutting. The coastal redwood (*Sequoia sempervirens*) is one of the few conifers which does this.

Using the methods illustrated in Fig. 4.7 woodsmen could maintain stands of trees indefinitely, even without seedlings. Modern methods of forest management are usually variants of *clear cutting, shelterwood* or *selection systems* which involve the growth of large numbers of seedlings, now often produced in enormous numbers in forest nurseries. If commercial seedlings are employed the trees are far more standardized, due to selection, than in older forests where individuals of such trees as *Quercus robur* show marked variation in size, leaf form and canopy shape.

Clear cutting involves harvesting trees of all sizes over a considerable area, a method frequently used with plantation monocultures. Sometimes such forests are allowed to regenerate by shooting from stumps or from seed; in the latter case trees are often cut down in strips or wedges so that seed can blow in from neighbouring stands. Clear cut areas are, however, more usually planted with seedlings, particularly in the case of conifers (Fig. 4.8) which are now often set out in Japanese paper pots.

Where scenic beauty is important, or where the forest is on steep slopes and prevents soil erosion or avalanches, *selection systems* come into their own. Here the aim is to maintain a balance between trees of all sizes, and often between different species; ideally the volume of timber felled is equal to the net increment each year. Unthrifty trees will be removed along with a number of others of various sizes, and the forest structure remains broadly the same for long periods of time. This system demands a high degree of skill on behalf of both management and workers, while the scattered logs are difficult to collect even with skidders. On the positive side, gaps in the canopy of

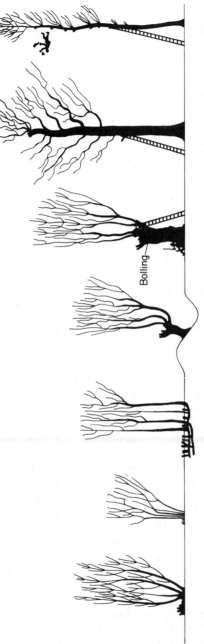

Bolling

Fig. 4.7 Methods of producing wood from trees. Left to right: coppice stool above ground (e.g. ash); coppice stool below ground (e.g. hazel); clone of suckers (e.g. elm); stub on boundary-bank; pollard; high pollard; shredded tree. The left-hand half of each has just been cut; the right-hand half is fully regenerated and is about to be cut again. (From Rackham.[21])

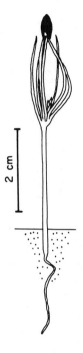

2 cm

Fig. 4.8 Young seedling of Scots pine (*Pinus sylvestris*). The hypocotyl has elongated and the tips of several cotyledons are still trapped within the testa. Three single needles borne on the developing plumule can just be seen.

protection forests using this system close swiftly, and the soil is never liable to severe erosion. Trees in such forests are wind firm and are said to be less liable to fire and pest damage,[173] but if a species is to arise from seed under such conditions it needs to be shade tolerant.

In *shelterwood systems* existing trees are harvested on two or more occasions, allowing the seedlings which will form the basis of the future woodland to become well established before the canopy is completely removed. In a previously poorly tended forest the first stage is to remove inferior trees so that seeds falling on the forest floor come from good quality parents. After some good seed years many of the parent trees are felled, thus providing an economic return and affording satisfactory light and moisture conditions for the developing seedlings. Finally, the last of the mature trees are removed when the seedlings are well established. With the shelterwood system commercial seedlings have to be used if natural regeneration is patchy, especially in the rather extreme variation known as the *seed tree system* where very few parent trees are left. These trees are vulnerable to wind blow, and offer little protection to the young seedlings which may be rapidly overgrown by weeds.

In the temperate zone there are now very few examples of truly wild or primaeval forests—*wildwood* in the sense of Rackham[20]—and soon there may be none. In the near future all tree communities are likely to become subject to one or other of the four main *silvicultural systems* described. Of these, selection systems give rise to forest most similar to wildwood, though the latter frequently contained more tree and shrub species. The chief differences lie in the possession by the wildwood of senescent trees, standing dead timber and decomposing logs, which encourage a diversity of birds, insects and other organisms. However, many semi-natural woodlands will continue to exist, and in these *gap regeneration* (see Section 5.2) is often similar to that in wildwood.

Silviculture treats forest trees as crops which are established, tended, harvested and then replaced by others. A *silvicultural system* encompasses (a) the regeneration of the trees, (b) the form of the crop produced, and (c) the orderly arrangement of the crops over the forest as a whole. The many different variants of the four main systems described above produce woodlands of distinctive character; the choice of which system to use is an important aspect of woodland management, particularly where soil and avalanche protection are involved. European foresters usually aim for yields which are regular and sustained rather than intermittent or spasmodic. From this concept of regularity has arisen the ideal of the *normal forest*, from which the same quantities of timber and other forest products can be taken in each year or period of years. In such a forest there is a complete succession of age classes; these classes are so balanced and distributed that as each class becomes mature it can be harvested (and then regenerated) to provide a similar yield to each of the classes which preceded it. In many parts of the world, however, forests are not being managed in this way and in others they are being destroyed rather than managed.

5

Succession

5.1 SUCCESSION AND CYCLIC CHANGE

Areas of bare ground are formed, for example, where glaciers are retreating, along rising coastlines, as landslip scars, at the bottom of drained lakes, and where severe flooding or fire has destroyed the previous vegetation. Such areas are usually rapidly colonized by organisms within reach of the bare substratum. As the vegetation develops it provides shade, enriches the soil with humus and, together with the associated animal communities, generally modifies the often harsh conditions originally present. This reaction with the environment allows more demanding species to establish, and the habitat becomes increasingly closed. Generally the original (pioneer) plants tend to be suppressed by competition from the mesophytes which, under the changed conditions, grow more vigorously than the pioneers. All this is part of *succession*: a non-seasonal directional change in the types and numbers of organisms present in a particular habitat over a period of time. Successional changes within plant communities provide a variety of niches for heterotrophs, so that, for example, successions of insects, birds and mammals or of soil fungi have been recognized as accompanying plant successions.

The classical concept of succession was developed by a number of workers, notably by Clements (1916),[64] who recognized six main phases in the process of succession:

1. *Nudation*, the production of an open area.
2. *Migration* of available species to the fresh habitat.
3. *Ecesis*, the adjustment of the plant to its new environment. This

involves the processes of germination (where spores or seeds are concerned), growth and reproduction.

4. *Competition* (both intra- and interspecific) between the organisms present in the habitat.

5. The *reaction* of plants and animals on the habitat, leading, for example, to the creation of the shade and nutrient-rich litter provided by young elm trees. Competition and reaction do not follow each other, they occur simultaneously.

6. Final *stabilization* of the community which reaches a climax at which it is held to be in equilibrium with its environment. *Climax* relates to the most complete adaptation of vegetation to the conditions of life found in the various climatic zones of the world.

The climatic climax is the only climax recognized by Clements,[65] a view often referred to as the *monoclimax theory*, though he noted the way in which soil, reaction, competition, migration barriers, and man could prevent the full development of the 'true' succession and so cause a number of 'subclimaxes'. Clements also viewed a plant formation as a supra-organism which arose, grew, matured and died. Tansley[26] placed greater emphasis on factors which could differentiate vegetation from the climatic climax, stabilizing it in corresponding edaphic, physiographic, biotic or anthropogenic climaxes (the *polyclimax theory*). Tansley drew attention to the dynamic nature of vegetation: 'each plant community has had an origin and will have a fate'. He realized that 'even climatic climax communities, though seemingly permanent so long as the existing climatic complex persists, may contain within them the seeds of their own decay', as when they cause changes in the soil which will eventually prevent the regeneration of the dominant species.

The six developmental phases described above constitute a *primary sere* in which climax vegetation, supposedly perfectly adapted to its environment, develops on an area of bare ground. Frequently, however, vegetation undergoes succession after being damaged but not destroyed. Such a *secondary sere* occurs, for example, when forest is clear felled and then abandoned in the hope that it will regenerate naturally. A *plagioclimax* develops when the vegetation is subject to some influence which deflects the progression of a sere in an unnatural way, such as the repeated selective felling of the most economically valuable species in a forest. The roles played by deer and other animals in deflecting forest successions can be demonstrated by *exclosure experiments*, as in northern Wisconsin, where protective legislation has led to high populations of white-tail deer (*Odocoileus virginianus*). These animals browse saplings of both sugar maple (*Acer saccharum*) and eastern hemlock (*Tsuga canadensis*), but the latter is more severely damaged. The rapid replacement of hemlock seedlings and saplings by sugar maple was reversed in trial plots from which the deer were excluded.

The climax concept poses many problems and is still vigorously discussed, for example, Kershaw,[134] Sprugel.[222] Clements[65] viewed climax as a self-reproducing equilibrium in which species composition and other properties of the ecosystem would be relatively constant through time. It is now clear that natural disturbance occurs far more frequently and is much more important in forest dynamics than was allowed for in the classic self-reproducing equilibrium-type climax (cf. Jones[130]). Indeed, in the cold damp climate of northern Finland old spruce stands become moribund; reproduction is poor even when gaps appear in the original canopy. Decomposition here is so slow that nutrients are not released in quantity until the site is burnt and normal regeneration becomes possible. In such an area a stable self-reproducing climax forest will never be achieved. Moreover, many North American forests previously though to be examples of climax vegetation are in fact large, wholly or partially even-aged stands which regenerated after fire (evidence for which is provided by charcoal in the soil), so the evidence they provide now has to be considered in an entirely different light. In recent years views have changed somewhat concerning the stability of climax forest; even the forested areas of the tropics are no longer believed to be as unchanging as previously thought.

Gales often modify the structure of forests. As long ago as 1913 Cooper[68] found 'a mosaic or patchwork which is in a state of constant change' on the Isle Royale, in the northwest of Lake Superior, where old windthrows regenerated as new ones developed. A similar structure is found in many forests; Sernander[214] described the mosaic found in old-growth Swedish spruce forests on unstable morainic soils as 'the storm-gap structure'. Figure 5.1a is a map of a typical area of the Fiby Forest, near Uppsala, which still possesses a structure very similar to that described by Sernander, whose efforts preserved it from felling. The radial increment diagram for a mature spruce shown in Fig. 5.1b illustrates the marked increase in width of the annual rings of this tree immediately after 1795, when very many mature trees were blown down.

Watt[236] investigated the relationships between the distribution patterns found in various plant communities and the processes by which they were produced. He described seven examples of mosaic vegetation in which the patches or phases are dynamically related to each other. In every instance the vegetation is interpretable as being in a state of **cyclic change** and the dominant species exhibits the phasic series pioneer, building, mature and degenerate during which its competitive ability changes. This series develops naturally in unmanaged woodlands, which frequently possess mosaic structure, but the same sequence is also exhibited by plantations, where it can be termed the *stand cycle*. During the **pioneer phase** of a woodland, tree seedlings frequently grow in an open area in which many herb species flourish. The canopy is closed by lateral contact between saplings early in the *building phase*, during which intra-specific competition is so intense that many trees are suppressed and die.[69] Accumulation of woody biomass reaches its peak in this phase during which, particularly in plantations of evergreen conifers, the ground flora is greatly diminished. In the *mature phase* competition between the trees is reduced and they bear their heaviest crops of seed. The canopy becomes less dense and shade tolerant herbs are able to establish. The *degenerate phase*, in which biomass accumulation is small and eventually negative, seldom occurs in commercial forests. Heart rots and other decay organisms reduce the quality and quantity of the wood. Branches die, trees often become stag-headed, dead organic matter accumulates in the ecosystem and herbs receive far more light (see Fig. 9.4).

In young stands of *Fagus sylvatica* on the South Downs there is intense shade and root competition between the young trees, whose initial high density decreases markedly as the woods age and a ground flora dominated by *Oxalis acetosella* develops where the soil, which rests on chalk, is not too shallow. Bramble later succeeds wood sorrel as the groundlayer dominant (Fig. 5.2) and Watt used this bare ground–*Oxalis acetosella*–*Rubus fruticosus* sequence to date stands of beechwoods growing on differing soils. The ground layer succession proceeds most rapidly in beechwoods on soils of the greatest depth and surface acidity, normally correlated with the highest humus content, lowest calcium carbonate level and closest texture.

Figure 5.3 shows the spatial distribution of bare, *Oxalis* and *Rubus* phases in an old unmanaged beechwood, together with the gap phase in which regeneration occurs following the death of old beech trees. The gaps (see Section 5.3) may at first be dominated by another kind of tree, such as ash, oak or birch, whose lighter shade allows young beech to grow more successfully than beneath *Fagus* itself. Such ancient woodlands with an uneven age structure give an idea of what primaeval wildwood was like and show the importance of cyclic change, often involving other tree species in gap regeneration, in maintaining temperate climax forests dominated by a single species. Though the mosaic pattern constantly changes, the overall species composition of a large area of such a forest remains broadly similar. However, as in many natural populations, particular age groups may be represented much more strongly than others. The events responsible for the existence of a large proportion of ancient trees in a semi-natural wood may have happened 200 or 300 years ago, when

(a)

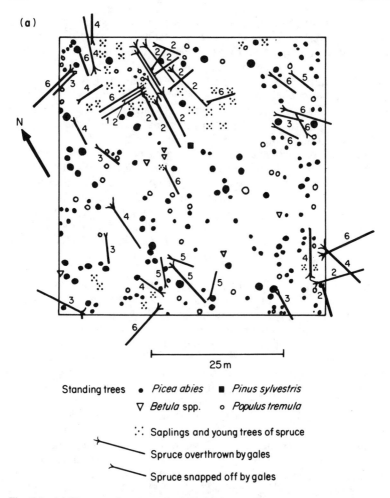

25 m

Standing trees   • *Picea abies*   ■ *Pinus sylvestris*

                  ▽ *Betula* spp.   ○ *Populus tremula*

                  ∴: Saplings and young trees of spruce

                  Spruce overthrown by gales

                  Spruce snapped off by gales

Fig. 5.1 **(a)** Diagram of an area of the Fiby Forest, near Uppsala, Sweden, showing 'storm gaps' resulting from the windthrow of Norway spruce (*Picea abies*) on boulder moraine. Storm gaps also develop on marly moraines. Seeds of spruce often germinate on the fallen trunks whose degree of decay (necrotization 1–6) is indicated. In stage 6 the area is usually entirely covered by a growth of moss, but a row of young trees may mark the line where the trunk fell and subsequently decayed. (Redrawn from Sernander.[214])

heavy masting and weather conducive to germination followed the death of many old trees from some general cause such as water stress.

Sprugel[222] describes a particularly regular type of cyclic change which occurs in balsam fir (*Abies balsamea*) forests at altitudes of

(b)

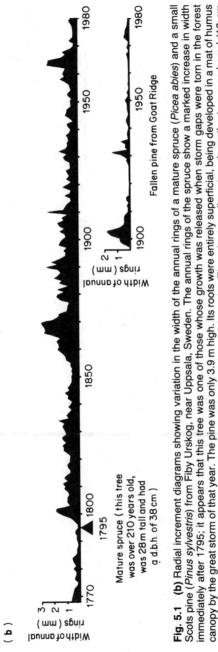

Width of annual rings (mm)

3
2
1

1770   1795   1800   1850   1900   1950   1980

Mature spruce (this tree
was over 210 years old,
was 28 m tall and had
a d.b.h. of 38 cm)

Width of annual rings (mm)

2
1

1900   1950   1980

Fallen pine from Goat Ridge

Fig. 5.1 (b) Radial increment diagrams showing variation in the width of the annual rings of a mature spruce (*Picea abies*) and a small Scots pine (*Pinus sylvestris*) from Fiby Urskog, near Uppsala, Sweden. The annual rings of the spruce show a marked increase in width immediately after 1795; it appears that this tree was one of those whose growth was released when storm gaps were torn in the forest canopy by the great storm of that year. The pine was only 3.9 m high. Its roots were entirely superficial, being developed in a mat of humus and vegetation (in which lichens were conspicuous) overlying solid granite. Though stem diameter where the tree was bored (10 cm above the ground) was only 6.5 cm, the increment core showed over 80 annual rings, some of them paper thin. (Unpublished data of H. Hytteborn and J. R. Packham.)

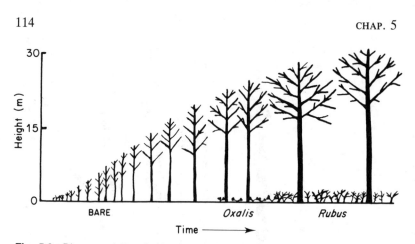

Fig. 5.2 Diagram of the phasic change during the life history of an even-aged beechwood (*Fagus sylvatica*), South Downs plateau, England. (Redrawn from Watt,[236] by courtesy of the *Journal of Ecology*.)

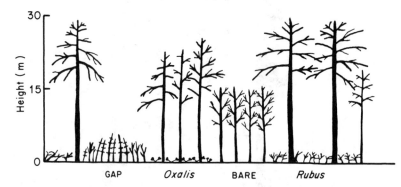

Fig. 5.3 The distribution of the phases in space when an old beechwood has been left to itself and has trees of all ages. Beech (*Fagus sylvatica*) is forming a reproduction circle in the gap (see Fig. 5.5). This typically has young ash (*Fraxinus excelsior*) in the centre. (Redrawn from Watt,[236] by courtesy of *Journal of Ecology*.)

over 1000 m in the north-eastern United States. Here aerial photographs show crescentic waves of dead trees which were at first thought to represent windthrown areas. Closer examination showed almost all the dead trees at the fronts of the crescents to be still standing; they did not fall until some time after death. In **wave regeneration** mature trees continually die off at the front edge of a wave, which lies behind an opening in the forest canopy and is exposed to the prevailing wind, while young trees spring up after the wave has passed on at a speed varying between 1 to 3 m yr⁻¹

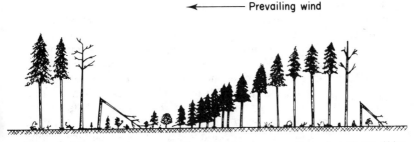

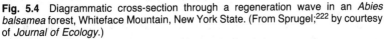

Fig. 5.4 Diagrammatic cross-section through a regeneration wave in an *Abies balsamea* forest, Whiteface Mountain, New York State. (From Sprugel;[222] by courtesy of *Journal of Ecology*.)

according to the degree of exposure (Fig. 5.4). Endogenous factors play a part in this rhythmic pattern. Balsam fir is moderately short-lived and becomes increasingly susceptible to stresses, particularly those caused by pathogens, at the age of 50–60 years. The trees bearing the brunt of the prevailing wind are very commonly partially senescent but are finally killed by environmental stress resulting from a loss of branches and needles in winter due to accumulations of rime-ice, death of needles owing to winter desiccation, and decreased primary productivity because of cooling of the leaves in summer. Their death releases the young saplings previously held in check by heavy shade and also exposes the trees immediately downwind to much greater environmental stress. Initiation of the individual waves is likely to occur when one, or a small group of trees, is killed by localized stress (e.g. windthrow, butt rot) exposing the arc of trees standing in the lee.

Regeneration waves in the *Abies balsamea* forests of New York, New Hampshire and Maine tend to follow each other at sixty year intervals. Very similar moving regeneration waves occur in *Abies vietchii* and *A. mariesii* forests at 2000–2700 m on several mountain ranges in Japan, but these firs grow more slowly and live longer (to about 100 years) than balsam fir so the waves tend to be further apart. In wave-regenerated forests there is an endless cycle in which the trees degenerate, die, regenerate, mature and degenerate again at any one point. The composition of the forest as a whole, however, remains relatively constant with time and the ecosystem is in a ***steady state***.

In a large steady state forest[222] features of the ecosystem such as net primary productivity, soil nitrate and species richness would show little or no variation with time, apart from seasonal changes. The 'steady state' theory takes into account the large-scale natural disturbances which occur in many forests, rather than assuming, as is implicit in the classical theory of climax, that tree-for-tree replacement is the normal pattern of ecosystem maintenance in all forest systems. It is unlikely that the maintenance mechanisms of all the varied types of forest are the same; there may indeed be some forests where large-scale disturbances are so rare that tree-for-tree replacement is the normal pattern of regeneration. The steady state concept, however, applies very well to forests in which such disturbances are a normal feature, including those which are fire-controlled, fire-susceptible, have a storm-gap structure, or are wave-regenerated. Such a system could also be expected to adapt well in the face of long term changes in the weather.

The changes which occur in the composition of communities associated with decomposition contrast with the autotrophic successions described in this chapter. A number of natural 'degradative successions' occur which end, not with a climax community, but a completely decomposed food material. The nature of these successions is discussed in Section 8.2.

5.2 THE MAINTENANCE OF SPECIES RICHNESS IN WOODLANDS

Woodlands vary in species richness, but many display a very great variety of plant life. What allows the development of the many-splendoured diversity of a temperate deciduous woodland or of a tropical forest? Competition between animals is often seen to be very direct; these mobile organisms frequently engage in physical combat or compete for the same food. This relates closely to the principle of *competitive exclusion* which was defined by Gause:[95] '. . . as a result of competition two similar species scarcely ever occupy similar niches, but displace each other in such a manner that each takes possession of certain peculiar kinds of food and modes of life in which it has an advantage over its competitor'. In so writing he was using the definition given by Elton:[84] 'the *niche* of an animal means its place in the biotic environment, its relations to food and enemies'. Zoologists generally accept the idea that in order to survive in a community at equilibrium every animal species must occupy a different niche. The full requirements of an animal are complex and it is easy to envisage many types of animal niche, whereas all photo-autotrophic plants need light, carbon dioxide, water and the same mineral nutrients, though their tolerances of various environmental conditions differ.

Woodland autotrophs, in contrast to animals, are sedentary when adult, so many of the most critical aspects of competition between them must concern the struggle to occupy any areas of ground which become bare. Mobility in green plants is usually restricted to the seeds or other propagules, which are dispersed in a variety of ways (Section 4.1). Mechanisms which contribute to plant diversity in woodlands without involving the *regeneration gap* are reviewed in Section 3.4. Grubb[103] shows that these alone are insufficient to provide an adequate explanation of why species richness can persist in plant communities; it is a failure to consider the nature of regeneration that has caused many to reject 'Gause's hypothesis' with respect to plants. Heterogeneity of the environment (physico-chemical and biotic) ensures that the replacement plant, or plants, which come to occupy the regeneration gap left when a plant dies may sometimes be of a species different from that present formerly. The replacement stage is thus crucial to our understanding of species diversity in plant communities, and to the basic processes of evolutionary divergence in plants.

Only when differences in their seeding patterns, germination and early life are considered is it possible to understand why so many species of essentially similar life-form, adult phenology and habitat-range persist together in species-rich communities. The size of the gap is itself important; when a large tree falls the gap produced is likely to be dominated next by a light-demanding species such as birch, pine or ash, whereas shade-tolerant species such as beech or western hemlock are more likely to be the next occupants where the gap in the canopy is small.

The successful invasion of a gap by a given species will be influenced by the timing of processes leading to the production of the means of vegetative reproduction (e.g. stolons, rhizomes, suckers, bulbils) or, more usually, of viable seed (flowering, pollination, setting of seed), its dispersal in space and time, requirements for germination (Section 4.1), establishment and onward growth. The orientation, size, shape, and time of formation of gaps help to provide heterogeneity in the environment, as do the nature of the soil surface, the litter, other plants, animals, fungi, bacteria and viruses present. All stages and processes leading to the replacement of a mature tree or other plant by another are important, though as Grubb[103] remarks 'The idea that all these stages are important in the maintenance of species-richness has been all too often ignored'.

Foresters realized early the importance of differences in regeneration requirements; at first tolerance to shade received emphasis but later differences were recognized in the ability to tolerate root competition. Aubréville[40] suggested that any one tree species never regenerated under itself in the African rain forests that he had studied. This is not true of forest trees in general, though direct regeneration beneath a complete canopy of the parent tree does not occur in some species.

Three factors are particularly significant in controlling the sequence of events during the colonization of a gap developed in *Fagus sylvatica* woodland:[235]

1. The age of the woodland. If the wood is not completely mature but still has much ash and oak there will be plenty of shrubs and herbs to colonize the gap. Later in the succession, when the beech is almost pure, the lower strata may be largely suppressed or even absent. If bramble (*Rubus fruticosus* agg.) colonizes the woodland floor at about the time that the beech begins to bear seed it may grow so luxuriantly in the gap as to prevent regeneration unless cut over. In a natural forest, however, the passage of large mammals would probably damage the bramble cover sufficiently for ash or oak seedlings to grow up and at least partially suppress the bramble, thus enabling beech to develop again.

2. The size of the gap is important because beech mast formed in high forest drops almost vertically and is largely confined to the margins of wide gaps, the centres of which are often occupied by a dense growth of common ash (Fig. 5.5) whose seed is wind dispersed. The occasional beech seedling has little chance of establishing in the central core of ash until the taller growth and deeper shade of the young peripheral beech, together with the gradual extension of the parent beech canopy, tend to suppress the more light-demanding ash. The outcome varies, but in at least some cases the ash in the centre of the gap grows upwards fast enough to avoid suppression. In narrow gaps the whole floor can be seeded by the beech whose seedlings and saplings may not meet with competition from any other tree.

3. The time when the gap is formed in relation to a full-mast year. If the beeches have just seeded heavily their seedlings can establish themselves before a serious competitor, such as bramble, can fill the gap. When beechwoods are managed on the selection system it is important to fell and extract mature trees in winters when there is plenty of viable mast in the soil. Even when this operation was carried out 30 years previously, mapping of the surviving, relatively young, trees often provides evidence of the original reproduction circles.

Seed availability is crucial to the subsequent development of the regeneration gap. In practice early successional species usually appear soon after woodlands are disturbed by fire, cultivation, severe thinning or windthrow. There is strong evidence that these plants often develop from seeds which have long been buried in the soil. For example, investigations of mineral soil cores (taken after careful removal of up to 8 cm of litter and humus) from 16 sites in successional field and forest stands in Harvard Forest, Massachusetts,

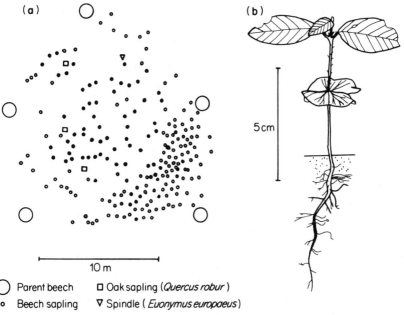

(a)

○ Parent beech   □ Oak sapling (*Quercus robur*)
o Beech sapling   ▽ Spindle (*Euonymus europaeus*)
● Ash sapling

Fig. 5.5. **(a)** Reproduction circle of beech (*Fagus sylvatica*) from Fig. 5.3. The gap is in beech associes (sere 2) and has ash in the centre and a peripheral zone of young beech. Beech has epigeal germination; the two semi-circular cotyledons of the seedling **(b)** are photosynthetically active for a considerable period. ((a) Redrawn from Watt,[235] by courtesy of *Journal of Ecology*.)

showed that seeds of many field species germinated in virtually all the soils tested. The number of species present as viable seed was not greatly different whether the soil came from recently abandoned cultivated fields, dense *Pinus strobus* plantations devoid of ground cover, or an 80-year-old *P. strobus* stand with a hardwood under-storey which represented the mature phase of the secondary succession from old field. Seed populations beneath *Pinus resinosa* and *Picea rubens* were similar to those under *Pinus strobus*.[146]

Seeds of late successional and climax species, together with those of most trees, tend to be deposited in surface litter and humus. Many are carried into forest stands by wind; birds and mammals transport others. Nevertheless, woodland floors frequently contain viable seeds of many successional species from pioneer to climax. This can be of commercial importance as in the control of blister rust in the western white pine (*Pinus monticola*) in North America where *Ribes* spp., alternate hosts of the fungal pathogen, developed again after systematic eradication, cutting of old-growth forests and burning of slash. Viable seeds present in the soil were favoured by humus reduction and the increased light and temperature.[172] Various species of *Rubus* frequently establish rapidly when European and North American woodlands are disturbed. The fact that forest soils contain so many of their seeds, which are widely dispersed and remain viable after passing through the gut of many birds and mammals, is a major contribution to the success of this genus.

5.3 FOREST CHANGE AND SERAL WOODLANDS

It must be very unusual for the condition of any substantial area of vegetation to remain static; change is ever present. Similarly the fact that a particular type of vegetation has developed in a certain way in one instance is no guarantee that a similar succession would develop from the same starting point at another time, or in another place, even if conditions were only slightly different. Fascinating though it is to reconstruct the ways in which forests have developed, one must not think of such successional schemes as being immutable; future forests may well evolve differently even if left undisturbed. This section is concerned with the changes which have occurred in recent times in an ancient and relatively stable forest, and also with the development of seral woodlands. All the examples considered involve change, usually of mangement but in one case of climate.

Change in an ancient Polish forest

Well established and apparently non-seral forests may show evidence of marked changes in the proportions of the dominant trees, a feature which can often be detected by measuring the stem diameters of the trees (Fig. 5.6). A good example is afforded by a typical area of the National Park created by the Polish Government in the forest of Białowieża in 1923. At about this time[186] there were many large old trees of *Tilia cordata* (small-leaved lime) but virtually no young ones. In contrast, hornbeam and Norway maple were regenerating, though not so strongly as Norway spruce. The species present vary with the soils but almost half the wooded area of the Park is now covered by Querceto-Carpinetum in which the main tree species are *Carpinus betulus, Tilia cordata, Quercus robur, Acer platanoides, Ulmus glabra* and *Picea abies*. The forest is primary in the sense that most of it has had a virtually uninterrupted tree-cover since prehistoric times. A survey in 1973 showed an almost continuous canopy of hornbeam with tall emergent trees of small-leaved lime, common oak and Norway spruce (Fig. 5.7). Small-leaved lime now regenerates freely. Groups of seedlings, saplings and young trees are common both in

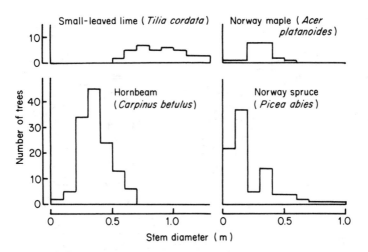

Fig. 5.6 Frequency of trees in successive diameter-classes for the principal species in a typical plot of one hectare in the Białowieża Forest, Poland, before 1928. (Histograms redrawn from Pigott;[186] by courtesy of The Royal Society.)

gaps and beneath the main canopy; those of lime probably all date from later than 1923 so there is a discontinuity in the distribution of the diameter classes of this tree (Fig. 5.8).

As with many forest trees the amount of fruit produced by *Tilia cordata* varies widely from year to year. The direct influence of climate is most marked at the northern limit of distribution, which is reached in northern England but extends further north in Finland and Sweden. At its northern English limit the species flowers in July and August, but produces only small quantities of fertile seed and then only in very warm summers such as that of 1976. This is caused by failure of fertilization in the cool oceanic climate of Britain. In the more continental climate of Finland fertilization normally occurs but the seeds of northern trees fail to complete their development by autumn. Fruiting is prolific and much more frequent in central Europe and commences when the trees are more than 25 years old. In Russia *T. cordata* produces the best quality seed in the upper part of the crown; initiation of inflorescences and formation of fruit occur only on unshaded branches. This is true even in the Białowieża Forest where July and August are normally warm and sunny with mean air temperatures of 19–20° C. In the unbroken forest the production of fertile fruit during 1973 was almost confined to the emergent crowns of old trees, around which quite high densities of seedlings are visible even in August.

Although rooting by wild pigs (*Sus scrofa*) usually kills existing

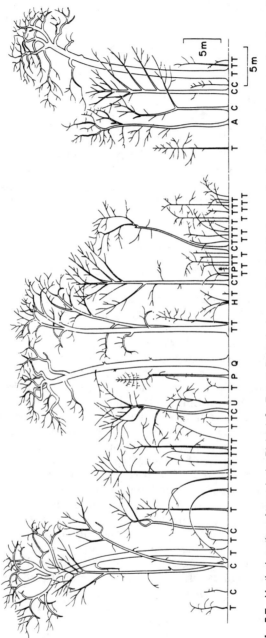

Fig. 5.7 Vertical section of trees in the Białowieża Forest, Poland, along a strip of width 2 m passing through 2 main groups of saplings of *Tilia cordata*. **T**, *Tilia cordata*; **C**, *Carpinus betulus*; **A**, *Acer platanoides*; **U**, *Ulmus glabra*; **Q**, *Quercus robur*; **H**, *Corylus avellana*; **P**, *Picea abies*. (From Pigott;[186] by courtesy of The Royal Society.)

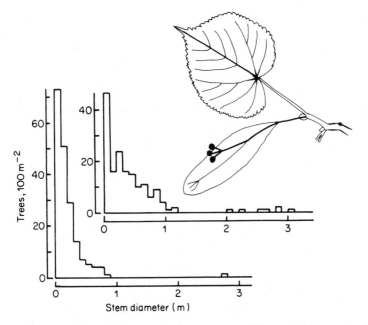

Fig. 5.8 Frequency of trees of small-leaved lime (*Tilia cordata*) in successive girth-classes in two plots, each of 0.25 ha, recorded from the Białowieża Forest in 1973. Note the large bracteole to which the flower buds are attached. (Histograms redrawn from Pigott;[186] by courtesy of The Royal Society.)

plants, it often improves conditions for the subsequent establishment of tree seedlings by exposing mineral soil. Solitary boars or family groups destroy the herbaceous vegetation, remove the litter and tear up rhizomes or stolons of *Aegopodium podagraria*, *Asarum euro-paeum*, *Lamiastrum galeobdolon* and *Stellaria holostea*. Pigott[186] noted that the patches disturbed in this way were similar in size to those occupied by groups of tree seedlings, and that the pigs might destroy the surface roots of trees and temporarily eliminate root competition as in trenched-plot experiments.

Tree seedlings develop beneath the tree canopy as well as where there are gaps. Measurements made in August indicated that the irradiance beneath the general canopy was greater than that known to be necessary (c. 200–300 kJ m^{-2} d^{-1}) for the growth of the seedlings of small-leaved lime, wych elm and hornbeam. A very deeply shaded site beneath an even-aged stand of lime gave values of less than 200 kJ m^{-2} d^{-1}. Seedlings of lime were completely absent from this and other very heavily shaded areas though scattered patches of wood sorrel and asarabacca (*Asarum europaeum*) occurred. Groups of young tree seedlings in the gaps often contain more than one species: if such groups later consist of only one species this must be the result of competition. Groups growing beneath shade, however, usually consist of a single species. This may be due to different requirements for germination, but arises partly from the uneven distribution of the seed parents and the large variations in the amount of fruit produced in particular years by individual trees. Limited seed availability may well lead to an area being colonized by a single species though the conditions within it are suitable for the seedlings of several.

Certain herbs can largely prevent the establishment of particular species of tree seedlings. Common stinging nettle (*Urtica dioica*) frequently establishes and grows vigorously in gaps, where the soluble phosphate in the top 5 cm of soil of the area tested was higher than beneath the canopy. Hornbeam seedlings were absent from all the examined regions where stinging nettle was growing, while lime seedlings were very sparse where nettles grew vigorously. Well established wych elm seedlings were found in all the nettle clumps, growing at very low irradiance. This is interesting as *Ulmus glabra* seedlings of English origin tend, if anything, to be less tolerant of shade than those of *Tilia cordata*. The relative susceptibilities of various species of tree seedlings to fungal disease and predation by invertebrates may be an important factor in their survival under the moist shaded conditions of nettle clumps.

Tilia cordata is more abundant in the central region, which includes the National Park, than elsewhere in the Białowieża forest. In 1928 Paczoski attributed this to the tree's sensitivity to exploitation, the central area having been least heavily managed. Much of the forest away from the National Park had the same herbaceous vegetation, differing only in the much smaller proportion of *T. cordata* and a corresponding increase in *Quercus robur* and *Acer platanoides*. The gap in the regeneration of *Tilia cordata* extends backwards from about 1923 to before 1870, a period when the area was maintained as a hunting reserve for the Czars. During this period the number of carnivores was low and many deer and European bison were kept for hunting: if this helped cause the failure of regeneration in small-leaved lime it did not prevent that of other trees.

Vigorous regeneration of lime since 1923 has caused the proportion of young trees in the population to become very high, so the forest still has features derived from selective thinning. Its previous condition represented a *plagioclimax* in which the proportion of limes was kept at an unusually low level by some factor connected with the management at that time.

In the oak-lime-hornbeam forest *Tilia cordata* appears to be the potential dominant. The mature trees are long-lived and very tall, and the species is very shade tolerant when young. Hornbeam is shorter-lived and forms a lower canopy; it is likely to be displaced, at least for a time, from its present predominant role. In the National Park *Quercus robur* exists as large isolated trees; though seedlings occur sparsely in gaps, young trees and saplings are almost absent so the situation with regard to this species has scarcely changed since 1930. In contrast, oaks of all ages are present in oak-lime-hornbeam forest outside the Park and in association with *Pinus sylvestris* and *Picea abies* within it. Even though this area contains some of the least disturbed mixed forest in the European lowlands it is clearly not in equilibrium, and retains characteristics originating from the silvicultural treatment which ceased entirely in 1923.

Development of woodland on chalk soils

Management is even more important in chalk grassland which soon reverts to scrub in the absence of mowing or heavy grazing by cattle, sheep and rabbits. Table 5.1 illustrates some of the main features involved in the eventual succession to beechwood on the chalk soils

Table 5.1   Seres of woody vegetation on chalk soils. (After Tansley,[26] by courtesy of Cambridge University Press.)

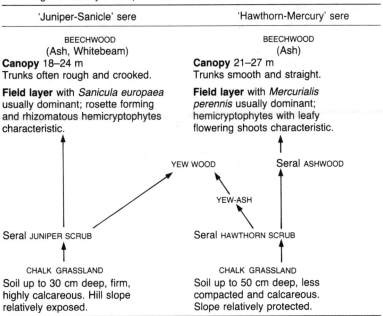

'Juniper-Sanicle' sere	'Hawthorn-Mercury' sere
BEECHWOOD (Ash, Whitebeam) **Canopy** 18–24 m Trunks often rough and crooked.	BEECHWOOD (Ash) **Canopy** 21–27 m Trunks smooth and straight.
Field layer with *Sanicula europaea* usually dominant; rosette forming and rhizomatous hemicryptophytes characteristic.	**Field layer** with *Mercurialis perennis* usually dominant; hemicryptophytes with leafy flowering shoots characteristic.

YEW WOOD   Seral ASHWOOD

YEW-ASH

Seral JUNIPER SCRUB   Seral HAWTHORN SCRUB

| CHALK GRASSLAND
Soil up to 30 cm deep, firm, highly calcareous. Hill slope relatively exposed. | CHALK GRASSLAND
Soil up to 50 cm deep, less compacted and calcareous. Slope relatively protected. |

of the Chiltern escarpments; the sequence on the South Downs is similar. The hawthorn (*Crataegus monogyna*) sere typically develops on the gentler, more sheltered slopes of the relatively soft Middle Chalk where the soil is moist, quite deep and can support luxuriant growth. The firmer and shallower soil of the juniper (*Juniperus communis*) sere frequently develops on the harder strata of the Upper Chalk, has a lower humus content in the surface layers, a lower water-holding capacity, and sparser leaf litter under the mature beechwood. A major difference between the two seres is that the beech colonizes juniper scrub directly, whereas seral ashwood often, and on the South Downs usually, succeeds hawthorn scrub before the beech enters the succession.

The habit of the juniper bushes shows two extremes. One is erect and averages 1.8–2.4 m high (though an exceptional 6 m has been recorded), the other low and widespreading. Hawthorn is the most widespread dominant in English scrub, flourishing on many soil types and occurring in the succession to oakwood as well as to beechwood. Dogwood (*Cornus sanguinea*), privet (*Ligustrum vulgare*), blackthorn (*Prunus spinosa*), buckthorn (*Rhamnus catharticus*) and wayfaring tree (*Viburnum lantana*) are very constant in chalk scrub, which has by far the most species of any British scrub type. Brambles and various species of *Rosa* are often pioneers. Spindle (*Euonymus europaeus*) and elder (*Sambucus nigra*) are also characteristic; field maple and hazel flourish particularly on deeper soils towards the bottoms of slopes, while *Clematis vitalba* is the characteristic and often luxuriant woody climber.

Whitebeam (*Sorbus aria*) is one of the commonest trees in chalk scrub and frequently persists in the canopy of the mature beechwood, as can the less abundant gean (*Prunus avium*). Pedunculate oak (*Quercus robur*) is unable to form trees of more than 4 m on the shallow chalk soils though its seedlings are widespread. Common ash and beech have a high constancy in chalk scrub, though ash is much commoner on the South Downs than in the Chilterns. Yew (*Taxus baccata*) colonizes chalk scrub very readily. Individual trees frequently live to a great age, excluding competition from other trees and shrubs by means of the very deep shade which they cast. Dead (relict) trees and bushes of scrub species such as whitebeam and juniper can often be found in yew woods, as at Kingley Vale near Chichester. This, the finest yew wood in Europe, is a fitting memorial to Sir Arthur Tansley, the father of British ecology. Besides the pure yew wood, mixed yew-ash woods also occur on the chalk escarpment, with fine old oak and yew growing on the loam of the valley bottom.

When beech directly colonizes juniper scrub on the exposed slopes of the Chilterns it rapidly kills the pioneer bushes, which are intolerant of shade, and forms closed beechwood. The transition from hawthorn scrub is more gradual. Any juniper present is soon shaded out, while hawthorn gradually decreases in abundance. Bramble, hazel and elder tend to remain as woodland species appear in the field layer. While *Sanicula europaea* is more constant on the shallow soils of the juniper sere, which will eventually give rise to a 'sanicle' beechwood, and *Mercurialis perennis* on the deeper soils of the hawthorn sere where a 'mercury' beechwood will develop, there is no profound difference between the field layers of the two seres. *Zerna ramosa* is more frequent in immature sanicle woods, and enchanter's nightshade (*Circaea lutetiana*) slightly more so in immature mercury woods.

In ash scrub on the deeper chalk soils hemicryptophytes with basal rosettes, such as *Fragaria vesca* and *Viola hirta*, are later displaced by mercury with its tall leafy shoots. Seral ashwood contains many field layer species characteristic of mature mercury beechwood, which will later develop in its place.

The relationships shown in Table 5.1 were worked out between the two World Wars by Dr A. S. Watt at a time when grazing by rabbits was intense and sheep were reared on most of the South Downs. Changing agricultural practices and the outbreak of myxomatosis, which greatly reduced the rabbit pressure for at least ten years from 1953 onwards, allowed woody vegetation to develop in many areas, notably the hawthorn-ash-bramble scrub on the steeper slopes of the Downs inland from Brighton. At Kingley Vale, juniper has been adversely affected by the reduction in grazing and young plants are much less common than previously. Though most of the gentler slopes are currently employed for cereal growing or dairying, some of the steeper sites have been largely abandoned and may become covered by woodland again.

Development of coniferous forest on glacial moraine

Successions from bare moraine to mature conifer forest afford striking illustrations of primary seres in which changes in the vegetation cover are accompanied by major alterations in soil conditions. A sequence of this type occurs in areas left bare by retreating ice in Glacier Bay, south-east Alaska, where climax forest develops in about 250 years. Ring counts show the oldest trees on the last morainic ridge to be about 200 years old; the maximum age of trees on the moraines decreases progressively as the glacier is approached. The oldest trees in the area are over 600 years old and grow in places beyond the furthest reach of glacial activity. The stages of succession are shown in Table 5.2; on well drained slopes the climax vegetation is coniferous forest dominated by *Picea sitchensis* with some *Tsuga*

Table 5.2 Succession from bare moraine to mature spruce forest in the Glacier Bay region, south-east Alaska.

Sphagnum dominated◄── ── ──SITKA SPRUCE FOREST
MUSKEG in poorly   Initially pure—later with western and mountain
drained areas   hemlock

↑

ALDER (*Alnus crispa*) thickets with scattered
cottonwood (*Populus trichocarpa*)

↑

WILLOW STAGE (*Salix barclayi, S. sitchensis, S. alexensis*)
These are at first prostrate but become erect and form dense scrub

↑

PIONEER STAGE Moraine colonized by *Rhacomitrium canescens, R. lanuginosum, Epilobium latifolium, Equisetum variegatum, Dryas drummondii* and *Salix arctica.*

heterophylla and *T. mertensiana*. Where the ground is flat, or has only a gentle slope, water-filled *Sphagnum* comes to dominate the moss mat and the forest floor becomes soggy. Occasional scattered individuals of lodgepole pine (*Pinus contorta*) are the only trees which can tolerate the poor aeration of the resulting muskeg.

Marble is present in the area and the soil parent material has a pH of 8.0–8.4. Figure 5.9 shows the rates at which the pH of this material falls when left bare or covered by different types of vegetation. Alder has a strongly acidifying effect, lowering the pH of the surface soil from approximately 8.0 to 5.0 within 30–50 years. It then remains at about the same as spruce invades—the pH values of the leaf litter of alder and spruce are similar. The nodules on the alder roots contain microorganisms (actinomycetes) which fix atmospheric nitrogen; the resulting increase in soil nitrogen is probably crucial to the initial establishment of the spruce, and soil nitrogen values decline somewhat after the elimination of alder. The gradual accumulation of soil carbon is important in creating a good crumb structure, which assists soil aeration and the movement of soil water.

Old field successions: monolayer and multilayer trees
Many of the principles governing forest succession are illustrated by the 'old field' sequences which developed as the American west opened up in the nineteenth century, and many eastern farms were abandoned. Natural regeneration was swift, even though the farmers had destroyed almost all the pre-colonial mixed conifer-hardwood forest. The resulting successions demonstrate the importance of the

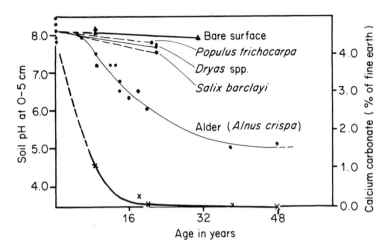

Fig. 5.9 Rate of change of reaction in the 0–5 cm horizon relative to type of vegetation cover. Change in calcium carbonate content (×) under *Alnus crispa* is shown by the lowermost curve. (Redrawn from Crocker and Major,[70] courtesy of *Journal of Ecology*.)

geometrical arrangements of tree leaves in suiting various trees to different light and water regimes, and thus to different stages in the sequence. Trees[114, 115] may be considered to have two main patterns of leaf arrangement, the multilayer and the monolayer; the optimal arrangement for intercepting and utilizing light depends on the amount of light reaching the tree, whose number of leaf layers can be estimated using a light meter technique. Many tree leaves in temperate areas can reach about 90% of their maximal rate of photosynthesis when they are receiving as little as 25% of full sunlight. When incident light is less than this, **monolayer** species, in which there is a single layer of leaves in a shell round the tree, are the most efficient, intercepting all the available light at its highest intensity. In crowded stands of trees such as the sugar maple and the American beech (*Fagus grandifolia*) there may be just one unit of leaf area for each unit of ground area beneath the tree, i.e. LAI is one. This is a very efficient arrangement in late successional species which produce dense foliage at the branch tips. Sugar maple and American beech both cast heavy shade and can come to dominate secondary forest.

Multilayered trees on the other hand produce leaves along those interior branches which receive enough light to be above compensation point, as well as at the tips of well lit branches. Trees of this form, including bigtooth aspen (*Populus grandidentata*), grey birch

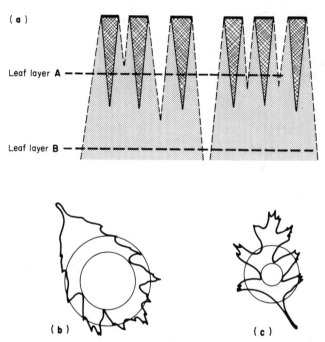

Fig. 5.10 The adaptive geometry of trees. **(a)** The shadow of a leaf layer. The umbra of each of the leaves in the highest layer is shown hatched. Leaves in this top layer would at a particular time completely obscure the sun from parts of leaves in a layer at **A**, but not from any part of a layer at **B**. **(b)**, **(c)** Leaves of black oak (*Quercus velutina*). Leaf **(b)** from a shaded branch near the ground and **(c)** from the top of the crown. Leaves of seedlings of this American tree have lobes proportionately smaller than those of **(b)**. The small circle is the largest circle that can be inscribed in each leaf. The larger circle has the same surface area as the leaf. The relative sizes of the two circles show how well lobing adapts the leaf for a multilayered distribution. (From Horn.[114] Copyright © 1971 by Princeton University Press, reprinted by permission of Princeton University Press.)

(*Betula populifolia*) and eastern red cedar (*Juniperus virginiana*), are best able to utilize the abundant light available at the start of an old field succession when they can grow more rapidly than the monolayer species. In this early seral stage the pioneer multilayer forms may be expected to dominate the hot, dry and sunny canopy, while mono-layer shrubs and herbs are likely to be the successful forms in the understorey which is cooler, moister and shadier. The late succes-sional monolayer species have seedlings which can develop in such an understorey, eventually ousting the pioneer multilayer species beneath which they establish. Seedlings of the multilayer forms are at a disadvantage in such an understorey and are usually shaded out.

Horn[114] describes the theoretical basis of the ways in which leaf size and distribution influence photosynthetic efficiency and drought resistance. The average length of the *umbra* of a leaf (the shadow within which the sun is hidden) is effectively proportional to the diameter of the largest circle which can be inscribed within the leaf (Fig. 5.10). The distance at which the shadow of a circle vanishes is about 50 to 70 times its diameter with the sun at its zenith on a clear day, whereas under uniformly cloudy conditions light comes from a solid 180°, and the shadow of a circle disappears at a distance equal to its diameter. If no leaves are to be in total shade, the minimum distance between the layers of multilayer trees in sunny climates is thus much greater than in cloudy ones, assuming leaf size to be constant. Conversely leaf size can be much greater for a given inter-layer distance in a cloudy climate than a sunny one. Light intercepted by the shoot but not reflected, transmitted, or used in photosynthesis, must be dissipated as heat. In a monolayer this heat load is concentrated in a single layer of leaves, but in a multilayer it is spread over several layers so this form is more resistant to drought. Further, the small size of the leaves of multilayer plants increases the efficiency with which accumulated heat is carried away by convection currents. Horn[114] argues that as leaves with a high heat load must transpire at a greater rate than those with a low one, water loss per unit of photosynthesis would be greater for a monolayer than a multilayer tree.

On these general theories we can expect—when soils are reasonably moist and light is the limiting factor—multilayer trees to invade open fields, for the seedlings of monolayer trees to develop beneath them and for the climax monolayer trees to cast so dense a shade that even their own seedlings would have great difficulty in establishing. This may well lead to a senile forest in which trees can establish only in gaps left by the decline and death of individuals which have lived for hundreds of years. In xeric successions, however, drought will prevent monolayer trees from competing effectively with multilayer species at late stages in the sequence.

In most forests the distribution of trees is influenced by so wide a variety of abiotic and biotic factors that diversity is maintained. There are also multilayer trees, including *Sequoia sempervirens, Sequoiadendron giganteum,* a fire-dependent species,[23] and *Pinus strobus,* that are extremely persistent in the later stages of the succession as well as being very efficient pioneers. Thus, although we can undoubtedly gain valuable insight from generalizing theories such as those of Horn, it is important to consider the behaviour of all the individual species in attempts to understand the mechanisms of forest succession.

5.4 ORIGIN OF BRITISH WOODLANDS AND THEIR FLORAS

Because of their east-west alignment, the European mountain chains prevented easy migrations of trees and other plants to and from refuges south of the Alps and Pyrenees during the Ice Age which began at the beginning of the Quaternary. In North America the major mountain ranges run north-south so that there, as in eastern Asia, the major elements of the rich Arcto-Tertiary forests were able to retreat south along continental migration routes, whereas in western Eurasia these complex forests were destroyed by the ice. Today we can only fully appreciate their former magnificence by visiting the mixed mesophytic forests of the Southern Appalachians or eastern Asia, areas far richer in tree and understorey species than any other temperate forests.

Interglacial sequences

At the start of each interglacial period the ice sheets wane in response to a gradual rise in temperature which reaches its peak at the *climatic optimum* and then declines. Annual precipitation increases as the temperature rises, but is then often maintained at a high level for most of the interglacial period. Heavy leaching under cold conditions, in which chemical weathering proceeds slowly, causes the amounts of available mineral nutrients in the soil to dwindle, particularly in upland areas, as the interglacial draws towards its end. Between glaciations plants which survived in refuges in the south, or on elevated areas which escaped the ice, have recolonized areas devastated by glacial incursions.

The trees which recolonized the country during the interglacials came from areas far to the south and east. As one glaciation succeeded another the indigenous tree flora became more impoverished. Examples of losses include Norway maple (*Acer platanoides*) and Norway spruce which both grew in Britain during the last complete interglacial, the Ipswichian, and silver fir (*Abies alba*) present in the previous Hoxnian interglacial. *Pterocarya* was present in the Hoxnian, and occurred with *Carya* in the early Pleistocene.

Evidence of these previous floras comes from fossils found in sedimentary deposits, especially *microfossils* in the form of pollen grains. The exine (outer coat) of these grains is extremely resistant to decay (especially in acid media), and much of our knowledge of Quaternary floras[9, 19] is derived from the pollen complement of cores

extracted from peat bogs, lakes and estuarine muds, often supplemented by **macrofossils** including wood, bark, leaves, bud-scales,
fruits and seeds. The cores are laboriously studied, layer by layer,
and reveal changes in the pattern of pollen deposition, and hence of
the previous plant population, with time. Pollen analysis (**palynology**)
involves many problems of interpretation; anemophilous plants
produce far more pollen than those which are entomophilous, and
some pollen grains preserve better than others. Wetland species
growing close to the deposit are over-represented, while the reverse
is true of plants at a distance from it. Discontinuities in the deposition
of the sedimentary material cause the record to be incomplete, and
care must be taken that the fossils are contemporaneous with the
deposits in which they are found, rather than derived from those of
another age.

Pollen diagrams for the last three complete British interglacials,
the **Cromerian, Hoxnian** and **Ipswichian,** provide evidence of the
plants, and consequently the climates, which characterized them. In
each Zone I, the **pre-temperate zone**, boreal trees—*Betula* and
Pinus—are present together with light-demanding herbs and shrubs,
especially members of the Ericaceae. Zone II, the **early temperate
zone**, is dominated by trees of the mixed oak forest (M.O.F.)—
Quercus, Ulmus, Fraxinus, Corylus—and the humus type improves
to mull. During the period in which Zone III, the **late temperate**,
deposits are laid down, forest trees such as *Carpinus, Abies, Picea*
and perhaps *Tsuga* increase in importance at the expense of the
M.O.F. In the **post-temperate zone** of climatic deterioration (IV) the
dominant tree genera are boreal (*Betula, Pinus, Picea*) and mor is the
characteristic humus type. The forest thins and non-tree pollen types
are frequent, especially those associated with damp heathland. The
next glaciation approaches and the vegetation is reduced to treeless
tundra.

Various points of ecological interest arise from our knowledge of
previous interglacials. Several exotic trees, including the commercially important conifers *Picea abies, Sequoia*, and *Tsuga*, formerly
indigenous in previous interglacials under climates like those of
today, can be expected to become fully naturalized when planted in
appropriate areas.[69] Impoverishment of the woodland flora has other
consequences; in former times the presence of a greater number of
competing species led to the more rigorous zonation of what tend
now to be rather broad habitat types.

Flandrian events

The ecological events of the present interglacial (Table 5.3) form a
sequence which so far has many similarities to those of the previous

three. Early in this century a careful analysis of the stratigraphy of Scandinavian peat bogs and lakes enabled Blytt and Sernander to interpret it as consisting of five post-glacial climatic periods. After the sub-arctic *Pre-Boreal* came the warm dry *Boreal* period, which was succeeded by the warm, wet oceanic climate of the *Atlantic* period. This gave way to the *Sub-Boreal* which was considered to have experienced a warm, dry continental climate, in contrast to the cold, wet oceanic climate of the *Sub-Atlantic* period that still continues. Von Post began the pollen-zone scheme in southern Sweden and the Blytt and Sernander scheme, with which it was soon correlated, proved so convenient that it has been retained as a chronological system even though the original climatic interpretation given above has not proved entirely accurate. In the following account of the development of the vegetation the pollen zones are indicated by Roman numerals.

The Lower (I) and Upper (III) Dryas periods represent the end of the Devensian (= Weichselian) glacial in which the country was covered by herbaceous vegetation. During the Allerød interstadial (II), a brief period of warming, and again in the Pre-Boreal (IV) at the start of the Flandrian, the climate improved sufficiently for birches (*Betula pendula* and *B. pubescens*) to form the first wood-lands. At this time only a few of the major broadleaved genera associated with temperate climates such as the hornbeam, sweet chestnut, beech, oak, lime and elm survived in southern Europe. In Britain birch and pine, which now occur relatively early in the succession to climax woodland, remained dominant until the end of the Boreal though the amount of hazel increased greatly. The junction between pollen zones V and VI is based on the general replacement of birch by pine, but it was in zone VI that the mixed oak forest (M.O.F.) began with the first major establishment of oak and elm as forest trees in Britain. The M.O.F. began in the south, presumably on the better soils.

Pollen analysis of 'moorlog'—freshwater peats dredged from the

---

Table 5.3 Correlation table for the end of the last (Devensian) glacial period and the present interglacial. (Based on Godwin,[9] by courtesy of Cambridge University Press.) Radiocarbon years correspond well with those determined by tree-ring chronology (dendrochronology) up to 2000 years ago. They then begin to diverge with the age as determined by ring counts, being up to 900 years greater in 3000 B.C. than given by radiocarbon dating. The difference is thought to have resulted from changes in the concentration of C^{14} in the atmosphere. B.P. ('Before Present') radiocarbon datings take the present as A.D. 1950.

DATE		VEGETATION			ARCHAEOLOGY		CLIMATE		
Radiocarbon years	Pollen Zones	Ireland	BRITISH ISLES	N. Scotland	Forest cover	Cultures		Blytt & Sernander periods	
B.P. 0 —	VIII	Alder–birch–oak	ALDER–BIRCH–OAK ((BEECH))	Lightly wooded heath	Clearing of forest by man	Norman	Warm spell	SUB-ATLANTIC	FLANDRIAN
						Anglo-Saxon			
— 2000						Romano-British			
	VIIb	Alder–oak	ALDER–OAK–LIME (Elm decline)			Iron Age (Plough)	Rapid deterioration		
						Bronze Age (Hoe)	Colder and drier	SUB-BOREAL	
— 4000						Neolithic (Flint axes)			
							Climatic optimum		
— 6000	VIIa	Alder–oak–elm–pine	ALDER–OAK–ELM–LIME	Pine–birch–alder / Pine–birch		Mesolithic (Hunter)	Warm and wet	ATLANTIC	
— 8000	VIb c ... a	Hazel–pine	PINE–HAZEL (M.O.F.)	Birch–hazel			Warmer and drier	BOREAL	
	V	Hazel–birch	HAZEL–BIRCH–PINE	Juniper–		Proto-maglemosian			
— 10 000	IV	Birch	BIRCH–(PINE)	Empetrum				PRE-BOREAL	
	III	Salix herbacea			Grass-sedge	Upper Palaeolithic	Cold	UPPER DRYAS	LATE DEVENSIAN
	II	Birch			and		Milder	ALLERØD	
— 12 000					open vegetation		Cold	LOWER DRYAS	
	I	Salix herbacea							

sea floor—indicates that the southern part of the North Sea basin was above sea level during zone IV, the Pre-Boreal. During the Boreal there was a rapid and sustained restoration of water from the world's icesheets to the oceans. This led to the separation of Britain from continental Europe by the English Channel in about 5500 B.C. The Irish Sea was either widened or separated Ireland from Britain at the same time. As the sea spread the climate became more oceanic and in the Atlantic period (zone VIIa in Britain) heavy rainfall accompanied the trend to greater warmth. The English Channel effectively ended the northward migration of plants to Britain; since its formation almost all woodland species which have established here have been introduced by man. However, the Atlantic saw the territorial expansion of the more thermophilous species which had already arrived and mixed oak forest became the climax vegetation of much of lowland Britain. The length of the *climatic optimum* of the present interglacial is in dispute but it certainly includes the whole of the Atlantic period. The regional variation of the primaeval forest is shown in Fig. 5.11, just before the onset of the elm decline at the beginning of the Sub-Boreal. The diagram shows the large area dominated by small-leaved lime (*Tilia cordata*), whose importance at this time has been revealed by the work of Birks *et al.*[47] on some 140 pollen profiles from all over the British Isles. Lime is extensively pollinated by insects and its pollen is not so widely dispersed by wind as that of other forest trees; examination of peat-bog cores originally gave an exaggerated impression of the significance of oak.

The picture of the prehistoric forests—Wildwood in the sense of Rackham[20]—which has been revealed is of considerable complexity. Alder (*Alnus glutinosa*) was present on damp land almost throughout the area, having reached Ireland just before the Boreal rise in sea level when lime had got no further than the Lowland Zone of England. The four regional types of 'dry-land' tree assemblages were each a mosaic of local forest variants. Traces of some of them still persist: in the birch-pine dominated region of the Scottish Highlands the patchwork of pinewoods and oakwoods still present around Loch Maree dates from as long ago as 7000 B.C. Though a few of the ancient Scottish Highland pinewoods still persist today, the Scots pine as a native tree is extinct south of Scotland and in Ireland. Evidence for the domination of elm and hazel in the east of Ireland is firm, while that for Cornwall and southwest Wales is tentative. Perhaps the most significant contrast, one still partially reflected in the semi-natural woodlands that yet remain, is between the Highland area dominated by oak and hazel and the Lowland Zone in which lime (*Tilia cordata* with some *T. platyphyllos*) was almost certainly the most important tree, being associated with oak, hazel, and

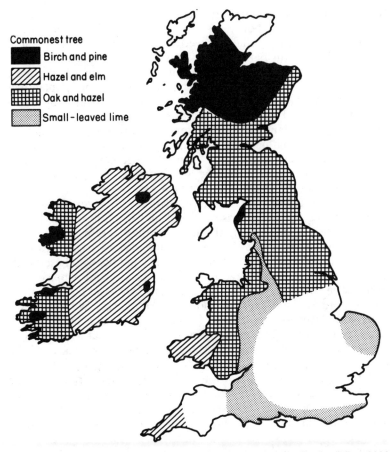

Commonest tree

■ Birch and pine

▨ Hazel and elm

▦ Oak and hazel

▨ Small-leaved lime

Fig. 5.11 Regional variation in the Wildwood just before the Elm Decline (about 3000 radiocarbon years B.C.). Derived from Birks and others (1975). No information exists for blank areas. (From Rackham.[20])

various others including ash in Somerset and pine in the Breckland of East Anglia. This lowland mosaic was the most complex of the four main types of Wildwood found in Britain. Native lime has become much rarer in the last 5000 years though it is more common[20] than had been supposed. Lack of suitable pollen profiles renders speculative discussion of such questions as whether the hornbeam woods of Essex and Suffolk, the beechwoods of the South Downs and Chilterns, and the ash and maple (*Acer campestre*) woods of the Midlands were already in existence at the end of the Atlantic period.

Influence of man on Flandrian forests

Until 5000 radio-carbon years ago the development of the forests of the Flandrian interglacial followed a pattern very similar to that of the preceding warm periods. Since then the influence of man has become overwhelming, particularly in Great Britain where forest clearance was so extensive that even after the widespread plantings of the present century only 8.8% of the country is covered by woodland. The charcoal and pollen records of the Landnam clearances[121] provide early evidence of the clearance of forest areas for shifting cultivation by Neolithic man. The elm decline itself probably marks the first major intervention by man; this decrease in elm pollen resulted, at least in part, from the lopping of elm branches for cattle fodder, possibly by shredding (Section 4.5).

Man has practised woodmanship in Britain for a very long time. The beginning of the increasingly cool and dry Sub-Boreal period approximately coincided with the arrival of the Neolithic peoples who used flint axes. The earliest of the Neolithic trackways laid across the Somerset Levels dates from about 4000 B.C. and the wood used in its construction appears to have been grown in a mixed coppice on a rather long rotation. The Bronze Age and Iron Age peoples introduced more efficient axes, the hoe and the plough. Woodland was felled and burnt to provide land for grazing as well as arable crops. Even so, when the Roman occupation ended in about 300 A.D. it is thought that out of a total of some 23 million hectares in Great Britain, the amount of land utilized for grazing was no more than one million hectares with rather less used for cultivation. Since then man has been far more destructive of the woodland cover. In Britain only fragments of the original forest cover remain; even in North America and continental Europe permanent clearance has been very extensive.

The Saxons were able to cultivate the heavy clays on which much of the mixed oak forest had stood and at the time of the Norman Conquest[69] four million hectares were in cultivation. At this time swine still fed in quantity on acorns and beech mast; the emphasis placed on the right of *pannage* for these domestic pigs suggests that the climate was more favourable for oak and beech than it is now, though it became even better in the thirteenth century, the Golden Age of British agriculture.

The ancient forests of England were large tracts of land bearing trees and undergrowth in many places, but frequently with considerable areas of pasture and, as in many other countries, subject to special laws. In England such 'Forests' were all royal; similar tracts of land controlled by nobles were called chases (e.g. Cannock Chase), and at one time about a fifth of England was covered by forest and chases though much of this area was not wooded. In the Middle Ages the word came to apply to the 'waste of the Forest' which was the area under Forest jurisdiction that was not farmland, private woodland or built up. Here farm animals were grazed, timber obtained from trees, wood from pollards, and poles from coppices. Venison was also produced, a function later taken over by enclosed parks in which deer still flourish. Now, however, the primary difference between forests and woodlands would be taken by many as simply one of scale; certainly most man-made forests are huge plantations with large areas of even age and often monocultures at that. The importance of woodland as a resource was well understood in mediaeval times; the way in which man has influenced the woodland landscapes of Britain is described by Rackham,[20] who shows how woodland archaeology coordinates the evidence provided by documents, the timbers of old buildings, and the remnants of ancient trees, woodlands, ditches and boundary banks.

5.5   THE ECOLOGY OF COPPICING

Coppicing ceased in most British woodlands after the second World War, but we have descriptions of commercial *coppice cycles* in Hertfordshire by Salisbury[203] and in Gamlingay Wood, Cambridgeshire, by Adamson.[30] Though many management practices result in a simplification of woodland ecosystems, coppicing actively encourages variety and, largely for this reason, has been revived in a number of woodlands now run as nature reserves, such as Hayley Wood in Cambridgeshire. Within a particular wood, different stages of a coppicing cycle provide a wide variety of structural and climatic conditions, so that the wood as a whole supports a *high diversity of species*. Old coppiced woodlands, such as Bradfield Woods in which coppicing has been uninterrupted, may contain more than 300 species of herbs, while certain Kent woods are partially dependent on coppice management for their rich insect and bird faunas.

Coppicing involves the felling of the underwood in autumn and winter and its most obvious effect is on shade. As this varies at different times of year the effect on a particular species is related to both its tolerance of shade and its phenology (see Sections 2.4 and 4.4). Rackham[191] estimates that coppicing '(a) increases summer light at least 20-fold, (b) increases spring light roughly twofold, and (c) extends the period of spring light by about three weeks (because the remaining shade is produced by standard trees which come into leaf later than small coppice)' in a typical British site. These increases in the amount of light reaching the ground layer after cutting the coppice enable many established herbs to grow more vigorously, while other species enter and become established. The exuberant flowering of vernal species such as primrose and wood anemone is an obvious feature during the first two or three years after cutting, for instance in oakwoods on clays or loams, while later in the year violets, red campion, yellow archangel, foxglove and rosebay willow-herb may flourish, the last being further favoured on burnt areas. As the coppice canopy closes the increased shading and crowding are tolerated by most of these species, although flowering may not be nearly so prolific. Others, however, may die out.

In Ham Street NNR, Kent, Ford and Newbould[91] recorded the greatest number of species of herbs (30) in areas of *Castanea sativa* coppice which had been cut 5 years previously, but thereafter lack of space prevented further colonization and the total number of species declined towards the end of the 12–17 year cycle. Components of the '*shade flora*' such as bracken, bramble and bluebell persisted through-out the cycle, showing maximum above-ground production when the canopy was removed, except for bluebell which was most productive after canopy closure in year 7. Bluebell is a special case, being a sun plant which photosynthesizes vigorously before the flushing of the tree canopy (see Section 2.4). Wood sage (*Teucrium scorodonia*), on the other hand, was abundant in areas examined 2 and 5 years after felling, but absent from later stages. Figure 5.12 shows fresh growth in a recently coppiced *Castanea sativa* woodland in West Sussex.

Felling the underwood also influences the bryophytes which are, in general, very good indicators of small scale mosaic patterns involving soil pH, levels of mineral nutrients, humidity and illumination. After coppicing the relative humidity (RH) of the air is decreased, while irradiation and the temperature range are increased. This has a differential effect on the growth of those bryophytes which are either able to invade or are present already. Gimingham and Birse[96] found that the sequence—dendroid forms (e.g. *Thamnium alopecurum* and *Mnium undulatum*) and thalloid mats (e.g. *Pellia epiphylla*):rough mats (e.g. *Eurhynchium striatum*):smooth mats (e.g. *Hypnum cupressiforme*):short turfs (e.g. *Ceratodon purpureus*) and small cushions (e.g. *Orthotrichum anomalum*)—occurred along a gradient in which light intensity increased and atmospheric RH decreased. This sequence helps us to interpret the striking contrasts in growth-form distribution (see Section 2.2) which may be seen when tracing bryophyte communities along a stream which runs through both felled and unfelled regions of a wood.

The liverwort *Pellia epiphylla* is favoured, like the moss *Mnium hornum*, by surface acidity, whereas *Pellia fabbroniana* is calcicole. *Hookeria lucens*, a moss of heavily shaded moist places, such as the deeply incised Seckley Ravine, Wyre Forest, is particularly susceptible to environmental change; exposure to direct sunlight kills it. Rackham[191] records an interesting bryophyte community in Hayley Wood on the rugged bases of old ash stools. These bear species such as *Lejeunea cavifolia, Porella platyphylla, Omalia trichomanoides* and *Neckera complanata*, for which Cambridgeshire is otherwise too dry.

In a mature compartment moisture is mainly lost through the transpiration of the standard trees and large coppice. When the large coppice is felled the water 'saved' is probably lost by increased transpiration from the ground vegetation, new coppice and the standards, all of which are more exposed to the sun than before and around which the wind can now eddy freely. Standard trees and ground vegetation in the experimentally coppiced areas of Hayley Wood often show more severe symptoms of drought damage than do those in the uncoppiced wood. Small seedlings, especially those of rushes, are particularly vulnerable to drought in the first year after felling. The successions of ground layer species which have developed in this wood since felling of coppice plots began again in 1964 are described in detail by Rackham.[191] They have been largely unpredictable, varying greatly from year to year—partly because of variations in the weather—and even within plots. Enormous quantities of rushes (*Juncus* spp.) have come up in some years. Rushes do not grow in the surrounding uncoppiced woodland; the seeds involved may have been produced by plants which grew after the last coppicing 50–90 years ago, buried, and then disturbed by the felling operations which exposed them to the light necessary for germination.

The wood is famous for its large populations of oxlips (*Primula elatior*); flowering in this species often increases seven-fold in the second spring after coppicing, but here its leaves and flowers are frequently eaten by fallow deer which also graze shoots developing on coppiced ash. The ash are now pollarded so that the young shoots are out of reach, while deer have been excluded from the best oxlip area by a high fence similar to those used in Sweden to prevent elk wandering across major roads.

In the Wyre Forest[204] most of the woods, in which *Quercus petraea* was then the most important tree, were coppiced on a compartment system at approximately 16–18 year intervals. Each area was clear cut except for the few seeding trees. In some places there were two ages of coppice, with the general matrix being on a shorter rotation than the more sparsely scattered oaks which were cut at longer intervals. The larger coppice stems were used for pit props, while some of the branches were rent and used to make oak baskets. An interesting succession developed on the old hearths used for the production of charcoal from the smaller cord-wood (2.5–10 cm in diameter). Recent hearths were blackened areas devoid of vegetation, but these were soon colonized, being especially suitable for the development of seedling trees so that old hearths were frequently covered by a thicket of shrubs and trees. Hearth sites were favourable to plant growth in several respects, being initially devoid of competition and having a surface soil enriched with carbonates, nitrates and phosphates, as well as a pH above that of the surrounding area.

Marchantia polymorpha, Funaria hygrometrica and *Ceratodon purpureus* often occurred in great profusion during the early colonization of a hearth, as they do today on the nutrient-rich sites of minor fires left after coppicing. Even in older phases when many woodland herbs, shrubs and trees had invaded, the more calcicole character of the hearth vegetation remained evident and species such as wood sanicle (*Sanicula europaea*) were often present, though absent from the surrounding vegetation.

Paris quadrifolia, most orchids and a few other plants, seem not to increase after coppicing,[191] while in *Mercurialis perennis*[203] the dry weight per unit area actually declines. The coppice cycle, when uncomplicated by grazing, benefits very many herb species in turn and its effect in restricting the dominance of dog's mercury— so common in well-drained neglected woodland—also encourages variety.

Many insects are known to require climatic or biotic features which can be provided by coppicing. Sunny glades and woodland edges are frequented by numerous species of butterfly, including the rare heath fritillary (*Melitaea athalia*) which now occurs in less than a dozen sites in Britain. This is a weak flying species which appears to be particularly dependent on coppiced woodlands; its larval food plant, common cow-wheat (*Melampyrum pratense*), tends to die out as the canopy closes. Other insects are attracted to small, sheltered clearings, and in general the habitat diversity associated with coppicing would be expected to support a corresponding diversity of insects.

Clearings with insects in turn attract certain birds such as grasshopper warblers, nightjars and tree pipits, while other species may be favoured by cover for nesting or feeding, or by the structural diversity of a particular stage of the cycle—for example scrub-like structure tends to support the largest number of breeding birds. In Ham Street NNR, the density of nightingales was found to be correlated with the presence of oak standards, and also with the age of the hornbeam coppice, which was most favoured when 5–8 years old, but quite unsuitable when older than 15 years, presumably because of the virtual absence of a ground flora.

The decline in the area of British forests which were effectively coppiced after 1945 was related to high labour costs and declining markets for the charcoal, poles, stakes, bobbins and tannin pro-

Fig. 5.12 Coppiced sweet chestnut (*Castanea sativa*) near Chithurst, West Sussex. These trees had been cut to the ground a year previously, leaving a stool from which fresh shoots have arisen. The previous coppicing cycle lasted 15 years. (Photograph by John R. Packham.)

duced. It is encouraging to note that markets, including the renewed use of cordwood for fuel, are now being found for the products of areas coppiced for conservation, while in Holland the subsidy formerly granted to owners converting woodlands from coppices to plantations has been withdrawn as coppices are needed for recreational use.

6

The Exploitation of Living Autotrophs

6.1 THE ROLE OF HETEROTROPHS IN WOODLAND ECOSYSTEMS

The tissues and exudates of trees and other green plants, rich in energy and nutrients, provide potential food for heterotrophs, ranging in size from microorganisms to birds and mammals. These may exploit the autotrophs either directly or, as with carnivores and fungivores, indirectly, via other heterotrophs. Many of the species composing this plant-dependent web affect green plants adversely, for example, through feeding or trampling, but the balance is redressed by pollinators and dispersers of fruits and seeds, and, of wider significance, by nutrient cycling (see Section 9.5).

The *grazing chain* (*herbivore subsystem*) starts with living tissues of autotrophs, the first link of primary consumers including exudate-feeders, herbivorous animals and parasitic plants. Their counterparts in the *decomposer chain* are detritivores and decomposer microbes. Certain carnivores act as links between the two chains, and eventually the dead remains of autotrophs and of heterotrophs, together with faeces, are mineralized by decomposers.

This chapter considers various aspects of the exploitation of living autotrophs, including instances where the same organism proceeds to feed on tissues which it has killed. Decomposition of dead remains is discussed in Chapter 8, with particular reference to soil organisms.

6.2 EPIPHYTIC MICROORGANISMS

The surfaces of living plants provide a substratum for autotrophic algae and lichens, and also support a varied heterotrophic microflora of bacteria, yeasts and filamentous fungi. Species found on or in seeds and buds provide an inoculum for the *phylloplane* (leaf surface),[77] but the *rhizoplane* (root surface) community is mainly derived from the soil. Some of these epiphytes subsist on dead tissues, such as sloughed cells which accompany even the earliest stages of root growth, while others feed on plant exudates and animal products, including the sugary excreta, or honeydew, of aphids.

Root exudates are mainly produced from the elongating region a few centimetres from the tip, and also from lateral roots, root hairs and senescing or damaged tissues. Compounds identified from these exudates include sugars, amino acids, enzymes, growth factors and cyst-nematode hatching factors. Exudates are believed to stimulate the germination of fungal propagules, young roots being particularly susceptible to colonization by saprophytes and pathogens. Selected bacterial species also build up on the young root surface, which provides numerous crevices as microhabitats. Some species invade and disrupt the epidermal and cortical cells, leading to sloughing of debris.[199]

Rhizoplane microorganisms may compete with roots for essential elements, but others, such as *Rhizobium* and ectotrophic mycorrhizas, are beneficial to higher plants (see Section 9.5). Nitrogen-fixing actinomycetes on tropical leaves provide another example of a symbiotic relationship. In contrast, certain microbes penetrate the surface defences of leaves, by means of enzymes such as pectinases, and exploit living tissues. As well as pathogenic bacteria and fungi, there are many weak parasites, some of which cause no visible disease symptoms, while others can invade only already damaged or senescing tissues. Senescence involves a lowering of defences against attack, as well as a greater release of exudates, so that species diversity normally increases with ageing. The successions of organisms which have been recorded during the lives of leaves presumably reflect the changing availability of different nutrients. *Aureobasidium pullulans* is a hyphomycete which has been reported from buds and leaves of a large number of coniferous and broad-leaved species. This fungus grows on and in sycamore leaves for the first two months after the buds open, usually without necrosis, and then survives as resting chlamydospores.[190] Among the species colonizing mature sycamore leaves another hyphomycete, *Epicoccum nigrum*, is active until leaf-fall but invades internal tissues only during senescence.

Senescence is probably hastened by the activities of many of these epiphytes, particularly in the case of pathogens, and the fact that decomposition starts in the seedling stage illustrates the difficulty of separating grazing and decomposer chains.

6.3   FOREST PATHOGENS

Tree disorders can be caused by abiotic factors such as frost, lightning, wind, unsuitable light levels, variable soil water content, drought and mineral deficiencies as well as by pathogens, of which the most serious are fungi. Unhealthy trees succumb more easily to disease than those which are vigorous and fast-growing. Thus *Betula pendula* succumbs more readily to drought when infected with the bracket fungus *Piptoporus betulinus* than when uninfected. Conversely, trees well suited to their physical and chemical environments withstand the attacks of disease organisms better than those which are not.

Diseases frequently influence the productivity of forests and alter the species composition of mixed woodland communities. Particular species are seldom completely eliminated by a disease, but their frequency and importance may be greatly reduced. In the early years of this century, for example, the American chestnut (*Castanea dentata*) was reduced from one of the most important upper-canopy species in the Appalachian forest to the status of an understorey shrub by a fungal pathogen. Diseases of the major trees and shrubs are particularly important in that these are the dominant plants of woodlands, moderating the habitats of other organisms in major respects. A full account of any microbial disease should include details of the pathogen and its host (or hosts), the symptoms, development and distribution of the disease, the damage which it causes and methods of control. Such an approach is adopted by Peace[18] in dealing with the pathology of trees and shrubs; Browne[58] has provided an account of animal pests and plant pathogens of plantation trees. This is a major subject in its own right; we are concerned with its importance in forest ecosystems and the main types of disease caused, though Section 6.4 treats the ecology of Dutch elm disease in detail. Nursery diseases influence trees at the seedling stage where 'damping off', which is often caused by *Pythium* spp. and *Rhizoctonia solani*, is an important cause of loss. The other main groups of fungal diseases attack the roots, the leaves and young shoots or the stems.

Fungal diebacks

Stem diseases of the bark and cambium such as that caused by the ascomycete *Endothia parasitica* in *Castanea dentata* often cause wilting and dieback of the whole crown, or of branches, if the shoot concerned is completely girdled. *Endothia parasitica*, the Asiatic Blight fungus, was noticed on trees in New York Zoological Park in 1904, having apparently entered America on Asian chestnut trees imported from Japan. Within two or three decades the American chestnut was destroyed as a commercial crop over the whole of its natural range in eastern U.S.A. The fungus is spread by sticky orange spores which ooze from the pycnidia and are carried long distances by insects and birds, including migratory woodpeckers, and also spread by wind-borne ascospores shot into the air from perithecia. Cases where vigorous recovery shoots arise immediately below the lesions, or where the cankers heal in instances where the fungus fails to girdle the shoot, indicate the acquisition of at least some field resistance to the fungus. American attempts to combat Chestnut Blight have been largely concerned with the development of disease-resistant hybrids by crossing Asiatic species such as *Castanea mollissima* and *C. crenata* with the American chestnut. In Italy trees of *C. sativa* are felled before the fungus reaches the base of the trunk. The uninjured root stock coppices freely; any sprouts which become infected are also cut back. When healthy coppice results the trees can be allowed to develop to high forest.

Fungal infection of trees often occurs through wounds made by insects, such as the twolined chestnut borer (*Agrilus bilineatus*) with Chestnut Blight and beech scale (*Cryptococcus fagi*) in the case of Beech Snap, now causing damage in beech plantations in S. England. *Nectria coccinea* which causes Beech Snap is endemic on *Fagus sylvatica* in Europe. It is also spreading on American beech (*F. grandifolia*) following the accidental introduction of the beech scale into Nova Scotia about 1890.

The destruction of the American chestnut by *Endothia parasitica* is an example of a severe ecological imbalance between an exotic parasite with high reproductive ability combined with severe pathogenicity and a new host plant. Similar situations involving different trees and pathogens will doubtless arise in the future, and in view of this it is significant that the remission of Chestnut Blight on *Castanea sativa* first noted in Italy in 1951 resulted from a loss of virulence by the parasite. Hypovirulent (H) strains almost white in colour have since been isolated from cankers undergoing spontaneous healing, whereas cultures of the normal virulent (V) strains isolated from severely damaged trees were orange in colour and had more abundant conidia. By plating conidia from pigmented 'JR' hypovirulent cultures separate V and H strains were segregated. The growth of hypovirulent H strains in the same trees as those parasitized by V strains caused the disease to regress, and this 'exclusive hypovirulence' probably results from a change in the V strain after hyphal anastomosis between the two strains. Hypovirulence was transferred into American strains of *Endothia parasitica* by repeated co-inoculations of the host tree with an American V and a French H strain. American H strains are much more effective in reducing the activity of American V strains than the original French form,[127] so that the phenomenon of hypovirulence may serve as a basis for the biological control of Chestnut Blight in N. America.

Brunchorstia dieback has long been an occasional cause of damage to pine, especially Corsican pine (*Pinus nigra*), in the northern and wetter parts of Britain. Buds infected during the summer die in the following winter and the older shoots may die back progressively during the ensuing May and June. During 1979 many Scots pine trees in the Scottish border counties died from attacks begun in the previous year. Other diebacks in 7- to 20-year-old plantations of Scots and Corsican pine in the English Midlands during 1979 had symptoms resembling those of *Brunchorstia*, with buds failing to flush in spring. The fungus consistently isolated from the dying branches, however, was *Cenangium ferruginosum*, a common saprophyte on pines in the U.K. although weakly pathogenic in North America and parts of Europe. It had not previously been considered to act as a pathogen in Britain; in this instance severe spring weather may have disposed the pines to fungal attack.

Root rots

Fomes annosus (*Heterobasidion annosum*) causes Fomes root rot which kills conifers and occasionally deciduous trees, being one of the most important forest pathogens in Britain, especially on alkaline soils. The orange-brown fruit body of this bracket fungus, which is also a cause of butt-rot, is perennial, has a white margin and is formed close to the ground. Cut stumps are easily infected by its basidiospores and the fungus spreads into the attached root system, passing by root to root contact into the healthy trees. Modern methods of control are aimed at preventing infection of the cut stump by treatment with urea, creosote or sodium nitrite which act as disinfectants. The difficulty is that a badly knocked stump or root will have fresh surfaces exposed so that *F. annosus* can enter and form a fresh focus of disease. An interesting alternative treatment is to inoculate stumps with spores of the saprophytic basidiomycete *Peniophora gigantea* which competes with the parasite, rotting the *Pinus* stumps and preventing successful colonization by *F. annosus*. This method of biological control, which destroys the substrate instead of just capping it off, was developed by Rishbeth[194] who prepared and packeted suspensions containing the oidia; this control is now used by the Forestry Commission in whose woodlands *Peniophora gigantea* can often be seen looking like spilt candle wax on the dead stumps.

Fomes annosus does not grow freely in soil, but a number of other root fungi such as *Fomes lignosus* and *Armillaria mellea* spread through it by means of bootlace-like rhizomorphs (tough masses of entwined hyphae) provided the fungus has a source of nourishment. The black rhizomorphs of *A. mellea* can extend more than five metres from a fallen log and enable this basidiomycete, whose fruiting bodies disappear with the first frosts, to reach and destroy a wide range of herbaceous and woody hosts. Honey Fungus has a world-wide distribution and the tree genera in which it causes Armillaria root rot include *Pinus, Picea, Larix, Castanea, Fraxinus, Quercus, Salix* and *Taxus. Armillaria* often kills small trees outright but death may be ultimately caused by drought, waterlogging, windrock, or other adverse factors which the tree could have withstood had its root system been complete.

The colonization by fungi of hardwood stumps is affected by the type of chemical treatment used to control regrowth. Treating the stumps with 2,4,5-T encourages the establishment of *Chondrostereum purpureum*, which infects the cut surfaces and rots the wood relatively slowly. This fungus is often replaced by *Armillaria mellea* which colonizes the stumps by means of its rhizomorphs. Ammonium sulphamate, on the other hand,[195] is translocated in the stumps and generally favours species causing rapid decay, such as *Bjerkandera adusta (Polyporus adustus)* and *Coriolus (Polystictus) versicolor*, some of which compete well with *Armillaria*. This treatment ensures rapid killing of stump roots and is an effective way of preventing honey fungus causing serious damage. Rishbeth subsequently investigated the possibilities of a more direct biological control using inocula. Any saprophytic fungus to be used as an inoculum would have to tolerate ammonium sulphamate in order to colonize the treated stumps without delay. It would also have to rot the roots rapidly and compete sufficiently well to prevent early replacement by other fungi; *C. versicolor* seems to be effective in a variety of tree species.

Non-fungal pathogens

A number of non-fungal tree diseases are of importance. Elm phloem necrosis, for example, is caused by a mycoplasma and has resulted in severe losses of American elm (*Ulmus americana*) and winged elm (*U. alata*) in the U.S.A. Early symptoms are similar to those of Dutch elm and other vascular diseases; trees often die in the year in which they are first infected. Viruses cause many tree diseases including elm scorch and oak ringspot. Wetwood of elm results from infection by the anaerobic bacterium *Erwinia nimipressuralis* which produces methane and can cause sufficient pressure to split the trunk releasing a watery 'slime flux'. Many woody plants are attacked by stubby or corky root nematodes; growth in Douglas fir is greatly reduced by *Xiphinema baleri*.

Importance of forest pathogens

In the constant battle against forest pathogens there are always areas where particular species are causing unusually heavy damage, or where the entry of exotic parasites would cause severe problems. The present activities of *Phytophthora cinnamomi*, which is slowly working through large areas of Australian *Eucalyptus* forest, show it to be one of the most ecologically damaging pathogens, killing most native trees, understorey and ground cover plants. This phycomycete has an almost world-wide distribution in temperate and tropical regions, growing on a wide range of conifers, broad-leaved trees, shrubs, and herbaceous plants. The zoospores of *P. cinnamomi* show remarkably active chemotactic movements towards the growing regions of avocado roots in response to a root exudate, and cause lesions within days.

The genetic basis of a plant's resistance to a pathogen has important ecological consequences. Though vertical (*race specific*) *resistance* is very effective, breakdown, when it occurs, is usually complete. Horizontal (*race non-specific*) *resistance* usually develops selectively after exposure of the host to the disease and is commonly polygenic. This type of defence is at a lower level, but much more general and not liable to a complete and sudden breakdown. The employment of vertical resistance in new hybrids of short-lived crop plants is often an effective strategy. With trees horizontal resistance, already widespread in many natural populations, may ultimately be more beneficial.

6.4   DUTCH ELM DISEASE

Dutch elm disease[10] results from infection of the internal tissues of the trunk and branches of elms by *Ceratocystis ulmi*, an ascomycete spread by insects and sometimes by wind, which produces toxins that cause the wood parenchyma to exude gum leading to the formation of tyloses. These bladder-like intrusions pass through pits in the cell walls into the vessels, which become blocked causing the foliage to wilt. The disease, now rampant in the United Kingdom and North America, has in Britain been rapidly dispersed by the bark beetles *Scolytus scolytus* (*S. destructor*) and *S. multistriatus*. Aggressive strains of *Ceratocystis ulmi* attack *Ulmus americana* and the English elm (*U. procera*) very severely, wych elm (*U. glabra*) being a little more resistant. The foliage of diseased trees yellows and dies, often in mid summer, and trees showing such symptoms are often dead within a few weeks. The purified fungal toxins consist of a number of unusual glycopeptides capable of reducing water conduction in cuttings from elm seedlings.

The characteristics of *Ceratocystis ulmi* populations in Britain have been investigated by Brasier and Gibbs[53,54] who showed that the present epidemic was begun by an aggressive 'fluffy' strain, rather than the 'waxy' strain which is slow-growing, non-aggressive, has few aerial hyphae and appears to be a residuum of the 1930s epidemic, which killed 10–20% of elms in England. The fast-growing aggressive strain was imported into Britain on bark-bearing logs of Rock elm (*Ulmus thomasii*) from Toronto; its initial dispersal was probably accomplished by the North American bark beetle *Hylurgopinus rufipes* and by *Scolytus multistriatus* growing in galleries in the bark. In a typical infestation the beetles, carrying the spores of *Cerato-cystis*, fly to the crowns of adjacent healthy elms. The fungus is inoculated into the vascular tissues of the tree, at the junctions between the leaves and twigs and in the crotches of the twigs, during maturation feeding of the beetles when their gonads mature. Once the foliage has wilted the shoot tips curl over forming 'shepherds' crooks'. If an infected twig is cut through, black spots, marking areas containing tyloses and gum, can be seen in the youngest annual ring.

Fertilized female scolytids lay their eggs in galleries excavated under the bark of trunks and branches of trees affected by *C. ulmi*. (A rising watertable, attack by honey fungus or sheer old age may also render elms susceptible to attack; during 1976 beetles tried unsuccessfully to penetrate the bark of trees which were stressed by the effects of drought, but otherwise healthy.) The resulting larvae tunnel out further galleries (Fig. 6.1) and pass through five instars before pupation. Even after death of the tree, bark remains suitable for scolytid development for up to two years. *C. ulmi* may survive for many months as a saprophyte, its one sexual and two asexual phases sporulating luxuriantly in the galleries and in crevices in the bark. The beetles play a vital role in spreading *C. ulmi*; they carry spores on their antennae, mouthparts and legs but unless they create a feeding injury extending into the xylem infection will normally not occur. Ambrosia beetles form galleries inhabited by fungi in a similar way to the scolytids, but whereas they are dependent on the fungi, which they consume, the scolytids feed on components of the wood. Scolytids apparently do not eat *C. ulmi* and their relationship with the fungus seems to be coincidental.

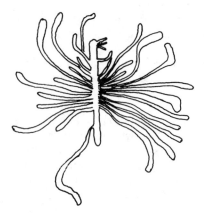

Fig. 6.1 The 'signature' of *Scolytus* engraved on elm sapwood. Note central chamber and radiating larval galleries.

Dutch elm disease is thought to have entered Europe from Asia during the first World War and was first described in the Netherlands in 1921. Epidemics of the disease might be prevented by controlling the vector, controlling the fungal pathogen, or replacing the existing elm population with hybrid trees bred to resist the disease. Crown spraying with insecticides to prevent maturation feeding and to kill the scolytid vectors cannot be recommended for general use. The nematode *Parasitaphelenchus oldhami* has little effect on either *S. multistriatus* or *S. scolytus*,[119] though it parasitizes both. However, it might eventually be possible to find an effective means of biological control. The '*cordon sanitaire*' policy is to remove dead and diseased trees promptly, and to prevent the movement or importation of diseased trunks. In 1976 there were few parts of southern England where elm disease was not extensive, but in East Sussex less than 20% of the original elm population was dead or dying. A *cordon sanitaire* policy operated in this area but not in West Sussex where over 80% of the trees were dead by 1976. The relatively light infection in East Anglia was probably related to the predominance of the more resistant smooth-leaved elm (*Ulmus carpinifolia*). As the fungus can spread via root grafts between trees whose trunks are ten metres apart, attempts to save healthy members of a partly diseased group may involve digging trenches and killing connecting roots. Protection of healthy trees by injection with systemic fungicides such as benomyl is only partially effective; it is expensive, has to be repeated every year, and damages the trunk.

Recent western European outbreaks of Dutch elm disease have been caused by two genetically distinct aggressive strains, one from North America and another, whose colonies are powdery and irregular in shape when grown on a culture plate, from central Europe or further east. The former passed from North America through the U.K. to France and Germany, while the latter caused outbreaks in Italy and Iran. Both were involved in the epidemics which occurred in Ireland during 1977. In view of the considerable variation exhibited by *Ceratocystis ulmi*, Brasier[52] suggests that new elms should be bred from stocks in the Himalayas or south-western China, where pathogenicity is not a problem; although the origin of Dutch elm disease seems to lie in this region, it also has the greatest diversity of elms in the world.

While the Dutch elm cultivars 'Commelin' and 'Groeneveld' are more resistant than British native elms they are attacked by the fluffy strain of *C. ulmi*. However, the search for resistant hybrid trees continues, and in the U.S.A. encouraging results have been achieved with hybrids from the crosses *Ulmus parvifolia* × *U. wallichiana* and *U. japonica* × *U. pumila*. Perhaps one of the best hopes for the survival of elms in Britain lies in a genetic change occurring in the fungus, leading to the fluffy strain becoming less pathogenic. There is also the possibility of the survival of at least some of the trees which develop from the stumps or suckers of felled trees.

Fungal diseases and insect pests are often of greater significance in plantations and regeneration forests having a very limited number of tree species than in more diverse natural systems. Even so, it seems likely that fungal epidemics occurred in the past and were responsible for widespread destruction of particular tree species. Indeed, the parasitic activities of an exceptionally aggressive strain of *C. ulmi* could cause the extinction of the elm itself, but not of the scolytid vectors which can develop in trees other than elms.[39] Relatively unaggressive strains such as the 'waxy' isolates of *C. ulmi* are, on the other hand, better adapted to continued parasitic life in that a large host tree population remains available to future generations of the fungus.

Dutch elm disease, together with *Scolytus multistriatus*, reached N. America, where the new aggressive strain later evolved, on European elm burl logs imported to manufacture veneer. It is ironic that a similar importation into Britain should have caused the death of 20 million elms, out of an original population of 30 million, between the beginning of the outbreak in the late 1960s and 1982 by which time the effects in the central and southern regions were very marked, posing severe problems with regard to falling trees and replanting. It also emphasizes the dangers of introducing more aggressive strains of existing pathogens into Britain, as well as such serious new diseases as American Oak Wilt (*Ceratocystis fagacearum*) and Chestnut Blight.

6.5   WOODLAND HERBIVORES

Certain mammals (and less importantly, birds) can cause serious damage to woodland herbs, shrubs and trees, by eating foliage, severing roots, stripping bark, and trampling or even felling whole plants. They also play an important role in woodland regeneration, as feeders on fruits, seeds and seedlings (Section 4.3).

Temperate forests lack specialized arboreal leaf-eating mammals, although the canopy-dwelling fat dormouse (*Glis glis*) includes tree leaves in its diet. Squirrels and various voles and mice, such as *Apodemus flavicollis*, feed on buds in spring, after the mast crop has been depleted. Grey squirrels (*Sciurus carolinensis*), introduced into Britain in 1876, often occur at much higher densities than in North America, where they are rarely pests. As a result, certain individuals are forced into sub-optimal territories, which they mark by chipping off bark. Large-scale removal of bark between May and July can kill susceptible hardwoods such as *Fagus sylvatica* and *Acer pseudoplatanus*. In Colorado, the porcupine *Erithezon epixanthum* feeds almost entirely on the phloem of *Pinus edulis*, selecting trees whose branches have high sugar concentrations, associated with attacks by root fungi.[221]

Many kinds of deer and other large herbivores rely on woody browse during the winter and dry seasons, and some show marked preferences for particular species. If populations are allowed to increase excessively, as when protected from predation, the consequences may be very marked. The eruption of mule deer (*Odocoileus hemionus hemionus*) on the Kaibab Plateau, Arizona, during the first quarter of this century, led to the virtual elimination of their preferred species of *Rubus* and *Salix*.

Deer also damage trees by fraying the bark with their antlers. In some species this occurs only when the velvet is being removed, and also at traditional rutting stands. Roe deer (*Capreolus capreolus*) bucks also cause widespread fraying during territorial disputes. Bark can be stripped off by deer and certain other mammals, including elephants, but the latter also push over whole trees to reach fruit, leaves and bark. The threatened reintroduction of beavers (*Castor fiber*) into Britain would at least provide the U.K. with an example of a tree-felling animal.

Turning now to invertebrates, Southwood,[218] in a discussion of the various chemical and physical hurdles facing potential insect feeders on angiosperms, points out that relatively few insect orders contain appreciable numbers of species which feed on or in foliage, the major woodland examples occurring within the Lepidoptera, Coleoptera, Diptera and Hymenoptera. Even these may have to adapt their feeding strategies to the phenology of the plants, since much of the greenery of the forest is only potential food, protected for most of the year by the defences of the trees.

Foliage-feeders may do no more than raise a pimple on a leaf surface, or they may cause reduced growth or even death of whole trees. Partial defoliation may alter light penetration and hence the performance of shrubs and herbs below, while wide-scale mortality of mature trees, followed by natural regeneration or replanting, will have far-reaching effects on the ecology of the community. Whatever the scale of the damage, in all cases energy and nutrients are moved from the tree to the animal, and so to diverse food webs.

Galls are abnormal growths, each of a characteristic form which results from the unique interaction between a particular species of plant and gall-causer. The latter may be a microbe, nematode, mite or insect, the gall providing food and protection for the developing organisms. Although in some instances, such as Knopper galls on acorns (Fig. 6.2) and certain adelgid galls on conifers, the plant is

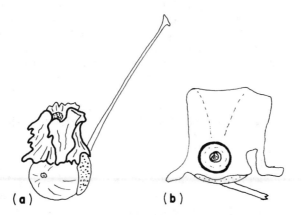

Fig. 6.2   Knopper gall (*Andricus quercus-calicis*): **(a)** on undistorted acorn; and **(b)** in section, showing larval cell above degenerate acorn. In late summer these galls are bright green and sticky; they later turn brown and woody. They were first recorded in Britain in 1961, and are a potential threat to seed collection stands, since acorns are usually destroyed. The sexual generation occupies 1 mm swellings on male catkins of *Quercus cerris*.

adversely affected, it is assumed that usually the relationship is harmless, even when for example the burden may reach several hundred spangle galls per oak leaf, covering 80% of the surface. Darlington[72] has suggested that galls benefit not only the animal but also the plant, by localizing damage rather than allowing a free range. They certainly benefit the communities of parasites and inquilines ('lodgers') within the galls, and also supplement the diet of birds such as tits.

Sycamore aphids (*Drepanosiphum platanoidis*) are an example of a more mobile burden, whose reproduction is favoured by the higher concentrations of soluble nitrogen in the phloem sap of actively growing or senescing leaves.[78] During midsummer, when gravid females are virtually absent, colonies tend to occur in the cooler lower canopy, under leaves sheltered from the wind. Their sugary excreta, or honeydew, support sooty moulds, which may interfere with photosynthesis, and also channel nutrients into the forest floor. The siphoning of energy into aphid populations is partially compensated by the production of leaves with a higher chlorophyll content, but reduced growth rates of leaves, stems or roots, recorded in sycamore and lime, are probably associated with the injection of growth substances in the aphids' saliva (Section 9.2). Various adelgids (which, like aphids, are true bugs, i.e. Homoptera) cause distortion of conifer needles, sometimes leading to defoliation, but spraying of plantations is usually not justified economically; it is a different matter in seed orchards and for nursery stock, while large-scale planting of the silver fir (*Abies alba*) in Britain has been thwarted by die-back caused by *Adelges nordmannianeae*.

As the leaves of dominant species in temperate woodlands age they not only become tougher but also tend to have increasing concentrations of resins, tannins or other compounds which are thought to defend them against various herbivores. Winter-moth caterpillars (*Operophtera brumata*) reared on oak leaves picked at the end of May were found to develop into smaller (and therefore less fertile) adults than those which fed on younger leaves, with lower tannin levels.[99] Development early in the season is typical of many Lepidoptera and Coleoptera with larvae feeding on oak or beech leaves. Among species which feed on older leaves, some complete their development in the following year, while others develop as leaf-miners in the tannin-free mesophyll (Fig. 6.3). Oaks and other broad-leaved trees in Britain are sometimes defoliated by caterpillars such as those of *Operophtera* and the green oak roller (*Tortrix viridana*). Damage was widespread in England and Wales in 1979 and 1980. In Chaddesley Woods, Worcs., at the end of May, 1980, after a month of high temperatures and virtually no rain, numerous oaks, hazels and even common ash were completely defoliated, although individual oaks which had only just begun to flush escaped attack. Falling frass was distinctly audible as it hit the bone-dry litter, and trunks were festooned with silken skeins produced by caterpillars descending to seek food or to pupate. Yet by mid-July these ravages were largely masked by lammas growth (see Section 9.2). Outbreaks

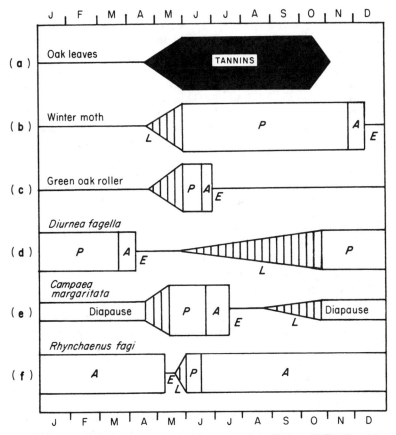

Fig. 6.3 Phenology of foliage-feeding insects on oak and beech. **(a)** Tannin content of leaves of *Quercus robur*. **(b)–(e)** Phenology of four species of Lepidoptera on oak (from Varley, G. C. in Petrusewicz[181]). **(f)** *Rhynchaenus fagi*; beech leaves are mined by the larvae and skeletonized by the adult weevils (data from Nielsen, B. O. (1978). *Natura Jutlandica*, **20**, 259–72.) **E**, egg; **P**, pupa; **A**, adult; **L**, larval growth periods, shaded.

of this kind are relatively minor compared with the plagues of gypsy moth caterpillars (*Porthetria dispar* = *Lymantria dispar*) in New England, which originated from small numbers introduced from Europe in the 1860s.

Yew (*Taxus baccata*) is an example of a tree with alkaloids in the foliage and seeds which are poisonous to Man and livestock, while β-ecdyson, a moulting hormone commonly found in gymnosperms, presumably disrupts development in herbivorous insects. Alkaloids, tannins and other 'defensive compounds' are at their greatest diversity in the tropics, a feature perhaps reflecting the wealth of potential herbivores. In general such plants are protected from defoliation, although certain animals may specialize in feeding on them, for example the proboscis monkey on tannin-rich foliage in Malaysian mangrove swamps. Plants growing on tropical white-sand soils are particularly rich in defensive compounds, for example, greenheart (*Ocotea*) and mora (*Dimorphandra*), whose timbers are extremely resistant to decay. The foliage of plants from New Jersey pine barrens has also been described as being 'unharvestable' by herbivores, and as yielding 'a medicine man's warehouse'.[123]

Further north, a native lepidopteran, the spruce budworm (*Choristoneura fumiferana*), normally occurs at low densities. Periodically it erupts to produce deadly conifer-defoliating epidemics which last 5–10 years; in Quebec, these are known to have occurred at 30- to 70-year intervals back to 1704. In the forests of New Brunswick, S.E. Canada, species diversity was gradually reduced by selective felling, leaving mainly birch and balsam fir (*Abies balsamea*), the latter being the conifer most seriously damaged by budworm. Extensive die-back of birches in the 1940s preceded a 1947 epidemic on the remaining conifers, supporting the idea that pest outbreaks are favoured by lower diversity. Continuous stands of mature balsam fir, a small tree very rich in resin, are most vulnerable possibly because evaporation rates within the canopy are particularly favourable to the caterpillars. The survival of the later larval stages is favoured by dry, sunny summers; a succession of these, as in the late 1900s and 1940s, can release a population from its low-level, endemic phase.

In the western United States, the bark of *Pinus contorta* is attacked by females of the mountain pine beetle (*Dendroctonus ponderosae*), thus liberating terpenes and an aggregating pheromone which attract additional egg-laying females.[31] If only small numbers are involved, eggs or larvae may be controlled by resin. Large-scale invasions girdle and kill trees, possibly through the action of blue-stain fungi, introduced by the beetles, which maintain moisture conditions favourable for larval development. Major infestations occur at 20- to 40-year intervals, devastating the largest trees over vast areas and thus altering community structure (see Section 7.4).

The generally low population densities of most forest insect pest species may be contrasted with the situation in agriculture, where many species are persistent pests. These endemic populations of forest insects were likened by Bevan[46] to 'a porpoise close behind us'. As an example of treading on the forester's tail, Bevan details the defoliation of Scots pine in the U.K. by pine looper caterpillars (*Bupalus piniaria*). This is a native species, but although periodic epidemics had been recorded in continental Europe for over a hundred years, large-scale damage was not seen in the U.K. until 1953, when it was reported from Cannock Chase and in Morayshire. Economic damage is most likely to occur in Scots pine, at the pole stage and later, growing on sandy soil in low rainfall areas; its absence from Thetford Chase has not been satisfactorily explained. Annual predictions of the likelihood of outbreaks, based on sampling of litter and soil for pupae, can be supplemented by egg counts. Aerial spraying has been used by the Forestry Commission against the young caterpillars on only four occasions (up to 1979). D.D.T. has been replaced by non-persistent tetrachlorvinphos and, more recently, by an insecticide which upsets moulting by preventing chitin deposition. Such treatments reduce populations to low, non-outbreak levels.

Pine looper caterpillars attack needles after buds have been formed, so that defoliated trees can flush again in the following year, and therefore recover from an attack, but this ability may be upset by drought or secondary pests. After the 1953 Cannock attack, 50 000 defoliated *Pinus sylvestris* were further exploited, as breeding sites, by pine shoot beetles (*Tomicus piniperda*; Fig. 6.4) which had previously existed at a low, endemic level in an apparently healthy forest. Usually this species frequents freshly-felled logs for breeding, attacks on living trees being limited to shoot-pruning due to maturation feeding; the '6-week rule' aims to remove such logs within 6 weeks of felling between March and June, before they can be exploited. Breeding in healthy trees is normally resisted by resin, but not in the case of *Bupalus*-weakened trees. Large areas of breeding material were also provided on Cannock by the New Year gales of 1976 and the fires of 1977. Even after removal of timber, however, replanting has its pest problems in the form of *Hylobius* (Fig. 6.4) and *Hylastes*, beetles which breed in the remaining stumps and then attack the stems and roots of seedlings, causing heavy mortality, unless protected by Lindane dips.

Another indigenous species, the pine beauty (*Panolis flammea*), known to be endemic throughout Britain and to have caused serious damage to Scots pine in Central Europe, has only recently become a pest of British forests. Since 1976 there have been annual defoliations of lodgepole pine (*Pinus contorta*) in various parts of Scotland, followed by death of terminal buds. The bacterial preparation *Bacillus thuringiensis*, which is specific against caterpillars, failed to reach young larvae feeding within needle tissues. Regular pupal surveys are now followed, where appropriate, by aerial applications of non-persistent insecticides such as fenitrothion, environmental hazards being further reduced by using target-specific spraying techniques.

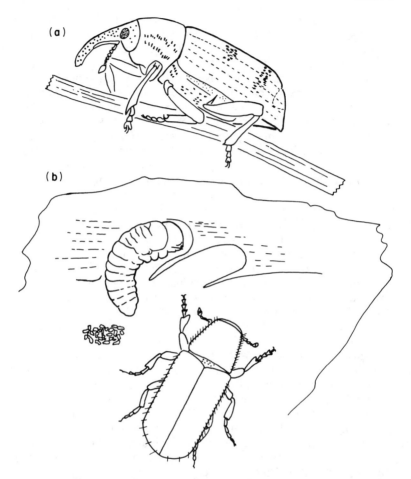

Fig. 6.4 Beetle pests from Cannock Forest, Staffs, June 1980. **(a)** *Hylobius abietis* (large pine weevil). Larvae develop in stumps and logs; adults damage bark of young pines. **(b)** *Tomicus piniperda* (pine-shoot beetle). Larva and adult under bark of a pine log, a potential source of infestation of weakened standing trees.

Woodwasps (Siricidae) are of little importance to conifers in Britain, unlike the situation following their introduction into Australia and New Zealand, where *Sirex noctilio* kills trees, especially *Pinus radiata*. Heavily trimmed or lopped trees are most likely to be killed; translocation, transpiration and phloem respiration rates are altered in these 'stressed' trees. Subsequent changes in bark permeability allow a greater loss of water vapour and volatile monoterpenes, thus attracting *Sirex* females. These introduce their eggs in mucus, as well as spores of the basidiomycete *Amylostereum areolatum*, beneath the bark. Fungus and mucus both cause further inhibition of translocation, so that more woodwasps are attracted. The fungus-softened wood provides food for the tunnelling larvae, but this fungal development is also the cause of death to the tree.[154]

As with pathogens, public health inspectors need to be particularly vigilant at ports and timber yards if the establishment of exotic pests, such as large bark beetles (*Dendroctonus* spp.) in Britain, is to be prevented. In addition, there is always the possibility of further pests arising from among the ranks of indigenous species.

In conclusion, whereas some tree species, especially in the tropics, are chemically protected from virtually all animal attack, others support a wide range of consumers, normally without obvious detrimental effects. On the other hand, certain interactions are more serious and may even be fatal to the tree.

7

Balanced Communities?

7.1 POPULATION FLUCTUATIONS: KEY-FACTOR ANALYSIS

It is often taken as axiomatic that there exists a 'Balance of Nature', at least in ecosystems with minimal human interference. In fact, such a balance has never been demonstrated for all the component plant and animal species of a particular community, studies usually being restricted to, at most, a few species. Before considering community interactions we will therefore concentrate on the population dynamics of individual animal species.

The numbers of individuals at a given stage in the life cycle usually fluctuate in successive generations, the amplitude varying in different species (Fig. 7.1). The major causes of inter-generation fluctuation in species with discrete, non-overlapping generations, can be determined by **key-factor analysis**.[28] Basically this involves following the progress through time of a single cohort (the progeny of a population born at approximately the same time) and so constructing an age-specific life-table, to show the numbers surviving at a particular time. The decrease in numbers at successive time intervals is a measure of mortality, including not only death but also other processes such as emigration which result in a decrease. If abundance is expressed in logarithms, the difference represents the killing power or k-value of the process or factors responsible for the measured mortality:

$$k\text{-value} = \log_{10}N_s - \log_{10}N_{s+1}$$

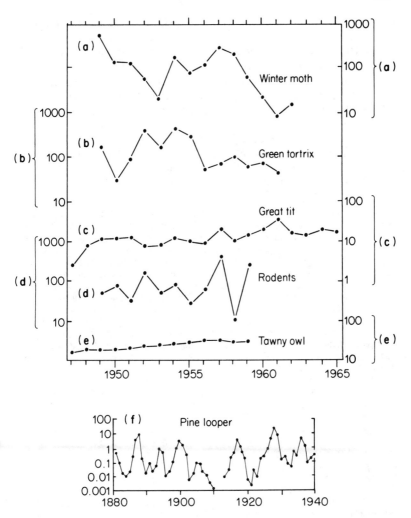

Fig. 7.1 Examples of population fluctuations. **(a)–(e)** at Wytham, Oxford: **(a)** *Operophtera brumata*, larvae per m^2; **(b)** *Tortrix viridana*, larvae per m^2; **(c)** *Parus major*, breeding pairs per 10 ha; **(d)** *Apodemus sylvaticus* plus *Clethrionomys glareolus* per 5 ha in June; **(e)** *Strix aluco*, pairs per 525 ha (= Wytham Estate). **(f)** At Letzlingen, Germany; pupae of *Bupalus piniaria* per m^2. (**(a)** and **(b)** from Varley;[231] **(c)** from Perrins;[179] **(d)** and **(e)** after Southern;[217] **(f)** from Varley, Gradwell and Hassell.[28])

where N_s and N_{s+1} are population densities at successive sampling occasions.

The total generation mortality, K, equals the sum of the individual, sequential k-values. The contribution of each to changes in K can be assessed by compiling a series of life tables for successive generations, in order to determine the k-value which is mainly responsible for inter-generation fluctuation: this is designated the *key factor*, being the key to change.

The results of Varley and Gradwell's classic work on winter moth (*Operophtera brumata*) at Wytham Wood, near Oxford, can be used to illustrate two methods of key-factor analysis. Sampling techniques and results are summarized in Table 7.1. and Fig. 7.2. Visual

Table 7.1 Life table for Winter moth at Wytham Wood, 1955–56 (from Varley, Gradwell and Hassell[28]). Actual samples yielded the values (numbers per m²) shown in bold type, from which the remainder are derived. Sampling was confined to five oak trees (*Quercus robur*), of total canopy area 282 m². The wingless females were trapped in November and December as they climbed up the trunks to lay their average complement of 150 eggs each. After feeding in April and May, caterpillars were collected as they descended on threads to pupate in the soil; they were examined to estimate numbers due to be killed by particular parasites, such as the tachinid fly *Cyzenis albicans*, whose eggs are ingested by caterpillars. The number of healthy pupae (15.0) is double the number of adult females emerging during the following winter, assuming a 1:1 sex ratio. Pupal parasitism was estimated by trapping the emerging adults of the wasp *Cratichneumon culex*. The remaining difference between healthy larvae (83.0) and healthy pupae was taken to have been caused by predation, acting before pupal parasitism.

	No. killed	No. live	Log no. live	k-value
Females climbing trees, 1955		**4.39**		
Maximum oviposition (= no. of females × 150)		658.0	2.82	
Fully grown larvae	551.6	**96.4**	1.98	$0.84 = k_1$
Attacked by *Cyzenis*	**6.2**	90.2	1.95	$0.03 = k_2$
Attacked by other parasites	**2.6**	87.6	1.94	$0.01 = k_3$
Infected by protozoan	**4.6**	83.0	1.92	$0.02 = k_4$
Pupae killed by predators	54.6	28.4	1.45	$0.47 = k_5$
Pupae killed by parasites	**13.4**	15.0	1.18	$0.27 = k_6$
				$1.64 = K$
Females climbing trees, 1956		**7.5**		

examination shows that changes in K are most closely correlated with changes in k_1, which is therefore the key factor for this population. In certain cases it may not be so easy to distinguish the key factor by visual correlation. The use of regressions of each k-value on the corresponding generation mortality, K, has therefore been proposed. The k-value with the highest regression coefficient (b, the slope), is the key factor (Fig. 7.2c).

The key factor for winter moth at Wytham, k_1, corresponds to the reduction in numbers, described as **winter disappearance**, between the

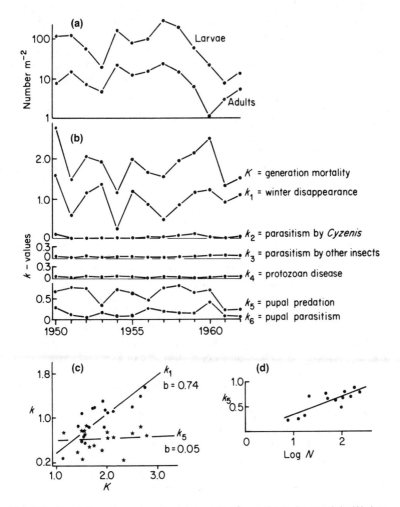

Fig. 7.2 Population dynamics of winter moth (*Operophtera brumata*) in Wytham Wood, Oxford. **(a)** Generation curves. **(b)** Graphical key-factor analysis. **(c)** Key-factor analysis by regression coefficients. **(d)** Density-dependent action of pupal predation (k_5). **((a), (b), (d)** from Varley, Gradwell and Hassell;[28] **(c)** from Podoler, H. and Rogers, D. (1975). *Journal of Animal Ecology*, **44**, 85–115.)

calculated initial population of eggs and the mature larvae which descend from the trees to pupate. Observations in the canopy showed that neither egg mortality nor feeding by birds on caterpillars contributed much to k_1. However, examination of individual trees revealed that winter disappearance was least on trees which flushed early, allowing the first instar larvae access to nutritious foliage of low tannin content (Fig. 6.3). Most larvae on late-flushing trees failed to find food and emigrated on silken threads, giving at least some a chance of surviving elsewhere. The degree of synchronization between egg hatching and bud burst is largely determined by the effects of spring temperatures on egg development, the time of flushing of individual trees being less dependent on the external environment. A similar relationship has been detected for *Tortrix viridana* infestations on oaks in the English Lake District.

The effects of parasites which attack winter moth caterpillars (k_2-k_4) showed very little variation from year to year (Fig. 7.2b), unlike pupal predation (k_5), which often varied in the opposite direction to k_1, suggesting a possible compensatory or regulatory role.

7.2 REGULATION

Regulation, in the sense of restoring a population towards its characteristic equilibrium level after disturbance, implies negative feedback, involving **density dependence**[22]. A density-dependent mortality process (e.g. disease, competition) or factor (e.g. a specific pathogen) has a **proportionately** more adverse effect on a high density population than on the same species when less abundant (Fig. 7.3). Although regulation depends on density dependence, density dependent processes are only regulatory if they are of sufficient magnitude and act at the right time to offset the effects of disturbance.

Varley and Gradwell tested for density-dependent relationships in their winter moth life-table data by plotting k-values against the logarithms of the population densities on which they acted. Only k_5, **pupal predation**, showed a positive regression which was statistically significant, indicating density dependence (Fig. 7.2d). The relative contributions of various beetles and small mammals to this predation are incompletely known. Somewhat surprisingly, larval parasitism does not appear to vary in a density-dependent fashion; although percentage parasitism by *Cyzenis* tends to be greater on trees with higher numbers of caterpillars, this is less likely in years when winter moths are generally abundant. The small effect of *Cyzenis* is largely a result of the strongly density dependent mortality experienced by both parasite and host as pupae in the soil. Winter moths introduced

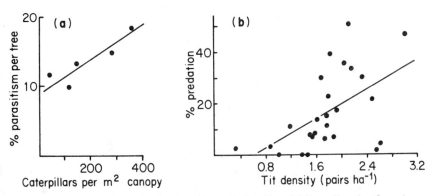

Fig. 7.3 Examples of density-dependent relationships. **(a)** Parasitism by *Cyzenis albicans* of winter moth caterpillars on five oak trees, Wytham, 1958 (from Hassell, M. P. (1980). *Journal of Animal Ecology*, **49**, 603–28). **(b)** Predation by weasels on nests of titmice (*Parus* spp.) in nestboxes, Wytham, 1947–1972. (From Dunn, E. (1977). *Journal of Animal Ecology*, **46**, 633–52.)

into Canada lacked the regulatory influence typical of Wytham populations, and increased to very high levels. Subsequent release of *Cyzenis* resulted in effective biological control.

7.3   DYNAMICS OF SPECIFIC WOODLAND ANIMALS

Pine looper and spruce budworm

In areas where *Bupalus piniaria* is a pest, pupal surveys reveal fluctuating populations with major peaks, several years apart, which represent potential outbreaks of loopers and possible defoliation in the following summer (Figs 7.1 and 7.4). Within a year or two, however, numbers fall again to a low, endemic level. Elsewhere, as for example at Thetford in East Anglia, average populations are much lower, and even relatively high counts do not lead to damaging outbreaks. This was the situation in the forest in the Netherlands where Klomp[139] studied changes in abundance of various stages of *Bupalus* over a 14-year period. The causes of death among early larval instars were not established, but the influence of weather on survival was assumed to be important; the extent of this mortality appeared to make a major contribution to the pattern of overall fluctuations. Among larger caterpillars, predation by tits and other birds was thought to be density-dependent, while the marked reduction in numbers between pupation and adult emergence was due mainly to parasites. In fact Klomp later suggested that parasitism, either by a tachinid fly or an ichneumonid wasp, was the key factor for *Bupalus* in this site (see[28]). Whatever the factors responsible for

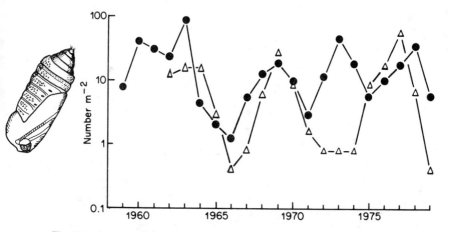

Fig. 7.4 Pupal counts of *Bupalus piniaria*, representing the highest count from any compartment at Cannock, Staffs, (●) and Tentsmuir, Fife (△).

change, populations never reached levels at which there was likely to be shortage of food.

In sites such as Cannock, outbreaks seem to occur when survival is particularly favoured by the weather, enabling populations to escape from the normal constraints of their enemies. The subsequent fall in numbers of pupae could be a consequence of larval competition for food, especially if trees are defoliated. The decline would be compounded by the production of smaller, less fecund adults, as a result of increased mutual interference between larvae at high densities (Fig. 7.5). Adult mortality and emigration would also affect the number of eggs laid.

The aim of control measures should be to time the application of insecticide so that the larval population is reduced by 80–90% before the caterpillars have become large enough to cause damage (Fig. 7.6b). The remaining larvae are then mopped up by parasites such as *Cratichneumon nigritarius*, so that populations return to endemic levels without the intervention of defoliation and possible subsequent attack by *Tomicus* (see Section 6.5). Our understanding even of this well known pest is, however, far from complete, since epidemics may collapse naturally, as in 1970 at Wykeham, Yorkshire, when a normally insignificant larval parasite is thought to have rendered spraying superfluous.

By way of comparison, the course of a typical epidemic of **spruce budworm**, and the effects of spraying, are shown in Fig. 7.6a. Data collected during the last 30 years have recently been incorporated into a complex simulation model, involving interactions between the

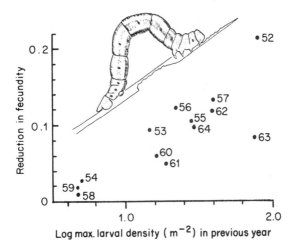

Fig. 7.5 Delayed density-dependent influence of larval density on fecundity in *Bupalus piniaria* at 'de Hoge Veluwe', in the Netherlands. (Modified from Dempster,[75] after Klomp.[139])

pest and its enemies, forest maturity, the weather and management practices.[180] This has helped to explain why outbreaks are triggered at particular stages of forest maturation, and why control measures applied against such outbreaks are locked into a fate like that of Sisyphus, who was punished in Hades by repeatedly having to push a huge stone uphill, only for it to roll down again. The vital role of avian predators is stressed, particularly if combined with the use of viruses rather than insecticides. The potential for natural control can be increased further by reducing effective forest maturity through particular logging strategies.

Aphids

Key-factor analysis has not been applied to aphids, because of the complexities associated with overlapping generations, polymorphism and migration. Dixon has studied the population dynamics of certain tree-dwelling species, especially the sycamore aphid, *Drepanosiphum platanoidis*, and has recently reviewed his findings.[80, 81] *D. plata-noidis* overwinters as eggs laid on sycamore twigs. Larvae which emerge from these eggs before the buds of a particular tree have expanded in spring are especially vulnerable to predation and to being dislodged by rain. However, if egg-hatch and bud-burst are synchronized, the larvae are able to feed on young leaves with a high amino-nitrogen content; these larvae develop into adults which are potentially larger, and so of a higher fecundity, although this may be

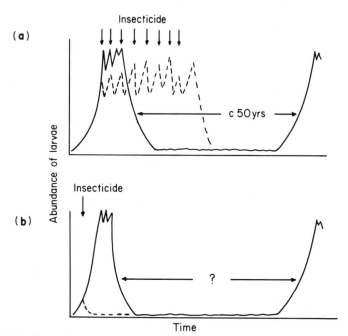

Fig. 7.6 Fluctuations of conifer pests treated with insecticide (---) and untreated (—). **(a)** Spruce budworm in New Brunswick; **(b)** pine looper in Britain. In contrast to results obtained with spruce budworm, high populations of pine looper can be rapidly reduced to low, endemic levels by a single application of insecticide. (From Way, M. J. and Bevan, D. (1977). In *Ecological Effects of Pesticides*. Perring, F. H. and Mellanby, K. (Eds), pp. 95–110. Academic Press. Reproduced by permission of the Council of the Linnean Society of London.)

diminished as a result of overcrowding. There are two further parthenogenetic generations before males and egg-laying females gradually appear among the late-summer population, so that some eggs can be produced even if there is an unusually early leaf-fall. An inverse relationship has been observed between the abundance of aphids colonizing the leaves in spring and the numbers of egg-laying females in the following autumn. This was once thought to be a consequence of the reproductive rate in early autumn being influenced by aphid-induced changes in the quality of the host plant. During the autumn, various nutrients are withdrawn into the trunk from the leaves of trees (see Section 9.5). Senescing leaves of infested sycamores retain more nitrogen, implying that less is available to aphids in the phloem (Fig. 7.7a). It has since been shown that autumnal fecundity is determined largely by the size of the second-generation adults, which is itself related to the degree of crowding

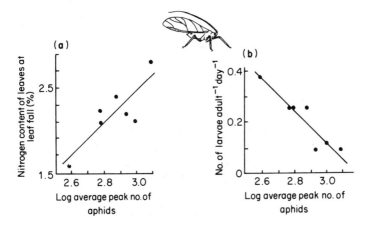

Fig. 7.7 Aspects of the population dynamics of sycamore aphids (*Drepanosiphum platanoidis*). **(a)** Relation between nitrogen content of leaves at leaf fall and spring–summer population density of aphids. **(b)** Fecundity between 15 July–15 August in relation to aphid abundance earlier in the year. Average peak number = $\frac{1}{2}$[(peak no. on buds + peak at budburst) 2 + summer peak]. (From Dixon.[81])

earlier in the summer (Fig. 7.7b). The timing of the autumn increase depends on the duration of the period of reproductive diapause during June and July, when virtually no larvae are produced, this aestivation being prolonged the more the aphids are crowded. At this time, when there may be a hundred or more adults per leaf, mutual disturbance results in reduced rates of feeding on leaves with a low nitrogen content. These density-dependent consequences of crowding are considered by Dixon to be capable of regulating populations of sycamore aphids, and in fact they tend to overcompensate for the disturbing effects of the weather, especially autumn winds. The action of parasites and predators, such as anthocorid bugs, is not considered to be regulatory; by killing large numbers of young aphids in those autumns when the fecundity of crowded populations is already low, they may merely add to the overcompensation. Similar mechanisms seem to apply to the lime aphid (*Eucallipterus tiliae*), where high densities lead also to increased migratory activity, while in this species and in the green spruce aphid (*Elatobium abietinum*) there is stronger evidence that aphid-induced changes in food quality are important in the population dynamics of aphids. In other parts of the world various arboreal aphids, including *E. tiliae* and the walnut aphid (*Chromaphis juglandicola*), have been controlled by parasites, showing that the role of natural enemies cannot be totally discounted when considering changes in aphid abundance.

Great tits

Among woodland vertebrates, long-term studies at Wytham have provided a wealth of data about populations of great tits,[179] small rodents and tawny owls,[217] and, to a lesser extent, weasels[136] (Fig. 7.1).

Great tits (*Parus major*) feed their young for about two weeks in the nest (built in a tree-hole or nesting box) and for a similar period after the young have fledged and left the nest. Spring temperatures affect the date when the first eggs are laid (Fig. 7.8a), basically through the availability of food such as March flies (*Bibio* spp.), needed for the production of eggs; an average clutch of 8–10 eggs in as many days is almost equivalent to doubling the females's body

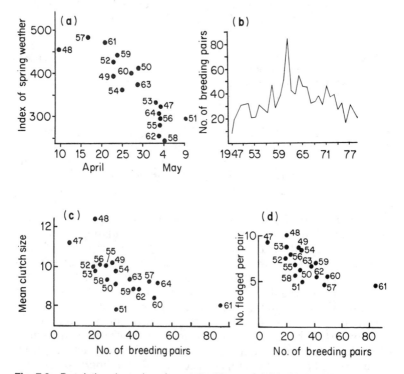

Fig. 7.8 Population dynamics of great tits (*Parus major*) in Marley Wood, Wytham, Oxford. **(a)** Average date of breeding, based on the first egg laid by each female, in relation to spring weather (index = daily max. + min. temperature (°C)/2 for 1 March–20 April). **(b)** Abundance of breeding adults, 1947–1979. **(c)** Influence of adult abundance on clutch size. **(d)** Density dependence of breeding success. **((a), (b)** From Perrins;[179] **(c), (d)** from Lack, D. (1966). *Population Studies of Birds.* Oxford University Press.)

weight. Hatching dates for eggs of moths such as *Operophtera* spp. and *Tortrix* spp. are also influenced by spring temperatures: the ensuing caterpillars provide the major source of food for the tit nestlings. Some correlation has been found between the time when caterpillars of early-summer species are most abundant (see Section 6.5), and the average date when nestlings are 11 days old and require the greatest number of food items. This peak feeding rate may involve the parents in as many as a thousand visits to the nest per day, yet it has been estimated that tits cull only 1–2% of the total caterpillar population. Young from early broods tend to be heavier than those reared later, and heavy fledglings are much more likely to survive and breed than are lighter birds. It is apparently advantageous for the tits to breed as early in the summer as the food supply for the females permits, thus producing the greatest number of offspring to survive the summer, when the young have to fend for themselves on small insects high in the canopy.

Between 1947 and 1968 in Marley Wood at Wytham the average number of fledglings per pair was six. Only about half the number of breeding adults died between one year and the next, so that if the breeding population was to be kept stable a marked reduction in the numbers of young before the following breeding season seemed inevitable. 'Mortality outside the breeding season' (i.e. between fledging and the setting up of breeding territories, which is usually in January) has been identified as the key factor for great tits in Marley Wood. Perrins[179] assumes that most of the decline in numbers of young birds is indeed mortality, occurring especially during the summer. The proportion of young which die is very much more variable than adult mortality. There was a positive correlation between survival of juveniles and the size of the mast crop of *Fagus sylvatica*, but this cannot be a direct causal relationship, since mast becomes available only after the survival rate has been determined; possibly mast crops are correlated with insect abundance during the summer. In contrast to this variable survival of young until the autumn, winter mortality is fairly constant from year to year, although during the severe winter of 1962–1963 the total population was reduced by 75%, and the young by 90%.

Disappearance need not necessarily imply death: it has been shown that some of the surplus of young birds could be accounted for by their emigrating to less suitable breeding sites such as hedgerows, having been unsuccessful in establishing woodland territories. Territorial behaviour does not set an upper limit to the number of breeding birds in a given area of woodland, but the size of individual territories seems to be related to the pressure exerted by intruders. Consequently there is an inverse relationship between average size of territory and the total woodland breeding population, the size of the latter being related in turn to two factors which determine breeding success: clutch size and hatching failure. Smaller territories generally provide less food for the female, while the time available for gathering food may be reduced by territorial disputes, the result being fewer eggs (Fig. 7.8c). Attacks on nests by weasels (*Mustela nivalis*) can lead to death of laying or incubating females, or of eggs or fledglings. The closer together the nest boxes at Wytham, the higher the proportion of nests attacked (Fig. 7.3b). Between 1947 and 1975, 23% of 4131 nests were attacked, but it is not known whether similar pressure is exerted on populations without nest boxes. The overall result is that more fledglings are produced per pair when the total breeding population is low than when it is high, an elegant example of a density-dependent relationship (Fig. 7.8d). Once on the wing, the young birds are still subject to predation: as many as 35% may be taken by sparrowhawks.

The flexibility of the territorial system in great tits permitted their breeding numbers at Wytham to fluctuate considerably over a 20-year period (Fig. 7.8b), as did numbers of woodmice and bank voles, the major food of strongly territorial tawny owls (Fig. 1.8).

Rodents, weasels and tawny owls

Woodmice (*Apodemus sylvaticus*) are strictly nocturnal, but bank voles (*Clethrionomys glareolus*) may also be active during the day. At Wytham, woodmice were found to subsist mainly on seeds, especially of oak and sycamore during the autumn. Voles ingested large amounts of green leaves from trees and shrubs, as well as seeds with soft testas, and also bark and leaf litter. In both species, the diet was supplemented in May by an influx of defoliating caterpillars. The breeding season normally extends from April to October, with four or five litters. Since populations are usually at their lowest level in the early summer, survival of young is probably poor at this time, but numbers typically pick up from midsummer, reaching a peak in autumn or early winter (Figs. 1.8 and 7.9). During the breeding season, there is a gradual change in age-structure and associated social behaviour, the older generation being replaced by younger and less antagonistic adults. *Overwintering survival* was broadly correlated with the size of the acorn crop of the previous autumn; a similar relationship between bank voles and ash seeds was observed in Lathkilldale.[90] Woodmice continued to breed into or even through the winter in 1956, 1958, 1962 and 1964 at Wytham: all were bumper years for acorns. Winter recruitment and improved survival resulted in the anomalous situation of the subsequent summer population being larger than that of the previous winter (Fig. 7.9). In years when

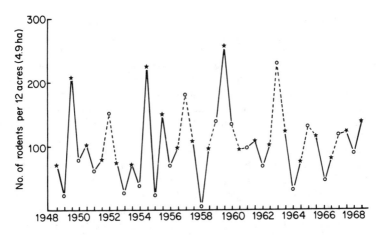

Fig. 7.9 Abundance of woodmice plus bank voles in Wytham Wood, estimated by live-trapping in December (★) and June (○). Interrupted lines indicate reversal of usual winter increase and summer decline. (From Southern.[217])

acorns were scarce, however, survival during the winter was poor, presumably reflecting competition for food.

Fluctuations in availability of acorns were thus primarily responsible for the considerable variation observed in the spring density of woodmice. However, this variation was found to be largely counteracted by a density-dependent postponement of the increase in numbers in late summer, this being later in years when spring numbers were high. The duration of this period of increase varied by as much as four months, and since numbers approximately double each month once it begins, this postponement had a considerable regulatory effect. Despite this regulation, numbers fluctuated markedly around a mean value of c. 20 ha^{-1}, and these small mammals were probably near the limit of their food supply on average one year out of two at Wytham.

It was concluded that weasels had no observable effect on rodent density or survival in Marley Wood,[136] in contrast to the control exerted on great tits. Apart from the influence of nest boxes on predation rates on tits, the major differences include predator/prey ratios, with many more rodents than tits per weasel, and the fact that the replacement of killed individuals occurs much more readily among the rodents, with their several litters, whereas lost clutches of eggs of tits are rarely replaced.

Weasels are opportunistic feeders, which are more likely to exploit birds' nests when rodent numbers are low. They expend considerable energy in hunting, especially for rodents, a food source for which they are most likely to be in competition with tawny owls (*Strix aluco*). Although they can exploit rodents, including young, in their tunnels (a resource denied to owls), they may occasionally be attacked by owls. Weasels usually breed only once in a lifetime which is not normally less than one year, in contrast to long-lived, *K*-selected owls, which employ a 'sit-and-wait' hunting strategy. Like weasels, owls appear to have little effect on the population density of rodents at Wytham, but they themselves are influenced by the abundance of rodents.

Between 1947 and 1959, the breeding success of tawny owls at Wytham was found to be closely linked to the abundance of woodmice and bankvoles, especially between about mid-March, when up to four eggs are usually laid, and mid-May, when the chicks can be left alone in the nest. During the summer, owls transfer their attention to other foods, such as moles, beetles and worms. In years when the combined density of the two species of rodent, assessed in June, was below the average of 20 ha^{-1}, owls failed to breed, or at best produced very few eggs (Fig. 7.10a). Success did not improve

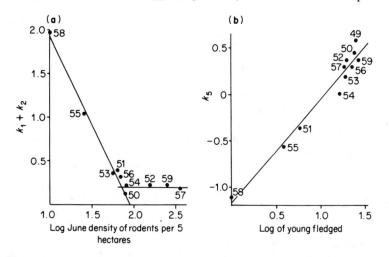

Fig. 7.10   Tawny owls (*Strix aluco*) on Wytham Estate. **(a)** Influence of rodent density on population losses through failure to breed (k_1) and to achieve maximum clutch size (k_2). **(b)** The density-dependent nature of overwinter disappearance (k_5). (From Southern.[217])

when prey densities were higher, probably because the owls could deal with only a certain number in a given time. Failure to breed was identified as the key factor at Wytham during 1947–1959. The number of pairs which failed to breed was rarely less than 30% of the total, and in 1958, when rodents were particularly scarce at Wytham, no owls bred at all. Hatching failure largely reflected desertion of eggs by females leaving the nest to supplement the food brought by their mates, while failure to fledge the young was also often a result of food shortages; in both instances, wet weather had a deleterious effect on hunting, the rodents being less audible in the sodden forest floor. The number of young fledged per year was usually $c.20$, except in 1951, 1955 and 1958, when rodent numbers were very low. The mean expectation of life is about five years, some adults occupying the same territory for more than seven years. Consequently, there are usually far more fledglings than are needed to compensate for the deaths of territory-holding adults.

Owlets which failed to find a vacant territory either died or emigrated, thus contributing to 'overwintering loss'. This loss varied from year to year in a density-dependent fashion, a greater proportion of owlets disappearing when their numbers were high, and with immigration in years when insufficient offspring were produced at Wytham (Fig. 7.10b). In contrast to the situation in great tits, recruitment to the adult population is limited by a remarkably rigid territorial system, which has persisted at Wytham with little change over many years. With $c.30$ breeding pairs, the average size of territory was $c.16$ ha, being greater in regions of denser cover. The chief benefit of this system is apparently that breeding success improves as the residents gain hunting experience within their territory. However, even experience cannot guarantee success every year.

Summary
From this review it can be seen that the breeding success of certain woodland animals depends on the synchronization of their life-cycles with food availability. Lean years may have far-reaching consequences, as when the acorn crop failed at Wytham in 1957: the following spring rodent numbers were at their lowest for the decade and tawny owls failed to breed. There is a variety of influences which can act as key factors, but even for the same species these may differ between sites and between years.

Although the significance of key factors is now generally recognized, there is less agreement about the occurrence of regulation in general, or of density dependence in particular cases (e.g. overwintering loss in tawny owls[75]). It is particularly difficult to assess the role of predators in regulation, as this requires long-term studies of changes in the proportion of prey killed as prey density alters. Winter moth populations were regulated at Wytham by predation on pupae, and in Nova Scotia by larval parasites, but there is insufficient evidence to decide whether predation by birds on pine looper caterpillars is density dependent. Among sycamore aphids and the various vertebrates studied at Wytham, regulation seems not to depend on natural enemies, with the exception, possibly artificial, of the box-nesting tits. In these species, and probably also in pine looper, the degree of crowding, itself often dependent on food availability, determines the extent of the subsequent input to the population, sometimes through behaviour-mediated changes in fecundity and timing of increases. Such populations are said to be largely self-regulated. Tawny owls, as top carnivores with virtually no enemies, exercise density-dependent control over membership of their exclusive territories.

The long-term studies at Wytham have recorded the gradual recovery of populations after climatically induced perturbations, such as the effects of the severe winter of 1946–1947. They also provided an opportunity to assess the effects of myxomatosis, which almost eliminated rabbits from Wytham in 1954. During the following year, foxes, owls and stoats fed increasingly on small mammals, while extensive attacks on birds' nests by weasels were first recorded in 1957. Myxomatosis caused a considerable upheaval, not only through its direct and indirect effects on animal populations, but also by removing the rabbit as a major obstacle to scrub regeneration.

7.4   CHANGES IN COMMUNITY STRUCTURE

The impact of such events as the 1976 drought on woodland communities is not yet fully known, but the likely effects of Dutch elm disease have been reviewed[39]. Of the 150 species of invertebrate associated with elm in Britain, only 38 are restricted to elm, including a gall mite and the white-letter hairstreak butterfly, which might become locally extinct. There is some evidence of regional shortages of nesting places for owls, and this would also be expected to apply to other birds which habitually used elms for nesting or roosting. Insects associated with bark beetle burrows have naturally increased, but the influence on decomposers is less clear. In shaded and damp situations they will be favoured by the increased availability of dead wood. In sites exposed to extreme insolation and desiccation, however, standing or fallen trees are virtually immune to attack, being likened by Elton[7] to kiln-dried timber. Truly woodland communities, as opposed to those of hedgerows and copses, should show little change, except where susceptible elms are locally abundant, as on scarp slopes of Jurassic limestone in the Cotswolds, where short-term reversion to scrub may be expected.

If bark beetles are to breed in them elms must be above a certain size, so it might be possible to perpetuate the species (and perhaps some of the community) by cutting back suckers before they become vulnerable. Similarly, mountain pine beetles tend to attack the largest diameter trees of *Pinus contorta* (lodgepole pine; see Section 6.5), so that infestations decline when few large trees are left alive.[31] In some regions of North America where lodgepole pine is seral, its survival and that of the beetles depends on fire, since otherwise the lodgepole pines are killed by beetles, and eventually succeeded by shade tolerant tree species including Douglas fir, a very large conifer with very thick bark. Extremely hot fires will kill even this species, while favouring seed release from the semi-serotinous (resin-sealed) cones of *P. contorta*. As the stand matures it becomes increasingly susceptible to beetle attack, producing the necessary tinder for further fires and the perpetuation by fire of *P. contorta*. This provides a clear example of the effects of biotic and abiotic factors on competitive interactions and hence on the structure of a woodland community.

7.5 DIVERSITY AND STABILITY

The idea that the balance of relatively simple communities of plants and animals is more easily upset, by destructive oscillations or invasions, than that of more diverse communities,[85] has become enshrined in the literature as 'complexity begets stability'[159] although Elton himself stressed that this needed verification. Elton assumed that in a species-rich community any species would accumulate enough enemies of different species to provide a complex system of checks and buffers against an abnormal increase in its numbers. In other words, stability was largely dependent on complexity of food-web organization.

Epidemics of pests or diseases provide an example of instability; they are normally thought to be typical of artificial monocultures rather than of natural stands, and to be more prevalent in non-tropical woodlands, although even tropical rain forests are not as free from pest outbreaks as used to be supposed. Foresters in temperate regions often succeed in maintaining the unnatural balance of monocultures until harvesting by the careful application of cultural practices, based on experience of the species selected for a particular site. Pest outbreaks are frequently associated with over-mature stands, or with inappropriate selection of species; recent increases in caterpillar attacks on immature conifers in Britain are partially a consequence of wide-scale planting since World War II, in sites for which experience was lacking. Outbreaks are not restricted to monocultures: in more diverse woodlands in temperate regions, pests such as spruce budworm are thought to maintain a fairly high level of diversity among trees by periodically devastating any species which tends to become dominant.[237]

The importance of disturbance in the regeneration of forest trees is discussed in Section 5.1. Although various mechanisms help to maintain species diversity, there are instances where succession leads to a climax dominated by one or a few species of tree. These communities may occur in areas where the climate is severe, as in the taiga. Elsewhere, soil conditions and the longevity of a particular species may lead to its becoming the climax dominant, as is the case with beech (*Fagus sylvatica*), a tree which suffers relatively little from insect pests, on the English chalk.

Tropical rain forest includes the most complex communities in existence. For example, the 17 km² of Barro Colorado Island, Panama, harbour over 700 species of trees, shrubs and lianas. Here the opportunity for diversification of feeding niches, provided not only by the great range of plants but also by the profusion of flowers and fruits, would be expected to result in extreme stability.

One theory which attempts to explain the diversity of tropical forests was proposed independently by Janzen and by Connell, and involves the participation of herbivores.[116] Seed predation by insects (many of which were assumed to be host-specific, e.g. bruchids in Costa Rica, see Section 4.3) and by more catholic vertebrates, killed virtually all seeds in the immediate vicinity of the parent tree. Similarly, any seedlings which managed to develop were more likely to be killed the closer they were to parental sources of host-specific defoliators (cf. oaks in the U.K.). Consequently only those seeds which were transported some way from the parent would have a significant chance of escaping discovery, germinating and surviving as seedlings. This led to the assumption that recruitment of new adults was possible only beyond a certain minimal distance (Fig. 7.11a).

It was predicted that this minimal distance effect would result in a low density of conspecifics, with adults tending to be spaced out, corresponding to the generally held view that tropical trees are thinly spread and fairly evenly spaced. So long as other species were able to colonize the minimal area denied to conspecific offspring, dominance by a single species should be prevented. However, Hubbell[116] has shown that nearest-neighbour distances between conspecific adults are insufficient for this spacing by predation to account for the observed numbers of co-existing species. Furthermore, experiments designed to assess the relationship between predation pressure, seed density and distance from the seed parent have rarely borne out the predictions of Janzen's original hypothesis.[66]

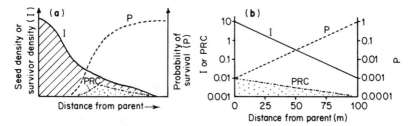

Fig. 7.11 Graphical models of the effects of seed or seedling predation on tree spacing. **(a)** Janzen's model, which suggests that recruitment of new adults (as shown by the population recruitment curve, PRC) occurs only beyond a certain minimal distance. **(b)** Hubbell's re-scaled model, which assumes that a small fraction of a large number of seeds next to the parent tree escapes predation. (From Hubbell.[116])

Hubbell stresses the high variability which characterizes the results of many of these experiments, and concludes that there may not necessarily be any clear relationship between seed predation and the spacing of trees. Within one site, the number of seeds produced by a species varies between individuals and between years, resulting in intraspecific variation of minimal distances and in the possibility of clumped patterns of dispersion. Surveys of two sites in Costa Rica showed that of the 114 tree species for which there were sufficient data all were either clumped or randomly dispersed, but none showed uniform spacing. The density distributions of young trees were equally revealing: some showed an exponential decrease away from the parent, others remained almost constant with distance, but very few showed a reduction close to the parent, as predicted by the seed-predation hypothesis. Re-scaling of Janzen's *seed-shadow model* (Fig. 7.11b) emphasizes the importance of the actual numbers of seeds surviving. Even if only a small proportion of the bulk of the seeds which fall near the parent manage to survive, they will contribute the largest numbers to the recruitment curve, so encouraging clumping.

Environmental heterogeneity is presumably responsible for the occupation of certain habitats by particular species, but specificity seems unlikely to be narrow enough to account for the co-existence of 100 tree species in a single hectare.[66] Factors leading to diversity in plant communities may (Section 5.2), or may not (Section 3.4), be associated with the concept of the regeneration gap. The regeneration of various species is favoured by the availability at particular times of gaps of different sizes. Connell[66] has suggested that species diversity will be highest either at an intermediate stage in succession after a large disturbance, or after smaller disturbances that are neither very frequent nor very infrequent ('intermediate disturbance'). Without these disturbances, such species-rich communities tend to evolve towards a lower diversity state or climax, which is much more widespread in the tropics than is often realized. Large areas of rain forest in Africa, South and Central America and S.E. Asia are dominated by a single species, for example ironwood, *Cynometra alexandri*, in the largest rainforest in Uganda.

There is still considerable disagreement concerning the connections between diversity and stability. The simple mathematical models and laboratory experiments quoted by Elton[85] support the idea of a positive relationship. However, May[159] has shown that a wide range of models suggests that as a system becomes more complex, with a richer structure of interdependence, so it becomes more dynamically fragile, tending to collapse if environmental or population characteristics undergo appreciable change. Complex tropical communities, although intrinsically fragile, may remain stable over very long periods, but are ill-equipped to withstand the perturbations imposed by man. Whatever the explanation of their diversity, we can ill afford to disrupt these unique communities with their myriads of species, many of which are undescribed or little known.

8

Death and Decay

8.1 DECOMPOSITION: RESOURCES AND PROCESSES

Within the forest whole organisms or their component tissues and organs are continually dying or being killed, thus providing the resources of energy and nutrients which sustain the decomposers, either directly or via members of the grazing chain. Instead of the word detritus (which has several meanings—including rock fragments) *necromass* will be used as a general term for this dead material, whatever its source: sloughed root cells or animal cuticles, dung and corpses, shed leaves, reproductive structures, branches and trunks, and, not least, standing dead matter. This chapter is largely concerned with decomposition of *litter* in the strict sense of shed plant remains.

Various agencies, acting simultaneously or in sequence on necromass, can bring about *chemical change* and *structural breakdown*, the twin facets of decomposition. Soluble components are leached out by rainwater, while degradation of chemical substrates is brought about mainly by catabolic activities of decomposers, especially fungi and bacteria, as well as by autolytic enzymes of the dead tissues and by fire. *Comminution* (fragmentation) can be caused by wind and rain, by freezing and thawing, or by movements of animals and plants; the feeding activities of many *detritivores* (used here in the broadest sense, to include decomposer animals which exist primarily on fungi or bacteria, as well as those which ingest necromass; see Swift et al.[25] for a more detailed terminology) are of importance in this respect. As time passes, the structural framework and chemical make-up are altered, and the necromass components are dispersed into the air, water or soil, or among members of the decomposer communities (Fig. 8.1). In this chapter emphasis is placed on how these organisms bring about decomposition, most of the quantitative aspects, including nutrient cycling, being discussed in Chapter 9.

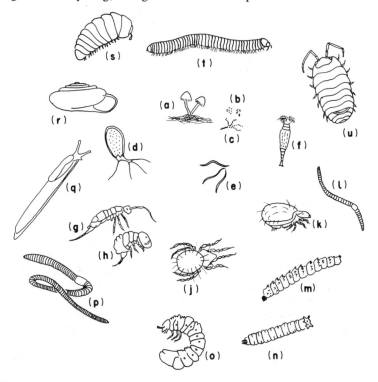

Fig. 8.1 Representatives of the major groups of decomposers in litter and soil (not drawn to same scale). **(a)–(c)** Microflora: **(a)** fungi; **(b)** bacteria; **(c)** actinomycetes. **(d)–(f)** Microfauna: **(d)** shelled amoeba; **(e)** nematodes; **(f)** rotifer. **(g)–(k)** Microarthropods: **(g)**, **(h)** Collembola (springtails); **(j)**, **(k)** Cryptostigmata (oribatid mites). **(l)–(u)** Mesofauna and macrofauna: **(l)** Enchytraeid (potworm); **(m)**, **(n)** Diptera larvae (bibionid and tipulid); **(o)** Scarabaeid beetle larva (white-grub); **(p)** lumbricid earthworm; **(q)**, **(r)** molluscs; **(s)**, **(t)** millipedes; **(u)** woodlouse. (For further details, see Wallwork, J. A. (1970). *Ecology of Soil Animals*. McGraw-Hill, London.)

That interacting agencies are involved in decomposition is suggested by the well known fact that, even under similar conditions, the leaves of, for example, ash and elder decompose more readily than those of oaks and conifers. Various authors have claimed that different features of leaves have an over-riding influence on decom-

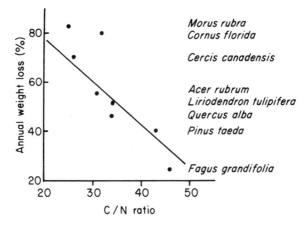

Fig. 8.2 The relationship between decomposition rate and C/N ratio of leaf litter of eight tree species on mull sites in Tennessee. $y = 113.2 - 1.75x$ ($P < 0.05$). (From Reichle, D. E. in Duvigneaud.[6] © UNESCO 1971. Reproduced by permission of UNESCO.)

position rates; these include toughness and thickness, content of calcium, carbohydrates or nitrogen, and the C/N ratio (Fig. 8.2). However, the demonstration of correlation between a single feature and rate of decomposition does not preclude the possibility of interaction (e.g. between softness and nitrogen content), while the ease of decomposition of leaves of certain species, especially relative to a particular group of decomposers, could be determined largely by features which differ from those of the majority. Nor does correlation imply causation, as Satchell and Lowe[208] pointed out when discussing the order of removal of leaf discs by *Lumbricus terrestris* from a range of different tree and shrub species. Palatability was correlated with nitrogen content, and with the amount of soluble carbohydrate present (Fig. 8.3a,b), but there was no evidence of how the worms made these distinctions: they were unable to differentiate between various concentrations of sucrose, and failed to discriminate between individual amino acids. On the other hand, the inverse relationship between palatability and polyphenol content (Fig. 8.3c) suggested a possible role for distasteful substances, and in this case different polyphenols were distinguished by the worms. Tannins seemed to be implicated (Fig. 8.3d), but discrimination still occurred in their absence, as with fresh elm, alder or sycamore, and also, with most species, after weathering for six weeks. The fact that paper discs soaked in leaf extracts were selected in the same order as unweathered leaf discs implied that differences in palatability were caused by unidentified compounds, possibly representing a balance between

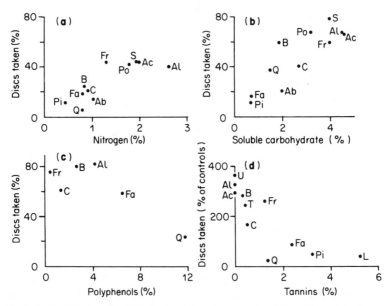

Fig. 8.3 Palatability of leaf litter to *Lumbricus terrestris*. Leaf discs (1 cm diameter) or needles (2 cm lengths) were placed on the surface of large bins of garden soil, containing *L. terrestris*, kept in a cellar. Relative palatability was assessed in terms of the proportion of discs of each species removed by the worms over a period of time (up to 33 days), or, as in **(d)**, as numbers removed compared to control discs of moist paper. Each of the four experiments was in a different year. Graphs show relation between palatability and chemical composition (% dry weight). **(a)** Nitrogen content. Nitrogen-rich species are generally more palatable, but alder and oak are less so than their nitrogen contents might suggest. **(b)** Soluble carbohydrate. **(c)** Total polyphenols (determined by the Folin procedure on 50% acetone extracts.) **(d)** Condensed plus hydrolysable tannins. Ab, *Abies grandis*; Ac, *Acer pseudoplatanus*; Al, *Alnus glutinosa*; B, *Betula verrucosa*; C, *Corylus avellana*; Fa, *Fagus sylvatica*; Fr, *Fraxinus excelsior*; L, *Larix decidua*; Pi, *Pinus sylvestris*; Q, *Quercus petraea*; S, *Sambucus nigra*; T, *Tilia europaea*; U, *Ulmus glabra*. (From data of Satchell and Lowe.[208])

distasteful and tasty. Weathering appeared to involve microbial breakdown of these compounds, rather than leaching. In this instance tasting is only the beginning of the process of decomposition, yet already it has involved chemical composition and the possible influence of microbes on the feeding of detritivores, features which commonly recur in studies of decomposition.

8.2 DEGRADATIVE SUCCESSIONS

As an individual unit of necromass progressively decays, there is a change in the availability of particular resources, such as energy or nutrients, or living space for feeding, shelter or oviposition. These changes are accompanied by qualitative and quantitative alterations in the species composition of the associated decomposer community. Ultimately the dead tissue loses its identity completely, its components being dispersed into the non-living environment and among the decomposers, which are then dependent on further supplies of necromass. This 'anticlimax' is in marked contrast to the situation during successions of autotrophs, where plant biomass increases until the climax community is reached; the diversity of heterotrophs associated with these 'classical' successions also tends to increase. Because of their dependence on diminishing resources, community changes occurring during the decomposition of units of necromass will be referred to as *degradative successions*.

The complexity and opacity of most natural forms of necromass, together with problems of isolating microorganisms and deciding when they have been growing actively (rather than existing as spores or other resting structures), have made it difficult to determine which decomposers are active within particular tissues at a given time, quite apart from the role that they play in decomposition.

Cellophane

Isolation and observation are made easier by using a simplified bait such as cellophane sheet, which can be buried in litter or soil for periods ranging from days to months.[230] Colonizing organisms can be picked off and cultured, or stained *in situ*. *Cellulases* are necessary for chemical decomposition; these are formed mainly by certain species of fungi (e.g. *Botryotrichum piluliferum*) although the characteristic trails formed by the rasping radulae ('tongues') of molluscs act as a reminder that many slugs and snails also produce cellulases. Fungal hyphae ramify over and within the sheets, clear areas around their active tips indicating sites of extracellular decomposition. The resultant sugars are absorbed by the hyphae, but also provide a potential food source for other organisms, such as sugar fungi (e.g. *Pythium oligandrum*), bacteria, protozoa and nematodes, most of which lack cellulases (Fig. 8.4). Alternatively, these organisms may feed on healthy or moribund hyphae or spores, which are also extensively grazed by arthropods, especially mites and Collembola. These animals, as well as segmented worms, may also ingest the permeated cellophane, which consequently gradually becomes dispersed. Such decomposers in turn may be consumed by carnivores, including nematode-trapping fungi, while corpses and faeces are further worked over, even long after the cellophane has disappeared.[105]

This fairly complex community constitutes a food web which is partially based on a very simple substrate. With the exception of the

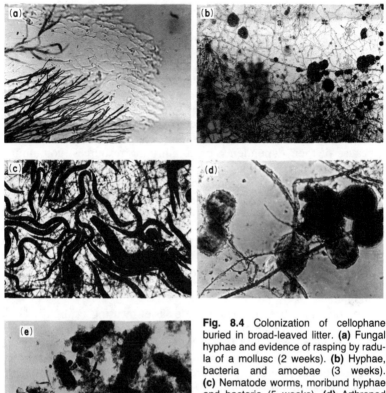

Fig. 8.4 Colonization of cellophane buried in broad-leaved litter. **(a)** Fungal hyphae and evidence of rasping by radula of a mollusc (2 weeks). **(b)** Hyphae, bacteria and amoebae (3 weeks). **(c)** Nematode worms, moribund hyphae and bacteria (5 weeks). **(d)** Arthropod faecal pellets (diameter 45 μm), hyphae and bacteria (13 weeks). **(e)** Disintegrating pellets (100 × 35 μm), with spores, worm chaetae and shelled amoebae (21 weeks). (Photographs **(d)**, **(e)** by Dr P. W. Murphy.)

breakdown of cellulose, the changes responsible for succession occur within and among the decomposers themselves, rather than in the cellophane. Nevertheless, this technique provides a further example of necromass requiring some form of *conditioning* (in this case by cellulolytic species) before certain organisms can make use of it. As well as fungal and bacterial grazers, most of the major groups of detritivores include species which ingest litter, and their distribution in the forest floor and their feeding and survival in the laboratory all indicate a preference for conditioned litter, often at a particular stage of decomposition. Similarly, certain phthiracarid mites ('hinged' oribatids; see Fig. 8.7c,e) normally lay their eggs on conifer needles, cones or beech cupules only after a period of microbial colonization. A closer look must therefore be taken at patterns of development of microorganisms on natural debris, in an attempt to generalize about these successions and their causes, as well as the roles and interactions of the constituent species. It should be borne in mind that natural plant debris differs from cellophane not only in its structural complexity, but also because it was once alive, and the cause of death, especially if parasitic microbes are involved, may predetermine the course of succession.

Conifer needles

The classic study of decomposition of needles of *Pinus sylvestris* by Kendrick (summarized by Millar[162]) concentrated mainly on fungi, which, rather than bacteria, were found to be favoured by the acid conditions of a Cheshire podzol site. The absence of lumbricid earthworms reduced disturbance to a minimum, so that the remains gradually progressed down through the sub-horizons of a mor-humus profile. A variety of isolation and observation techniques showed that certain species were characteristically abundant, and by implication active, at different stages of decomposition. The phylloplane microflora (see Section 6.2) included the ubiquitous *Aureobasidium pullulans*, as well as other primary saprophytes and parasites with a more restricted host range. The weakly pathogenic Ascomycete *Lophodermium pinastri* remained quiescent on healthy needles until senescence set in. During the first six months after needle fall, in the loosely textured and rather dry litter layer (L = A_{00}), cell contents were further decomposed by some of the phylloplane species. The litter-dwelling Ascomycete *Desmazierella acicola* then colonized the needles, being particularly active within the phloem during the two years or so in the F_1 (fermentation) layer, where the needles were more compacted and moist. Regions of internal attack were broken down further by **endophagous animals** (i.e. living within their food) such as the oribatid *Adoristes ovatus*, forming pellet-filled cavities in the mesophyll. Meanwhile, other microarthropods and enchytraeid worms grazed on hyphae or spores on the needle surface, including those of two species of Hyphomycete (*Sympodiella acicola* and *Helicoma monospora*) which replaced *Aureobasidium pullulans*. The needles were still superficially intact, but during the seven years in the F_2 layer the major fragmentation occurred, due mainly to animals. Fragments which had not previously been attacked internally were colonized by Basidiomycetes, including *Marasmius androsaceus* which can decompose cellulose and lignin, and by common soil fungi such as *Trichoderma* and *Penicillium*. The net result was the conversion of needles into an amorphous mixture of faeces, fungi and recalcitrant humus in the H layer. This was further processed by enchytraeids and chitinolytic fungi, the resulting ammonia enabling actinomycetes and bacteria to occupy more alkaline microsites.

The chemical and physical nature of the needles exerted a strongly selective influence on potential initial colonizers, so that most of the common primary saprophytes (see below) were excluded. Elsewhere, it has been shown that the relative competitive abilities of different species of fungi can be influenced by animals such as Collembola exerting differential grazing pressure, sometimes because certain fungi produce toxins. In turn, the particular species of pioneer may play a key role in the subsequent succession. For example, it was found that *Lophodermium pinastri* persisted until long after needle fall in Corsican pine, but with little evidence of other fungi or of noticeable decomposition. In contrast, needles infected with *Lophodermella* spp. were later colonized by fungi such as *Marasmius*, with appreciable depletion of cell walls. The relative importance of certain species can also be altered by changing the pH or nitrogen status of the litter. Consequently site characteristics, as well as different techniques, may account for some of the discrepancies between accounts of succession on litter of a particular species.

Broad leaves

The numerous studies of microorganisms associated with broad leaves have been summarized by Hudson,[117] Jensen[129] and Hayes.[111] Basically, Hudson recognizes three stages in these successions, comparable to the pine-needle situation. The first stage involves **colonization by phylloplane species**, some of which attack living tissues. The ascomycete fungus *Gnomonia errabunda* is specific to beech, acting as a parasite initially but persisting for several months on dead leaves, whereas other species may be less restricted but also less persistent.

Many saprophytes also occur in the phylloplane, being well placed to show appreciable activity during the second, or **senescent, stage**. **Common primary saprophytes**, with a wide host range, are particularly important here. They include the fungi *Aureobasidium pullulans, Epicoccum nigrum, Cladosporium herbarum, Alternaria tenuis* and *Botrytis cinerea*, and, in the Tropics, genera such as *Nigrospora* (only *A. pullulans*, however, occurs on pine needles). Restricted primary saprophytes, with limited host ranges, may also be present at this stage. Some of these parasites and primary saprophytes may persist after leaf fall, but the third, **dead, stage** is largely characterized by **secondary saprophytes**, including Basidiomycetes and various soil-inhabiting Mucorales and Penicillia.

Degradative changes

Swift[225] has pointed out that successions, in the strict sense of directional changes, occur only on individual units of organic matter, and that within a particular area of the forest floor community changes are cyclic, involving colonization and exploitation of a resource unit, followed by dispersal and recolonization of a new unit (see Fig. 8.5). Since studies of succession are normally based on samples of numerous units, the details of individual successions become blurred. The apparent importance of particular species or groups of microorganisms may be considerably coloured by the techniques used, and environmental differences between sites will also lead to varying results on the same type of resource (e.g. conifer needles). Nevertheless, it is widely believed that different resources

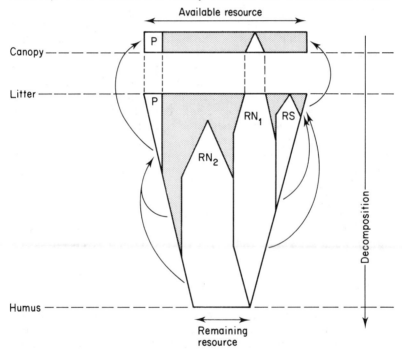

Fig. 8.5 Diagrammatic representation of successional changes within the fungal community on a 'typical' resource unit, such as a pine needle or beech leaf. Non-stippled areas represent extent of fungal occupation of the available resource; arrows indicate dispersal of propagules to other resource units. P = parasites, some of which persist after litter fall. RN₁ = primary resource-nonspecific saprophytes, some originating in the phylloplane. RS = resource-specific saprophytes. RN₂ = secondary resource-nonspecific saprophytes, which eventually replace the primary colonizers. This pattern may be disrupted if the unit is consumed by detritivores. (From Swift.[225])

have their own characteristic communities and successions, and that individual sequences are not determined by chance alone.

Assuming that degradative successions do occur, can we explain why? Microclimatic changes could have differential effects on microbial species, as in the case of fungi which colonize freshly fallen pine needles but become active only in the damper F_1 layer. As a more general explanation, however, changes in species composition could result from changing availability of resources, brought about by abiotic and biotic agencies and with the possibility of competition for these resources. Living space within a unit alters as tissues are penetrated and opened up, providing microhabitats for motile and non-motile organisms, as shown by endophagous fauna. Chemical resources, in the sense of energy and nutrient supplies, may be inaccessible to a particular species because they are masked physically or chemically (e.g. cellulose by lignin or tanned protein) or because the species lack the necessary enzymes, or as a result of some other difference in competitive ability compared with other species.

The observation by Garrett[94] that on herbivore dung the general succession passed from Phycomycetes to Ascomycetes to Basidiomycetes led to a functional explanation, based on the dominance of '*substrate groups*', *sugar fungi* being replaced by *cellulolytic species* and finally by *ligninolytic forms*, with secondary sugar fungi existing on the breakdown products of the last two groups. It is now realized that biochemical capabilities are not so strictly demarcated between the taxonomic groups, while sugar fungi are conspicuously absent from the initial stages of most successions. Cellulolytic ability seems more widespread than previously thought; there is, however, very little evidence of the role played by particular species, either individually or in combination, at particular stages of a given succession, for example little is known of the role of Basidiomycetes in needle decomposition. Enzyme complements presumably differ between species, but the availability of particular nutrients or the ability to tolerate polyphenols may be just as important as the possession of cellulases.

The order of disappearance of species from the community almost certainly reflects the results of competition for food resources, leaving the highly persistent Basidiomycetes, with their great diversity of enzymes, and the antibiotic-producing Penicillia. On the other hand, the order in which species appear may be largely a reflection of their characteristic distributions within the woodland: many of the initial colonizers are members of the phylloplane flora, well placed to exploit senescing leaves, while the aerial dispersal mechanisms of many primary saprophytes contrast with the passive, localized transfer of secondary saprophytes such as *Penicillium*.

Successions among detritivores

So far, discussion has centred on microbial successions. Anderson[33] recorded changes in numbers and species composition of various groups of animals found among beech and sweet chestnut leaves enclosed in mesh bags and placed in the forest floor of a *Castanea sativa* woodland in Kent. Some of these changes were seasonal, but some reflected changes in suitability of the leaves for colonization. During the first autumn and winter, gut contents of enchytraeids and chironomid (midge) larvae consisted mainly of fungal remains, as did those of oribatid mites, most of which belonged to three mycophagous species. Even phthiracaroids, which are normally considered to be litter ingesters, contained mainly fungal material at this time. From April onwards, the numbers of many of the mycophagous species declined, the increasing species diversity resulting partially from an influx of litter feeders. Certain species, such as the phthiracaroids, changed their feeding habits, concentrating on the conditioned litter (see Fig. 8.8). This change coincided with a reduction in polyphenol levels of the leaves which could have influenced the behaviour of those species of microbes and animals which are intolerant of tannins or other related compounds. The increase in species diversity to a maximum in the second autumn was assumed to accompany subdivision of food resources, and possibly increasing microhabitat complexity. In other words, a diversity of substrates and living places became available within and upon the leaves, including those provided by faeces and corpses.

Wood

The ecology of wood decomposition, recently reviewed by Käärik[132] and Swift,[226] provides further examples of successional changes, usually over periods of several years. Communities of animals associated with dying and dead wood are described by Elton,[7] faunal participation being of great importance in many types of wood decay.

Adjacent regions of an individual unit of necromass, such as a pine needle, can undergo different pathways of decay, and this is even more likely with woody remains, because of their sheer bulk. Heterogeneity is further increased by situation: dead trees may stand for many years, being slowly attacked by a small number of species (as shown by the sound heartwood of many elms felled five or more years after death due to *Ceratocystis ulmi*) in contrast to the greater diversity of organisms in the more equable climate of the forest floor. Nevertheless, some general observations can be made about wood decay, taking the scheme of Swift[226] as a framework (Fig. 8.6).

The *colonization stage* is characterized by death of the relatively few

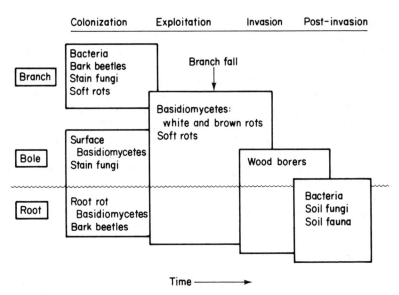

Fig. 8.6 Patterns of succession among the dominant organisms associated with decomposition of 'typical' woody material in Britain. (From Swift.[226])

living cells in wood, mainly in the inner bark and medullary rays. These cells 'defend' the adjacent dead wood which may be further protected by tough cell walls or by biologically active compounds (poisons or 'deterrents') in the heartwood. Breaching of these defences may be effected by certain organisms independently, but some are aided by wounding of tissues caused by wind, fire, frost, or other organisms (including Man). The Basidiomycetes *Fomes annosus* (*Heterobasidion annosum*) and *Armillaria mellea* are examples of fungi which can penetrate healthy tissues, causing root rot, and which can also colonize freshly cut stumps (see Section 6.3). Among insects, some termites (e.g. certain species of *Coptotermes*) habitually consume the wood of living trees, while bark beetles feed mainly on cell contents of tissues under the bark of living or recently felled trees. The introduction of spores of *Ceratocystis ulmi* during maturation feeding by elm bark beetles eventually leads to lowered resistance by the elms to oviposition and larval development (see Section 6.4).

Wounds on branches in the canopy may be colonized by bacteria, causing limited damage to the walls of ray parenchyma cells, as do soft-rot fungi, while cell contents are attacked by blue-stain fungi (often associated with *Tomicus* outbreaks, see Section 6.5). These primary attacks may facilitate invasion by wood-decaying Basidiomycetes, such as *Phellinus* spp., although more aggressive species, such as *Stereum* (*Chondrostereum*) *purpureum*, colonize freshly exposed surfaces and are inhibited by non-Basidiomycetes. Heart-rots (e.g. *Ganoderma applanatum*, responsible for the precarious state of many beech trees) often have their origins in wounds.

The **major decomposition stage** is dominated by the activities of Basidiomycetes and specialized woodboring insects which degrade cell walls. Some pioneer species of fungi may continue to attack dead wood, whereas others are replaced by saprophytes. Fungi causing white rot can attack both lignin and cellulose, either successively (e.g. *Fomes annosus*), or simultaneously (e.g. *Coriolus* (*Polystictus*) *versicolor*). In contrast, brown rot is characterized by patchy attack on cell-wall polysaccharides, leaving the lignin framework intact. White or brown rot may be accompanied by various Ascomycetes and Fungi imperfecti which slowly attack cellulose but not lignin, forming chains of cavities in tracheids and fibres, characteristic of soft rot.

Undecayed dead wood is attacked by certain termites and beetles, some of the latter producing their own cellulases (as in *Anobium punctatum*, the wood-worm, and certain cerambycids or timber beetles) while others are dependent on endosymbiotic yeasts or bacteria. Wood-boring 'ambrosia beetles' transmit specific fungi which grow on comminuted wood in the faeces and provide their main food source. Other insects, including many termites, characteristically feed on wood after a certain amount of microbial decay. It was found that invasion by wood-borers into branches of various broad-leaved species at the International Biological Programme site at Meathop, Cumbria, occurred about two years after branch fall, which was preceded by about six years of predominantly fungal decay.

Branches or stumps which are protected from desiccation by bark, moss or lichens may support a rich community of invertebrates, including many general litter dwellers such as molluscs, woodlice, millipedes, mites and spring-tails, and beetle and fly larvae, for example wireworms, stag beetles and leatherjackets. Some of these, such as insect larvae and mites, may burrow into the heartwood which is reduced to friable *frass*. The activities of the general soil fauna and microflora (e.g. Mucorales) dominate the **terminal stage** of wood decay, when the remains are finally comminuted and incorporated into the soil.

To summarize, although certain species of fungi and animals can bring about wood decay on their own, the process normally involves the integrated physical and chemical action of a succession of organisms. The structural complexity of woody remains, together with the diversity of associated organisms, make it difficult to explain why particular successions occur. However, the durability of these remains normally ensures an abundant supply of potential food resources, protected from climatic extremes, as well as refuges for hunters and hunted.

8.3   DIVERS DETRITIVORES

Several hundred species of microbes may be associated with the decomposition of a particular type of litter in a single temperate woodland. A square metre of the same forest floor might well contain more than a thousand species of animals, ranging in size from Protozoa to earthworms. Apart from carnivores and root-feeding herbivores, the majority are detritivores. Of those feeding among plant remains, some are *microphytophagous*, ingesting predominantly fungal hyphae, spores or bacterial colonies, but most subsist on decomposing higher plant litter, including varying amounts of micro-flora in their diet (*macrophytophagous*) (including the panphy-tophages of Luxton[149]). In culture, individual species often appear to display preference for particular microbes or leaves of particular species. However, within each feeding category, the gut contents of various species of animals taken from the forest floor usually appear remarkably similar to those of certain other species, which may even belong to different classes or phyla. This apparent *lack of food-niche differentiation* is in marked contrast to the specialization typical of herbivores.

Co-existence could be accounted for by surplus food, implying too much litter for too few detritivores. Fluctuations in space and time in amounts of litter do not necessarily coincide with variations in animal abundance, so that by chance certain populations may have plentiful resources. Alternatively, animal numbers could regularly be kept below the level at which interspecific competition for food occurs by the action of pathogens or predators, or, less dependably, by the influence of climatic factors. Very few quantitative data are available relating to such influences on abundance, let alone on competition. Intraspecific competition for other resources, such as oviposition sites, could also be intensified by climatic extremes; there is some evidence of higher mortality during the winter among mite eggs laid in beech cupules.

Assuming that variations do occur in the balance between supply and demand, what happens at those places and times with a shortage of food? *Interspecific competition* could be avoided by reducing the amount of overlap between various components of the niches of different species, especially when and where they feed, and what they feed on.

Separation in time occurs between species with markedly different phenologies, but overlap is particularly likely among those groups, such as many soil arthropods, which have developmental periods of a year or more. Time spent in moulting and other non-feeding phases such as diapause will reduce the number of potential competitors.

As regards *vertical distribution*, within the major groups of soil animals certain species are known to be characteristic of particular sub-horizons (Fig. 8.7), although others are more wide-ranging. Among oribatid mites this distribution has been correlated with that of 'preferred' food, whether specific microbes or particular stages of litter decay.[149] Within each sub-horizon at a single site, however, there are likely to be individuals of different species which have similar gut contents. The possibility of further partitioning of space within sub-horizons has been explored by Anderson,[35] who recognized two dozen microhabitats, ranging from intact leaves, twigs and roots to faeces and soil cavities, in gelatine-embedded sections from a range of humus forms under *Castanea sativa*. Species diversity was correlated with microhabitat diversity, but the precise requirements of individual species are insufficiently understood, partly because of failure to recognize and measure the components of living places which are crucial to the particular animals, rather than to the observer. However, on the assumption that species differ in these requirements, they can be visualized as being distributed throughout a vertical and horizontal mosaic of microhabitats, and so kept largely separate.

The gut contents of each individual will indicate some of the food resources available within recently visited microhabitats. These resources may change with time, as shown by phthiracaroids feeding on fungi and later on leaves (Fig. 8.8a). On the other hand, some may be common to various microhabitats, so explaining similar contents in different species. At times of increased likelihood of competition, as when frost, drought or flooding lead to a compression of the normal vertical distribution, feeding niches may become narrower, each species having its own feeding 'refuge', similar to the average components shown in Fig. 8.8b.

Finally, energy and nutrients could be shared between different species which ingest the same sort of food (and therefore have similar gut contents) by variation in *digestive abilities*. Unfortunately the techniques used to demonstrate the presence of certain enzymes, such as cellulases, often give equivocal results, and even if present, these enzymes may not be effective on natural litter. Nevertheless, possible digestive strategies may be envisaged.

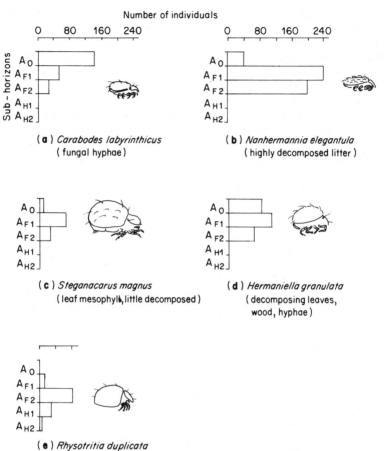

Fig. 8.7 Vertical distribution of adult oribatid mites from a *Castanea sativa* site at Blean Woods, Kent. The histograms represent the number observed in a total of 780 soil sections obtained from monthly samples between September 1967–August 1968. The major components of the gut contents of each species are indicated in parentheses. (From Anderson, J. M. (1971). In *Proceedings IVth International Colloquium for Soil Zoology*, pp. 257–72. I.N.R.A., Paris.)

Digestive strategies

Microphytophagous species feed predominantly on the microflora, whose protoplasm is exposed to digestive enzymes, either after cutting or chewing through hyphae or possibly by chemical penetration of, for example, spore walls. *Chitinases*, which have been demonstrated in microphytophagous oribatids,[149] presumably attack hyphal walls, while the possession of *trehalase* enables these mites to utilize the fungal storage compound, trehalose. It is, then, assumed that animals which 'specialize' on fungi or bacteria have the necessary enzymes to obtain their energy and nutrients from this diet.

For litter-ingesting species, the major components remaining in litter are cellulose and lignin, most of the more readily assimilable compounds having been 'mopped up' by herbivores and primary saprophytes. Molluscs, certain wood-boring beetles and at least one species of termite can decompose cellulose by means of their own *cellulases*, but these may be supplemented by microbial enzymes. In all other instances, decomposition of cellulose and lignin seems to be brought about by the *microflora*. A clearly *symbiotic relationship* is sometimes involved, such as with many termites and tipulid larvae (leatherjackets), in which certain species of microorganisms occur, often in a particular region of the gut.

Termites are known to derive most of their energy from the digestion of polysaccharides, especially cellulose and hemi-cellulose.[144] Symbiotic flagellates (or bacteria, in certain species) decompose cellulose anaerobically to acetic acid, which the termites absorb. The mechanism of lignin decomposition is obscure, since in fungi this is an aerobic process; species of the Basidiomycete *Termitomyces*, which grow on the fungus combs of members of one subfamily of termites, possibly attack lignin and expose cellulose to the gut symbionts, as well as being consumed themselves. Despite their symbiotic complements, many species of termites tend to feed on wood or other litter at a particular stage of decay. In some instances it is known that microbial conditioning involves the break-down of repellents or poisons; in others the microflora may provide vitamins or may even form the bulk of the diet.

Symbiotic bacteria have been found in larvae of *Tipula maxima* which apparently digest cellulose, for example in beech leaves, while wood-boring beetles either have endosymbionts or feed on ambrosia fungi. In other groups the microbial connection is more tenuous, although there is some evidence of characteristic gut floras in certain Collembola, oribatids, bibionid larvae (Diptera) and woodlice, perhaps involving the selection of certain ingested species.

The fact that litter feeders often show poor survival or cease feeding altogether after sterilization of their food suggests that they are somehow dependent on living microorganisms. These could form the major part of the assimilated diet, so that the habit of microbial browsing is merely extended into the substance of the litter. Some litter feeders can be reared on a purely fungal diet. The necessity for live microbes could imply that certain species of, for example,

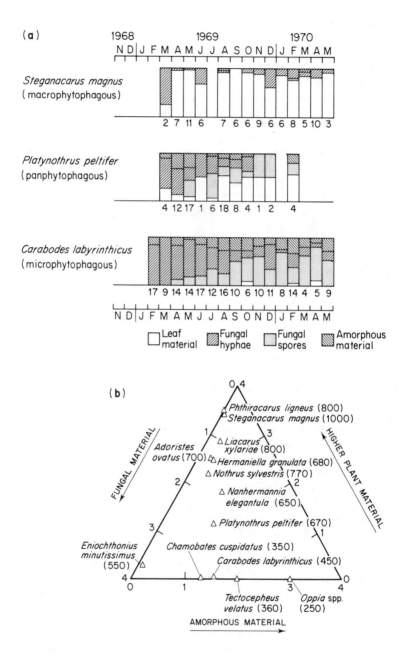

(a)

1968   1969   1970
N D J F M A M J J A S O N D J F M A M

Steganacarus magnus
(macrophytophagous)

2 7 11 6   7 6 6 9 6 6 8 5 10 3

Platynothrus peltifer
(panphytophagous)

4 12 17 1 6 18 8 4 1 2   4

Carabodes labyrinthicus
(microphytophagous)

17 9 14 14 17 12 16 10 6 10 11 8 14 4 5 9

N D J F M A M J J A S O N D J F M A M

☐ Leaf material   ▨ Fungal hyphae   ☐ Fungal spores   ▩ Amorphous material

(b)

0, 4

△ *Phthiracarus ligneus* (800)
△ *Steganacarus magnus* (1000)

FUNGAL MATERIAL   HIGHER PLANT MATERIAL

1   △ *Liacarus xylariae* (800)   3

Adoristes ovatus (700) △△ *Hermaniella granulata* (680)

△ *Nothrus sylvestris* (770)

2   △ *Nanhermannia elegantula* (650)   2

3   △ *Platynothrus peltifer* (670)   1

Eniochthonius minutissimus (550) △   *Chamobates cuspidatus* (350)   *Carabodes labyrinthicus* (450)

4   3   0
0   1   3   4

Tectocepheus velatus (360)   *Oppia* spp. (250)

AMORPHOUS MATERIAL

litter-dwelling bacteria multiply in the gut, among the comminuted litter, and are continually cropped, but only if further supplies are ingested; this seems to occur in at least one species of woodlouse,[193] and in the pill millipede, *Glomeris marginata*.[36] Certain macrophytophagous oribatid mites, such as phthiracaroids, lack chitinase and trehalase, but could presumably subsist on microbial protoplasm and the breakdown products (exometabolites) released by microbial activity in the litter. Cellulolytic activity, demonstrated in the intestine of certain woodlice, millipedes and, possibly, phthiracaroids, is again lost when the food litter is sterilized. Continuing microbial action may also be of importance in coprophagy; for example, certain millipedes resemble rabbits in needing to ingest their own faeces, in order to obtain sufficient energy and nutrients for normal growth. Feeding on the faeces of other species, with the possibility of differential digestion, provides a further way of sharing resources; this reworking of material, which does not occur in herbivore communities, may be one of the major factors accounting for the great diversity of the decomposition subsystem.

A wide variety of suggestions has, then, been made to account for avoidance of competition among detritivores, with their apparently rather generalized feeding habits. Experiments with single and mixed cultures of two species of oribatid showed that vertical distribution was more restricted in mixtures, but changes in microhabitat distribution and gut contents were more difficult to interpret.[34] Whatever the mechanisms of avoidance, detritivores have a part to play in decomposition, but just how important are they?

8.4 RELATIVE ROLES OF AGENTS OF DECAY

Except for the action of certain molluscs and insects which produce their own cellulases, major chemical changes in the composition of the necromass, especially its structural components such as lignin and cellulose, are effected by microbial enzymes. On the basis of

---

Fig. 8.8 Gut contents of oribatid mites from Blean Woods, Kent. Adult mites were recovered over a 20-month period from mesh bags buried in litter of *Fagus sylvatica* and *Castanea sativa*. Contents occurred as 1–3 discrete boluses, which were dissected and scored on a 0–4 scale, indicating the relative amounts of each of four major food materials. **(a)** Temporal variation in feeding by three species of oribatid from *Castanea* litter, showing the average composition of a bolus at each sampling occasion. The number of boluses examined is shown under the histograms. **(b)** Cumulative mean proportions of the three major food items in those species which were most abundant in the two types of litter during 20 months. Specialized feeders occur near the apices of the triangle, with more catholic species nearer the centre. Values in parentheses are body lengths (μm). (From Anderson.[33])

evidence presented in Chapter 9 the microflora is believed to account for about 80% of the energy flow within decomposer systems, with a relatively minor contribution from detritivores. However, many of these animals are described as wasteful feeders, egesting 85% or more by weight of their food as faeces, and this might be expected to influence decomposition processes. Animals enhance microbial activity in a number of ways, for example by aiding spore dispersal or by exposing necromass tissues to the microflora.

Spores and other propagules occur on and within the bodies of animals, and although some may be digested by particular species, others germinate freely. Some of these spores are transported from exhausted substrates to environments which are more favourable in terms of food availability or climate. Swift[225] has suggested that this method of transport is particularly important to fungal species within the forest floor.

Organisms with limited mobility, such as bacteria, could be introduced to otherwise inaccessible substrates by the feeding of animals, especially within tissues (as shown during acorn decay). Comminution greatly increases the surface area of exposed tissue: it has been estimated that the conversion of a 60 mm-long conifer needle into $10\,\mu m^3$ fragments by phthiracaroid mites results in a ten thousand-fold increase in surface area.[106] These tissues could be exploited by microbes either within the animal (in the case of species which can tolerate conditions in the gut) or after egestion. Faeces form foci of high nutrient status, with moisture-holding and pH characteristics which are often more favourable to microbes than the ingested litter. Consequently, microbial numbers and activity (e.g. respiration) are normally higher in faecal material (Fig. 8.9). There is now evidence of increased microbial activity, especially among bacteria, as a result of certain levels of grazing on faeces by arthropods. Browsing on litter might rejuvenate senescent microbial colonies, but could also destroy active hyphal tips.

These are some of the ways in which it has been proposed that detritivores help to unblock 'bottle-necks' in energy flow and nutrient cycling, thus contributing much more to soil metabolism than is indicated by their own energy requirements.[152] Nutrients are considered further in Chapter 9, and this section is concluded by reference to some quantitative studies of decomposition.

Decomposition rates are normally calculated from losses in weight of litter placed on or in the forest floor, whether loose, tethered or confined in meshbags. Disappearance of fragments from bags or lines, or deeper into the profile (as when dragged down by earthworms) results in exaggerated estimates. The relative importance of various agencies can be assessed by altering the influence of particu-

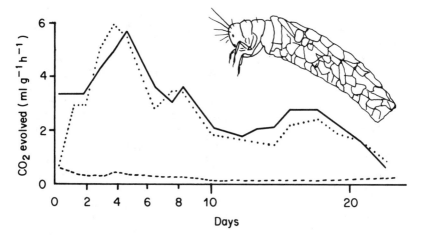

Fig. 8.9 Microbial respiration from food and faeces of larvae of the terrestrial caddis, *Enoicyla pusilla*, at 25°C. The similarity in activity on faecal pellets (——) and on oak leaves (···) ground to the same fragment size as in the pellets contrasts with that on entire leaves (– – –). (From Drift, J. van der and Witkamp, M (1959). *Archives Neerlandaises de Zoologie*, **13**, 486–92.)

lar groups, although absolute exclusion is rarely achieved.

Naphthalene has been used to reduce animal numbers. At Oak Ridge (Fig. 8.10b) the abundance of arthropods decreased by 82%, compared to control plots, Collembola being particularly affected. Bacterial populations in treated litter increased up to six-fold, probably because of the greater availability of corpses, but no changes were observed in amounts of fungal mycelium. Weight losses from litter bags in the two plots were not markedly different, in contrast to the results of Russian work using *Quercus robur*,[141] possibly reflecting differences in composition of the decomposer community, or a consequence of applying greater concentrations of naphthalene.

The significance of microarthropods in decomposition of oak leaves was demonstrated at Rothamsted when leaf discs disappeared more rapidly in soils treated with DDT than in controls; the differential effect of the insecticide on certain predators enabled Collembola populations to increase markedly.

Litter bags with different mesh sizes provide a means of distinguishing between the effects of leaching, microorganisms, mesofauna and macrofauna; in making quantitative comparisons between results from different bags, it is assumed that microbial decomposition and leaching are similar, whatever the mesh size. Results derived

from this method are somewhat equivocal (Fig. 8.10). Edwards and
Heath[82] recorded no loss in area of oak and beech leaf discs after nine
months in 3 μm-mesh bags in pasture soil. Losses from 0.5 mm bags
were associated with fragmentation by Collembola, Diptera larvae
and enchytraeids, which were supplemented appreciably by lumbricid earthworms in the 7 mm bags. On the other hand, lumbricids
caused little acceleration of decomposition of elm, ash, birch or lime.

In an Australian dry sclerophyll forest, with few earthworms or
arthropods, leaching and microorganisms accounted for 70% or more
of the weight loss from leaves of *Eucalyptus* spp. In wet forest, with
abundant detritivores, the contribution from megascolecid earthworms and macroarthropods was similar to that of leaching plus
microorganisms in the case of *E. delegatensis*, but not with *E.
pauciflora*, which apparently was not attacked by earthworms.[243]

Anderson[32] found no significant differences between weight losses
from bags of different mesh sizes, using *Fagus sylvatica* leaves in
either of two woodland sites, or with *Castanea sativa* leaves in the site
with a mor-like humus, suggesting that mycophagous species (such as
various mites), woodlice, millipedes and *Lumbricus rubellus* made
little contribution. Greater differences were recorded for leaves of
Castanea in the site with mull-like characteristics, presumably due to
Lumbricus terrestris (Fig. 8.10c,d). The use of aerially suspended
bags, in which microbial activity was assumed to be minimal,
suggested that a very large proportion of the weight losses could
result from leaching. There was no evidence of stimulation of
decomposition by mycophagous or litter feeding microarthropods,
although exploitation of their faeces was possibly hindered by the
retarded descent of bags and contents into the F_2 sub-horizon.

Relative importance thus varies with the type of necromass and
with the make-up of the decomposer community. Exclusion experiments yield the most extreme differences in mulls and similar sites
where earthworms or other macrofauna are typically plentiful. Even

---

Fig. 8.10 Rates of disappearance of leaf litter from mesh bags. **(a)** Leaf discs
(2.5 cm diam.) of oak (*Quercus* sp., ★) and beech (*Fagus sylvatica*, ●) in 7 mm (——)
and 0.5 mm (– –) mesh bags in newly cultivated pasture soil, with mull humus,
Rothamsted. Leaves were picked from trees in July. (Redrawn from Edwards and
Heath.[82]) **(b)** Leaves of white oak (*Quercus alba*), collected from trees at leaf-fall, in
2 mm mesh bags in *Q. alba* litter treated with 100 g of naphthalene per m[2] (★) and
untreated (●), Oak Ridge, Tennessee. (From Witkamp, M. and Crossley, D. A. (1966).
Pedobiologia, **6**, 293–303.) **(c), (d)** Leaf discs (2.5 cm diam.) of freshly fallen
sweet-chestnut (*Castanea sativa*) in 7 mm (●), 1 mm (○) and 48 μm (★) mesh bags in
litter of **(c)** a *Castanea* site with mor-like moder, and **(d)** a *Fagus sylvatica* site with
mull-like moder, both in Blean Woods, Kent. (Modified from Anderson.[32])

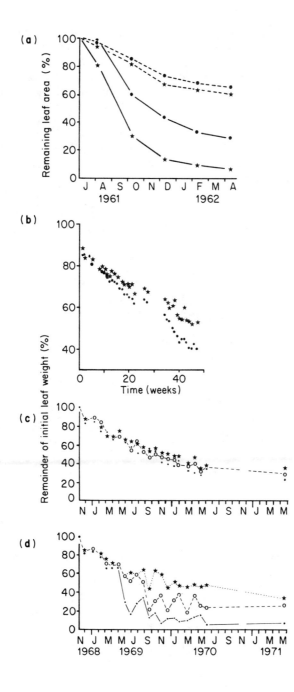

in sites where animals are unimportant in the initial decomposition of litter, evidence of increased decomposition rates might be expected among detritivore faeces. Respiratory activity has been shown to increase as certain faeces age, correlated with a build-up of bacteria in pellets of *Enoicyla* (Fig. 8.9) and of the pill millipede *Glomeris*. Nevertheless, decomposition rates of pellets of *Glomeris*, confined in bags at the litter surface, were similar to those of uningested leaves;[167] their fate might have been different deeper in the profile. Observations of faeces *in situ* (e.g. in sections) suggest that some, such as those of many termites and microbe-feeding Collembola, are much more resistant to microbial attack than those of other litter ingesters.[106]

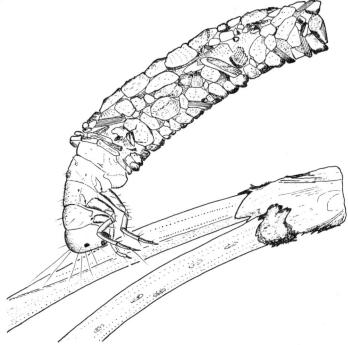

Fig. 8.11 Larva of *Enoicyla pusilla* on pine needle at Chaddesley Woods, Worcs.

The direct effect of most animals on litter decomposition in woodlands is therefore much smaller than that of the microflora and abiotic factors such as leaching. The influence of comminution and transport of materials into more climatically buffered regions of the forest floor is difficult to quantify, but is probably of considerable significance.

9

Energy Flow and Nutrient Cycling

9.1 BIOMASS AND PRODUCTIVITY OF AUTOTROPHS

There are various ways of taking stock of woodlands. Ecologists try to measure the weights and energy contents of various components of ecosystems, and also to determine and quantify pathways of energy flow and nutrient cycling, whereas foresters have traditionally assessed their forest stands, annual increments and yields in terms of trunk volume.

Estimates of amounts of living organic matter (*biomass*) present in trees, shrubs and herbs are complicated by the sheer bulk and heterogeneity of material. Conventionally, as in I.B.P. studies, woody structures such as branches are included in biomass estimates only if they bear living buds; however, standing deadwood and, in some instances, litter, are sometimes included in totals of biomass. Rather than use destructive sampling, which involves removing and weighing all plant material from a site, alternative methods are normally employed, especially if estimates are to be repeated. For example, aerial woody biomass of trees can be calculated by measuring trunk girth at 1.3 m above ground level, and referring to a regression of, for example, dry weight against girth, derived from destructive sampling of part of the site. Sampling of roots is extremely laborious, and often a nominal value of c. 20–30% of aerial biomass is used. Details of methods involved in woodland productivity studies are given by Newbould[166] and Pardé.[178] It should be borne in mind that many of the published data are based on approximations and assumptions, involving a range of techniques, so that they are not necessarily strictly comparable.

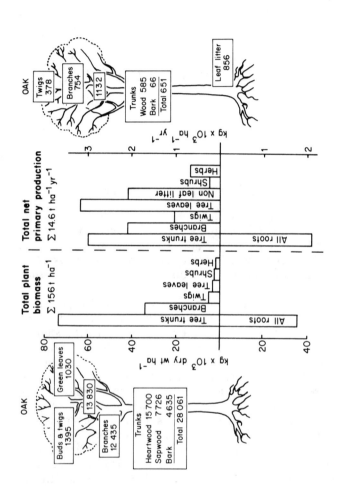

Fig. 9.1 Estimated values for plant biomass (kg ha⁻¹; to left of centre) and for net primary production (kg ha⁻¹ yr⁻¹; to right) in a mixed oakwood at Virelles-Blaimont, Belgium. Data for oak are given in the tree outlines. Number of trees per hectare: *Carpinus betulus* 1135, *Quercus robur* 195, *Fagus sylvatica* 87, *Acer campestre* 69. Shrubs include *Crataegus oxyacanthoides*, *Cornus sanguinea*, *Corylus avellana* and *Carpinus betulus*. For description of herb layer and soil, see Fig. 1.2. (From data of Froment *et al.* in Duvigneaud.[6]) © UNESCO 1971. Reproduced by permission of UNESCO.)

Labels within the figure:

Total plant biomass Σ 156 t ha⁻¹ — Tree trunks, Branches, Twigs, Tree leaves, Shrubs, Herbs, All roots

Total net primary production Σ 14.6 t ha⁻¹ yr⁻¹ — Tree trunks, Branches, Twigs, Tree leaves, Non leaf litter, Shrubs, Herbs, All roots

kg × 10³ dry wt ha⁻¹

kg × 10³ ha⁻¹ yr⁻¹

OAK (biomass): Buds & twigs 1395, Green leaves 1030, 13 830, Branches 12 435, Trunks: Heartwood 15 700, Sapwood 7726, Bark 4635, Total 28 061

OAK (production): Twigs 378, Branches 754, 1132, Trunks: Wood 585, Bark 66, Total 651, Leaf litter 856

The distribution of biomass among autotrophs in a Belgian broad-leaved woodland (whose dominant trees were c.75 years old) is shown in Fig. 9.1, while values from a range of sites are summarized in Fig. 9.2. Whittaker[239] states that biomasses of mature forests are

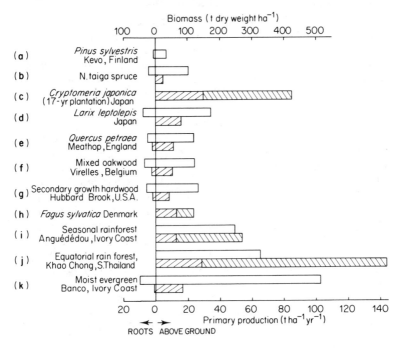

Fig. 9.2 Estimates of plant biomass (□), net primary production (▨) and gross primary production (▧), for a range of woodland ecosystems. (Data from **(a)** Kallio, P;[133] **(b)** Rodin, L. E. and Bazilevich, N. I.;[196] **(c)** Kira, T.;[137] **(d)** Satoo, R. in Duvigneaud,[6] pp. 191–205; **(e)** Satchell, J. E. in Duvigneaud,[6] pp. 619–30; **(f)** Duvigneaud, P. *et al.* in Duvigneaud,[6] pp. 259–70; **(g)** Bormann, F. H. *et al.*;[51] **(h)** Müller, D. and Nielsen, J. (1965). *Forstl. Forsøgsr. Danm.*, **29**, 69–160; **(i)**, **(j)**, **(k)** UNESCO.[27])

mostly in the range 200–600 t ha^{-1}; he gives mean values ranging from 200 t ha^{-1} for boreal forest, through 300–350 for temperate woodlands, to 450 t ha^{-1} for tropical rain forest. Estimates from the temperate rain forests of the Pacific Northwest include 1600 t ha^{-1} for Douglas fir (*Pseudotsuga menziesii*) and 2300 t ha^{-1} for coastal redwood (*Sequoia sempervirens*). High values for root biomass can be obtained by careful excavation; for example, figures of more than 200 t ha^{-1} have been recorded in Ghana and for *P. menziesii* in the Cascade Mountains.

Biomass is a static measure of the amount of matter present in living organisms at a particular occasion. Energy flows through this matter and production is added to it, so that biomass changes with time. Values for plants vary throughout the year, depending, for example, on the timing of incremental growth of stems and roots, and on the presence or absence of leaves or reproductive structures. As a stand matures, total biomass steadily increases to a maximum, with the weight of the trunks, which come to contain more and more dead heartwood, making a proportionately greater contribution in older trees. As crowns expand, the weight of leaves becomes maximal when the canopy closes, later declining as death and thinning reduce the number of trees.

Biomass on its own gives little indication of *productivity*, the rate of formation of organic matter. Estimates of woody biomass made a year apart yield values for annual increment, but give no information regarding losses caused by consumption of tissues by herbivores (including harvesting by man), and from litter formation, leachates or secretions. Consequently, *net primary production* (NPP; which represents the amount of assimilated organic matter remaining after the requirements of plant respiration have been met) can be assessed by estimating the extent of these losses and adding them to the annual increment, although leaching and secretion are usually, and consumption often, ignored. Once again regressions can be used, for example, NPP on girth.

Estimated values for NPP in woodlands are shown in Figs 9.1 and 9.2. The mean values in Table 9.1 need to be treated with caution, because of the techniques used and the number and types of sites

Table 9.1 Estimates of net primary production (t dry matter ha^{-1}yr^{-1}) in various woodland ecosystems; mean values, with number of sampled sites in parentheses, and estimated range of values.

	Japan[a]	Europe and[a] N. America	Tropics[b]	Range[c, d]
Boreal conifer	11.2 (74)	9.0 (19)		4–20
Deciduous broad-leaf	8.3 (48)	10.2 (57)		6–25
Temperate evergreen broad-leaf	20.2 (27)	7.0 (1)		
Pine	14.4 (42)	10.4 (15)		6–25
Temperate conifers	14.5 (67)	15.0 (5)		
Tropical forests			21.6 (13)	5–32

From (a) Kira[137] above ground values only; (b) Murphy, P. G. (1975). In *Primary Productivity of the Biosphere*, Lieth, H. and Whittaker, R. H. (Eds), pp. 217–31. Springer-Verlag, Berlin; (c) Whittaker;[239] (d) Swift, Heal and Anderson.[25]

sampled, but they show a general increase towards the equator, reflecting the influence of climate on production. The overlap between the ranges of the major forest biome types is partially explained by the effect of the *age of stand*. As shown in Fig. 9.3, NPP increases during the early stages of stand development, but subsequently declines, as the green tissues gradually fail to synthesize enough material for respiration and growth, especially of woody tissues. The proportion of photosynthate respired progressively increases until, in theory, none is available for growth, when NPP falls to zero. Corresponding changes take place in the production: biomass ratio (P:B) and its converse, the biomass accumulation ratio (B:P). Mean values for NPP over a large area therefore depend in part on the relative distributions of climax and early successional stages.

Gross primary production, representing total assimilation of organic matter (i.e. NPP plus plant respiration), is extremely difficult to estimate, and there are relatively few published data; some are given in Fig. 9.2, indicating the very high values, exceeding $100 \, t \, ha^{-1} \, yr^{-1}$, which can be achieved in parts of the tropics. The proportion used in plant respiration varies between $c.30–80\%$, increasing with temperature and with biomass accumulation ratio.[240] Temperate forests at early successional stages, with $c.40\%$ of production used in respiration, may therefore have values for NPP which are comparable to those of mature tropical rain forests, despite their gross production being less than half (Fig. 9.2); high temperatures are associated with respiratory losses of 75–80% (see Fig. 2.5), these being less at higher (and therefore cooler) altitudes.

Assessment of production in commercial forestry

Foresters are mainly concerned with the quality and rate of production of timber grown in the forest; consequently their assessments of productivity usually ignore many of the factors just considered. Many of the concepts involved in assessing tree growth are set out in forest management tables such as those used by the Forestry Commission.[104] Trees increase in fresh weight, dry weight, height and volume. Measurable volume, conventionally taken as being that of stemwood exceeding 7 cm diameter overbark, is the most meaningful measure in economic terms and the pattern of growth in an even-aged stand is usually described in terms of annual volume increment. Figure 9.4a shows that the *current annual increment* (*CAI*) increases for some years after planting and subsequently declines. CAI at *n* years is $a \, m^3 \, ha^{-1}$ while *b* is the *mean annual increment* (*MAI*), the average rate of increase from planting to a given point in time. At *forester's maturity*, where the two curves cross (*c*), the stand has the

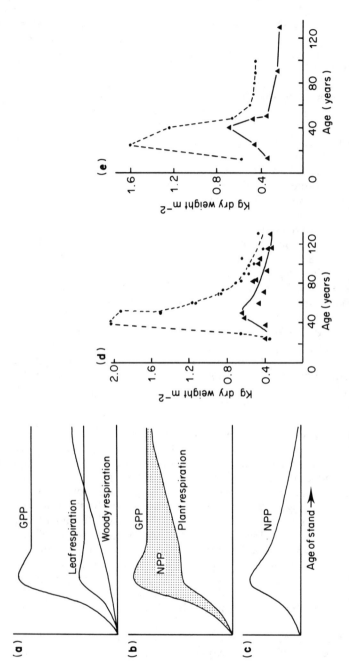

Fig. 9.3 Relationships between productivity and age of stand. **(a), (b), (c)** Hypothetical curves showing changes in gross primary production (GPP) and net primary production (NPP), the difference representing respiration. (From Duvigneaud.⁶) **(d), (e)** Net primary production (●) and annual litter fall (▲) in USSR. **(d)** Southern taiga spruce forests. **(e)** High oak forests, Voronezh. (From Rodin and Bazilevich.¹⁹⁶ © Translation (1967), Oliver and Boyd, Edinburgh.)

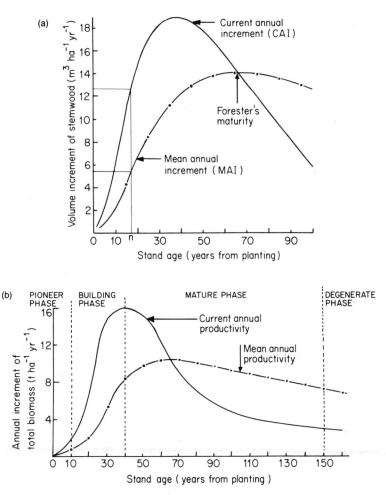

Fig. 9.4 **(a)** Patterns of volume increment in an even-aged stand of Scots pine (*Pinus sylvestris*) belonging to yield class 14. For symbols see text. Drawn from the data of Hamilton and Christie.[104] **(b)** Productivity changes with time in an even-aged stand of Scots pine. Commercial plantations would be felled well before the degenerate stage. (Redrawn from Cousens.[69])

maximum average rate of volume increment which can be achieved by a particular species on the site concerned. Theoretically the maximum average rate of volume production could be maintained in perpetuity by repeatedly felling the stand at this age and replanting with the same species.

The *yield class system* used in Britain is based on maximum MAI, i.e. the maximum average rate of volume production reached by a given species on a particular site, irrespective of when this occurs.[104] Maximum MAI under British conditions may be as low as 4 m³ ha⁻¹ for many hardwoods, larch and pines, but may exceed 30 m³ ha⁻¹ for grand fir. Each *yield class* represents the number of cubic metres (to the nearest even number) of timber produced per hectare at maximum MAI. Thus maximum MAI for a stand of trees in yield class 14 is greater than 13 m³ ha⁻¹ but less than 15 m³ ha⁻¹.

In any species, MAI reaches its maximum value at successively greater ages in the slower growing stands, as the yield class curves for oak (Fig. 9.5) illustrate. Maximum mean annual increments of different species are often of the same magnitude but reached at quite different times in the life of the tree, for example 35–40 years for poplar, 60 for Douglas fir and 80 for Norway spruce (trees in yield class 12 under British conditions).

The direct measurement of tree volume is time consuming. Fortunately there is a fairly close relationship between top height and the total cumulative volume production of a stand. *Top height* is the mean height of the 100 trees of the largest diameter at breast height (1.3 m) per hectare. Top height/age curves (i.e. *general yield class curves*), such as those given in Fig. 9.5, have been produced for all the major species planted in Britain. By entering top height in the appropriate year after planting, the practical forester can ascertain the general yield class of the stand. *Local yield classes* may be used for sites where, for example, a particular species at a given spacing tends to form trunks rather thinner or thicker in relation to top height than is normal.

Figure 9.5 contrasts the general yield class curves of oak with those of grand fir, which under British conditions grows faster than any other tree for which Hamilton and Christie[104] give data. Oak is a magnificient broadleaved deciduous tree, whose growth encourages the development of a diverse insect fauna and an attractive herb layer, but it grows far more slowly than most conifers and in Britain few commercial timber growers now plant it. Even with conifers, costing at compound interest over 50 years or so influences whether and when operations such as brashing and spraying are carried out: often owners have to cut their losses by 'premature felling'. Timber, especially in northern countries, tends to be a long-term, low return crop; indeed a cynic could say that the main advantage of softwoods in Britain is that they are less unprofitable than hardwoods.

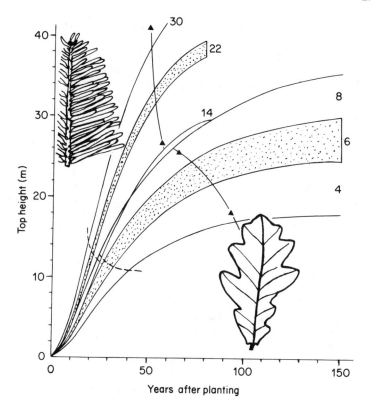

Fig. 9.5 General yield class curves for grand fir (*Abies grandis*) and native oak (*Quercus robur* and *Q. petraea*) under British conditions. The stippled areas represent the median yield classes for each species; the other figures indicate the lowest and highest general yield classes normally encountered. --- Time of first thinning, ▲–▲ age of maximum MAI. (Curves redrawn from Hamilton and Christie.[104])

9.2 SECONDARY PRODUCERS: THE HERBIVORE SUBSYSTEM

Values for biomass and production of woodland heterotrophs are even more difficult to estimate than for vegetation, but, however approximate, they are often used in attempting to quantify energy flow (for details of methodology, see[182, 184]). From figures published for the major forest types of the world,[239] the total animal biomass appears to be about a quarter of 1% of that of the world's forest vegetation. Only a small proportion of this biomass is represented by vertebrates, which contribute less than 10% to the total in European forests. The bulk is made up by invertebrates, most of which occur in litter and soil.

Quantitative data on feeding by woodland herbivores refer mainly to canopy-dwelling insects, especially phyllophagous (leaf-chewing) caterpillars and weevils. Some of these may occasionally cause widespread and severe defoliation, as on oak and other hardwoods in many parts of Britain in 1979 and 1980, but in general trees are subjected to chronic, low-level herbivory. Evidence of such activity occurs as holes in leaves, whose area is most readily measured at leaf-fall; in temperate broadleaved trees such holes commonly represent about 5% of the canopy leaf area. The corresponding consumption by insects (which may be less than the final hole area, because of leaf expansion and necrosis subsequent to feeding) is of the order of 1% of the net primary production of the trees,[169] and it is therefore usually assumed that the influence on trees is negligible. Even if trees are more severely defoliated, many species can produce at least a partial replacement, as shown by lammas shoots, although these in turn may be attacked, for example oak by mildew and caterpillars of the Buff-tip, *Phalera bucephala*. In July 1980 at Chaddesley NNR, Worcestershire, the canopy appeared to be fully developed in individual oaks which had been completely defoliated in May. Nevertheless, a study of *Quercus robur* at Wytham showed that the summer-wood increment of individual trees was less when caterpillars (mainly of winter moth and *Tortrix*) were abundant, despite lammas growth (Fig. 9.6a). Proportionate changes in growth of five oak trees and in their associated caterpillar populations are related in Fig. 9.6d. If a linear regression is assumed, radial growth of summer wood would have been 73% greater over the eight year period if there had been no caterpillars. In energy terms, such an increment loss is four times greater than the amount consumed, indicating that lammas shoots do not fully compensate for the damage. This is partially because of the timing of events: lammas growth in oaks may not be complete until July, so that the LAI is less than it would have been in undamaged canopy during the long days around midsummer. Consequently there is less photosynthate available for the summer increment, which is dependent on the productivity of foliage from May onwards (Fig. 9.6b,c). In addition, some of the energy and nutrients which would have been channelled into increment is expended on lammas growth. However, any undamaged foliage, including lammas shoots, can enable reserves to be laid down which contribute to spring increment and to the flushing of buds; such trees can potentially survive successive defoliations, although with little increment, as evidenced by a series of narrow annual rings, for example in many parts of southern England in the period 1917–1924.

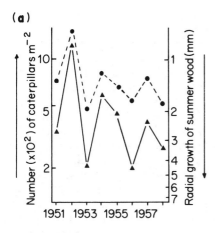

(a)

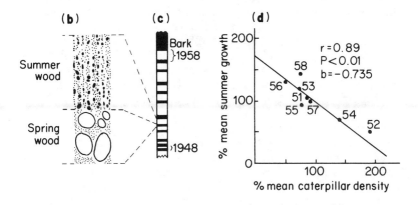

(b) **(c)** **(d)**

Fig. 9.6 The effect of partial defoliation by caterpillars on timber production by *Quercus robur* in Wytham Wood, Oxford. **(a)** Abundance of caterpillars (▲) and, on inverted scale, radial growth (●) of summer wood by one of five studied trees, showing significant negative correlation ($P < 0.01$). **(b)** The appearance of summer and spring wood, the latter with very large vessels. **(c)** An enlargement of an increment core taken from a single tree, showing variation in size of annual rings. **(d)** Regression of proportionate change in summer growth and in caterpillar density, based on means for five trees. Each tree's growth (or caterpillar density) in each year was expressed as a percentage of the mean summer growth of that tree over eight years; the mean value, for the five trees, of each of the two percentages is plotted for each year. (From Varley, G. C. and Gradwell, G. R. (1960). *Proceedings of the 11th International Congress of Entomology*, **2**, 211–4.)

In fact these attacks leave trees more vulnerable; successive defoliations of oaks in Hayley Wood, Cambridgeshire, between 1916 and 1925, were followed by death of one in four trees from mildew, honey fungus or competition from other trees.[191] Defoliation of beech by caterpillars of the pale tussock moth, *Dasychira pubibunda*, was found to have no measurable effect on incremental growth or production in a Danish site, probably because trees were attacked late in the summer.[170]

Deciduous conifers, such as *Larix* spp., also appear to be adapted to tolerate defoliation, which in effect brings about premature leaf fall. Stands of larch in Holland have survived after defoliation for nine consecutive years by web-spinning larch sawfly caterpillars (*Cephalcia lariciphila*), but this species killed many British trees in 1978, whereas normally damage is masked by fresh growth in late summer.

Timing is again important in *evergreen conifers*. Loss of needles may be less harmful if it occurs after the new buds have been formed, so that trees stripped of needles by pine looper caterpillars in late summer may be able to flush in the following year (but see Section 6.5 for the increased susceptibility of such trees to attack by *Tomicus*). Pine beauty caterpillars, feeding in midsummer on all ages of needles, eventually kill the cambium, so that buds fail to open. Among pine sawflies, larvae of *Diprion pini* also feed on various ages of needles, whereas *Neodiprion sertifer* leaves the current year's needles untouched; in Britain height growth may be checked by the first species, especially in young plantations, but in continental Europe both species are serious defoliators of pines. In North America the European spruce sawfly (*Gilpinia hercyniae*) feeds on older foliage, which has a lower photosynthetic capacity (Fig. 2.15). It kills the crown of the tree from the bottom; no buds are killed directly and no adventitious buds arise. The young, photosynthetically efficient, foliage remains active for longer, and after a sawfly infestation the very small amount of foliage remaining is mainly new growth in the tip of the crown. Trees can survive defoliation by sawfly of a severity which would cause death if the pest were spruce budworm (see Section 6.5), which tends to attack tree crowns from the top downwards, killing many buds and young shoots.

Sap-sucking insects would be expected to have a greater effect on plant growth, per unit of energy ingested, than leaf-chewing species, since they remove not only photosynthate but also considerable quantities of water and nutrients. Components of injected saliva could affect growth rates, while some species may facilitate entry by pathogens (e.g. *Nectria* by *Cryptococcus fagi*). Among pest species, adelgids can defoliate conifers, and the green spruce aphid (*Elatobium abietinum*) may reduce incremental growth by up to 30%. More detailed quantitative relationships between aphids and tree growth have been revealed for species occurring on sycamore and lime.

Sycamores infested with *Drepanosiphum platanoidis* have smaller leaves than usual. Dixon[79] found that the average size of mature leaves in two 10 m trees was negatively correlated with the abundance of aphids in spring. The average population of aphids during a seven-year period was estimated to effect a 48% reduction in leaf area of one of the two trees, suggesting the possibility of competition between the requirements of growing leaves and aphids for translocated nutrients. However, estimates of the amounts of energy and nitrogen removed by the aphids (based on analysis of honeydew production) showed that these fell far short of the amounts represented by the reduction in leaf area: energy consumption, for example, was only a third of the equivalent of the 'lost' leaf tissue. Dixon suggested that substances in aphid saliva, such as amino acids, indole acetic acid and phenolics, could reduce leaf growth, and a similar influence on xylem proliferation could provide a partial explanation for the observed reduction in the size of annual rings in infested trees, assuming that some is the result of reduced availability of photosynthate (cf. caterpillars feeding on oak leaves). In fact, the smaller leaves have a greater chlorophyll content, per unit area, than uninfested leaves, and infested leaves of saplings had a greater rate of net dry matter production. However, this is not reflected in the size of the annual rings, perhaps because this is a measure of the area of vessels required to supply a particular leaf area with water and salts. Whatever the reason, it has been estimated that the volume of stem wood could be increased by up to 280% per annum if there were no aphids.

Leaves of lime infested with *Eucallipterus tiliae* are of similar size to those of aphid-free plants, and there is no difference between the annual rings. Infested leaves contain less chlorophyll and fall earlier, suggesting damage by the aphids, and although aerial growth is unaffected, root growth may be completely inhibited; compensatory energy production is possible in the following year, when the leaves contain more chlorophyll, but only if aphids are absent.[147] Extrapolation of results from saplings indicates that the energy requirements of aphids on a mature lime (which may carry over a million aphids) are equivalent to 19% of net primary production.[148] Expressed in terms of ground area beneath the tree canopy, the energy consumed by aphids on lime is *c.*20 times the estimated consumption by phyllophagous caterpillars on oak at Wytham.

The channelling of production into reproduction may be hindered by herbivores, either because destruction of foliage reduces seed production, or because the seeds are consumed. In a Danish beechwood an average of 36% of the annual production of beech-mast endosperm was consumed by seed worms (see Section 4.3), corresponding to less than 0.001% of net primary production.[168] On the other hand annual rings of *Fagus sylvatica* may be about half their normal width during a heavy mast year, showing how photosynthate is redistributed within the tree itself.

Seed production represents potential regeneration but in fact most of the energy in seeds or seedlings is often diverted into the production of heterotrophs. In the same Danish beechwood, heavy defoliation of ash saplings by the lilac leaf miner (*Caloptilia syringella*), combined with repeated removal of terminal buds by roe deer, resulted in negligible growth of saplings which, although of maximum height 0.5 m, were up to 36 years old.[169] Quantitative estimates of consumption by vertebrate herbivores and their effects on seeds, saplings or mature trees are rare, but moose (*Alces alces*) were estimated to reduce production by young plants by 50% in a mixed forest near Moscow, mainly by decreasing growth rates rather than by direct losses due to consumption.

Whatever their effects on trees and other autotrophs, consumption by woodland herbivores probably rarely exceeds 10% of the net primary production. Even less is actually *assimilated*, and the proportion which becomes herbivore (or still less, carnivore) tissue is very small indeed. Values for assimilation/consumption efficiency (A/C) of woodland phyllophagous invertebrates are normally reckoned to be in the region of 20–30%, yielding 70–80% as faeces, destined for the decomposition subsystem. The corresponding value for vertebrate herbivores is about 50%, but in homoiotherms (warm-blooded animals) only 2% of this may pass into production, compared with 40% for invertebrates. In carnivores, A/C is typically in the region of 80%, but again homoiotherms 'lose' most of this energy in the form of respiratory heat.

Selected examples of *energy utilization* by woodland herbivores and carnivores are shown in Table 9.2. The values for *Operophtera*

Table 9.2 The fate of ingested food in various woodland animals.

Species	Food	A/C* (%)	P/A* (%)
(a) *Operophtera brumata* caterpillars	Hazel leaves	40	59
(b) *Heterocampa guttivita* caterpillars	Hardwood leaves	14	40
(c) *Drepanosiphum platanoidis* (aphid)	Sycamore leaves	9.5	44
(d) *Mitopus morio* (harvestman)	Various arthropods	47–74	–
(e) Salamanders	Insects	81	60
(f) Shrews	Insects	90	2
(g) Birds	Insects, fruits, seeds	30	2
(h) Chipmunks	Foliage, seeds, insects	82	2

* From basic energy-flow equations: $C = A + Fu$; $A = P + R$; where C = energy consumed (ingested), Fu = excreta, A = energy assimilated (i.e. digested and absorbed), P = energy in assimilated food used for tissue production, R = heat lost in respiration.

Data from (a) Smith, P. H. (1972). *Journal of Animal Ecology*, **41**, 567–87. (b), (e–h) From Hubbard Brook Forest, New Hampshire; Gosz *et al.*[97] (c) Dixon, A. F. G. in Phillipson.[184] (d) Phillipson, J. (1960). *Journal of Animal Ecology*, **29**, 299–307.

caterpillars indicate that these short-lived leaf feeders, which represent the sole growth phase of the individual, convert their food into body tissue with minimal loss as faeces or as metabolic activity. The much lower assimilation efficiency of aphids reflects the necessity to ingest an excess volume of phloem sap, primarily to obtain enough nitrogen. Lime aphids may not be particularly productive, but they bring about a massive flow of energy, turning over the energy equivalent of their average standing crop nearly 500 times during the year; most of this sap is siphoned on to leaves or litter below as honeydew.

Among the major vertebrates at Hubbard Brook, P/A values for shrews, birds and chipmunks indicate how little of the assimilated energy ends up as production in homoiotherms, in contrast to the situation in salamanders, whose metabolic rate is reduced during the winter, and which are more efficient converters of food into biomass. The maintenance of a high and relatively constant body temperature throughout the year in an animal as small as a shrew (adult weight 15 g) necessitates catching about 140 items of invertebrate prey per day, or one every five minutes during 12 hours' activity; this is equivalent to an intake of about one kilocalorie (4.2 kJ) of food energy per gram body weight per day.

The proverbial slowness of sloths reflects a low metabolic rate, which is further reduced at night when their body temperature is lowered.[128] Adult three-toed sloths (*Bradypus tridactylus*) spend most of their time among tree foliage, moving an average of 38 metres a day. An adult consumes *c*.5 g of fresh foliage per kilogram of body weight per day, an intake far below that needed by other mammals, such as monkeys, in tropical forests. Low levels of food consumption are undoubtedly among the factors which enable quite large sloth populations to exist in fairly limited territories.

Within the whole woodland ecosystem the amount of energy represented by production of herbivores and carnivores is far less than the 10% of net primary production which enters the grazing chain, most of which is 'lost', either from the chain, as faeces, or from the whole ecosystem, as respiratory heat. However, faeces, mucus, cast skins and dead bodies add to the decomposition subsystem a contribution which, although small compared to plant necromass, may be qualitatively and temporarily important to particular decomposers.

9.3 THE DECOMPOSITION SUBSYSTEM

Quantitative estimates of woodland necromass and its turnover are bedevilled by sampling problems, especially for roots and woody material, and also by the varying usage of terms such as litter, humus and soil organic matter. Data refer mainly to input in the form of aerial plant litter, usually ignoring standing deadwood, exudates, rainfall and leachates, animal products and even roots. Estimates of **annual litter fall** range from $c.1$ t ha^{-1} in arctic-alpine forests to 25 t ha^{-1} in certain tropical forests. A typical value for a temperate deciduous woodland is $c.4$ t ha^{-1} yr^{-1} (for reviews, see[5, 55, 111]). If all contributions from plants are included, then annual necromass input is closely related to net primary production; in climax forest, the two values theoretically differ only by the amount of plant production dissipated by the herbivore subsystem.

Litter input increases during the initial ageing of a stand (Fig. 9.3) but once the canopy has closed there may be little difference in litter production by stands with very different densities or ages of trees. Variation from year to year within a particular site (Fig. 9.7) results

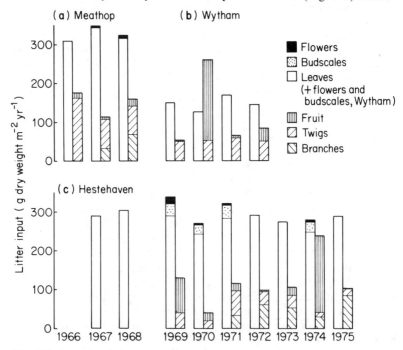

Fig. 9.7 Annual variation in litter input in three temperate broad-leaved woodlands. **(a)** Meathop, Cumbria, England: oak, ash, birch, hazel and sycamore. (Data from Sykes, J. M. and Bunce, R. G. H. (1970). *Oikos*, **21**, 326–9.) **(b)** Brogden's Belt, Wytham, Oxford, England: *Fagus sylvatica*. (Data from Phillipson *et al.*[185]) **(c)** Hestehaven, Denmark: *Fagus sylvatica*. (Data from Nielsen, B. O. (1977). *Forstl. Forsøgsv. Danm.*, **35**, 17–38.)

from the influence of factors such as the weather, pests and diseases on primary production; heavy investment in fruiting (e.g. mast years) or storm damage to trunks and branches make a substantial contribution to variation.

In cool temperate regions the most conspicuous seasonal variation in leaf fall occurs in deciduous trees, with major input in the autumn ('The Fall'). Storms or herbivores can cause the addition of green leaf material to the litter, and green leaves may also accompany the abscission of inflorescences (e.g. *Castanea sativa*). Temperate evergreen species typically shed leaves throughout the year, either irregularly (e.g. *Picea abies*), or with a peak in spring (e.g. *Quercus ilex* in the Mediterranean region, Fig. 9.8) or autumn (e.g. *Pinus sylvestris*), while *Cryptomeria japonica* is an example of a bimodal species in this respect. Certain tropical species also show bimodal behaviour, the leaves of *Terminalia catappa* being completely and quickly replaced by fresh growth twice a year. Even in those tropical rain forests where rainfall is almost uniformly distributed throughout the year there are numerous species which are deciduous, although some may be bare of leaves for only a few days. Leaf-fall is typically continuous in tropical forests, often with a sequential pattern of different species (Fig. 9.8b).

Input of non-leaf litter, especially bud scales, flowers and fruits, is also highly seasonal. The timing of litter fall is of significance, not only to the protection and development of seeds, but also to the activities of the decomposer community and the timing of nutrient release. The contribution made by the different parts of plants to total litter input varies widely with species and age, the percentage of non-leaf litter tending to increase as stands mature. Coppicing rejuvenates stands, so that leaf-litter production may be unusually heavy under coppice. Although fruits sometimes constitute nearly half the litter fall, woody remains usually make up the bulk of non-leaf litter, which itself forms on average c.30% of the litter. In terms of necromass, woody tissues probably represent a greater proportion than this; Swift[226] has suggested that twigs and branches may contribute c.40% of aerial production, with further input, so difficult to quantify, from standing dead trunks and dead roots. The percentage of aerial litter stemming from the field and ground layers may be as high as 50%, but 10% is probably a more typical value.

Whereas annual production of necromass tends to increase from the poles to the equator, the standing crop of necromass to which it is added shows the reverse, with greater accumulations at higher latitudes. Once a steady-state situation has been established, rates of input and depletion of necromass are virtually equal, but during the many years which may be taken to reach that state there can be an

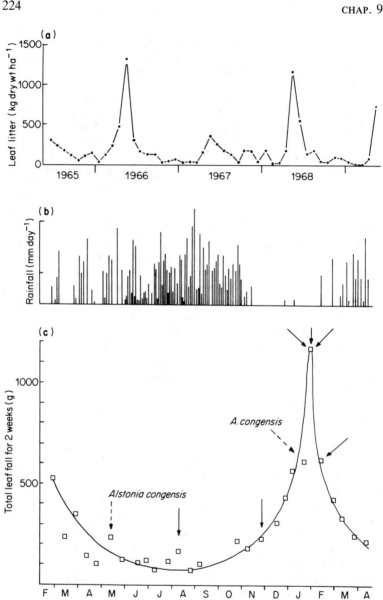

Fig. 9.8 Seasonal aspects of litter production. **(a)** Leaf fall in the evergreen *Quercus ilex* at Roquet, near Montpellier (from Lossaint, P. and Rapp, M.; in Duvigneaud.[6] © UNESCO 1971. Reproduced by permission of UNESCO.) **(b), (c)** Rainfall and leaf fall in a tropical forest at Ibadan, Nigeria. Arrows indicate maximum leaf-shedding for seven tree species, including bimodal *Alstonia congensis*. (From Madge.[155])

appreciable build-up to the standing crop of necromass characteristic of a site.

Generally, decomposition rates and turnover times are estimated for only part of the total necromass, such as aerial litter, leaves or wood. Decomposition often refers only to visible depletion from the standing crop, i.e. until components lose their identity when incorporated into humus, thus ignoring the later, and usually slower, stages of decay. Estimates of turnover which are based on ratios of input to necromass standing crop depend on the latter being in a steady state; even in an apparently mature woodland there can be considerable variation, both temporal and spatial, in the amounts of necromass present. In a 150-year-old beech site at Wytham, the decomposition rate of aerial litter, calculated from depletion and turnover times for miscellaneous debris, was found to be very similar to the mean annual litter input, suggesting a steady state,[185] whereas in Varley and Gradwell's oak site at Wytham, incremental growth is still occurring.

Most of the values for decomposition rates given in Table 9.3 are based on tethered or mesh-bagged litter, whose weight loss may include removal of large pieces, as by earthworms into their burrows,

Table 9.3 Estimates of rates of litter decomposition in woodlands.

Site	Type of litter	Decomposition rate ($mg\,g^{-1}\,yr^{-1}$, except b, c, e, f)		
(a) Kevo, Finland	Pinus sylvestris needles	180		
	Betula tortuosa leaves	270		
	Pinus sylvestris wood	50		
(b) Delamere, England	Pinus sylvestris needles	240 in 2 years		
		(Mull)	(Moder)	
(c) English Lake District	Betula pendula leaves	830	260	in 6 months
	Tilia cordata leaves	560	230	
	Quercus petraea leaves	260	230	
	Quercus robur leaves	170	170	
(d) Meathop, England	Hardwood branches in canopy	80		
	in litter	170		
(e) Ibadan, Nigeria	Leaves of five species of trees, mixed dry lowland forest	$6-15\,mg\,g^{-1}\,day^{-1}$		
(f) Banco, Ivory Coast	Tree leaves, moist evergreen forest	$13\,mg\,g^{-1}\,day^{-1}$		

Data from (a) Kallio;[133] (b) Kendrick, W. B. (1959). *Canadian Journal of Botany*, **37**, 907–12; (c) Bocock, K. L. and Gilbert, O. J. W. (d) Swift;[226] (e) Madge;[155] (f) Bernhard (1970) from UNESCO.[27]

so over-estimating decay rates during these earlier stages. This can be avoided by measuring CO_2 production associated with decomposition, but this fails to take account of leaching, and is complicated by respiration of living roots. Nevertheless, Table 9.3 gives some idea of the variation which occurs within and between sites. The fact that these values roughly parallel latitudinal changes in net primary production suggests that climatic factors have a major influence on decomposition. The ease of decomposition of the various components of necromass, and their relative contribution to the total, are also of importance. Most tropical forest leaves disappear completely within six months, whereas conifer needles may take more than a decade to do so in cool temperate or boreal sites.

In attempts to assess the quantitative role of the various agents of decomposition, the contribution made by different groups of organisms can be estimated in terms of one or more of the components of the basic energy-flow equations, referred to in Table 9.2. Despite the problems of extrapolating from the laboratory to woodland conditions, values for consumption suggest that in some sites litter input may be sufficient to satisfy the requirements of one or two groups of animals, but not all of them, let alone the fungi and bacteria. For example, oribatid mites were estimated to require half the annual litter input of 300 g m^{-2} in a Belgian oak woodland,[44] while if *Lumbricus terrestris* fed at the optimal rate of 27 mg g^{-1} body weight per day, the entire annual leaf fall at Merlewood Lodge Wood, Cumbria, would have been ingested in three months.[207] This apparent paradox is partially explained by the widespread incidence of *coprophagy*. This involves the reworking of litter which is ingested but only partially digested, the resultant faeces being re-ingested, with the possibility of repetition of the process through a succession of organisms (including coprophilous members of the microflora). This reprocessing can occur only if digestion is less than perfect, as is implied by the generalization that detritivores are wasteful feeders, passing out 80–95% of their ingested food as faeces. In fact, there are numerous reports of animals such as snails, woodlice and termites with assimilation efficiencies (A/C) of 40% or more; fungal-feeding springtails and oribatids have achieved values of 60–70%, and up to 69% has been claimed for the litter-feeding oribatid *Steganacarus magnus*, in contrast to earlier values of 10–15% (Table 9.4). Nevertheless, slow-moving litter consumers, such as certain oribatids with up to 15 pellets per mite per day, produce veritable dung heaps, constituting potential resources for coprophages.[106]

Caution should also be exercised when generalizing about the fate of assimilated energy. A 'typical' value for the proportion going into *production* of tissues in detritivores and microbes is 40% but the few

Table 9.4 Assimilation and production in adult oribatid mites (from Luxton[150]).

Species	Food	Temperature (°C)	A/C (%)	P/A (%)
Carabodes labyrinthicus	Fungal hyphae	10	40	–
Damaeus clavipes	Fungal hyphae	15	62	83.5
Steganacarus magnus	Leaf litter	18	41–69	92

published data (Table 9.4) indicate a wide range, even within the same group: thus whereas 5% was once considered a realistic figure for oribatids, more recent estimates for two species of these mites are as high as 92%. Whether this represents tissues of growing individuals or reproductive products, it constitutes a considerable immobilization of energy and nutrients, possibly of value during moulting and other non-feeding periods.

Despite uncertainties about the proportion of energy which is respired, and because of the relative ease of determining respiration rates, *population metabolism* is the most widely used measure of a population's contribution to energy flow. The results of laboratory determinations of respiration rates for various species over a range of temperatures and individual body weights can be applied to quantitative estimates of the composition of woodland populations sampled throughout the year. Estimated values for annual respiration rates of woodland detritivores, in kJ m^{-2}, include an average of 125 for oribatid mites from various Belgian sites,[45] 144 for termites in Malaysian rainforest,[244] and 630 for enchytraeids in a Douglas fir plantation in North Wales, where litter input was equivalent to 5670 kJ m^{-2} yr^{-1}.[171]

Data for the decomposition subsystem at Meathop (Fig. 9.10) suggest that 83% of the respiration is accounted for by activities of the microflora, although it must be stressed that estimates of the amounts of metabolically active microbial protoplasm are notoriously liable to error. However, this value for the microflora is almost the same as that obtained by Macfadyen[153] in a grazed meadow, indicating the over-riding importance of microbes in energy flow. Comparable data from other woodland sites are not yet available, but estimates can be made by applying generalized values for respiration to field population data. For example, in temperate woodlands it has been suggested that the scarcity of large decomposers, such as lumbricid earthworms, woodlice and millipedes, in mor (as compared with mull) sites, is compensated by the relatively greater activity of nematodes, enchytraeids and microarthropods.[153] Estimates for sites in Japan and S.E. Asia indicated that an increasing proportion of detritivore respiration could be attributed to large decomposers along a temperature gradient from alpine coniferous shrub sites to tropical rain forest;[138] the shortage of soil organic matter in the latter is thought to be inimicable to many of the smaller animals. The fact that the ratio of soil fauna respiration to litter input was small in the rain forest seemed to imply a relatively small role for animals in decomposition there. Other authors, however, have suggested that there is an increasing contribution by soil fauna to community metabolism on passing from boreal regions to tropical rain forests.[25] Although more sites need to be studied in detail, in general it can be assumed that decomposer energetics are dominated by microbial activity.

9.4   ENERGY FLOW THROUGH WOODLAND ECOSYSTEMS

Having considered the components of primary production and the dissipation of energy in woodlands, it would now seem appropriate to combine the various parts into an overall view of individual ecosystems. Unfortunately this is not yet possible, data being particularly incomplete for tropical forests. A few examples from temperate woodlands give some idea of the relative importance of the different subsystems and the fate of energy, but even these involve the use of unproven assumptions.

Provisional energy flow values for Hubbard Brook Forest, New Hampshire, are summarized in Fig. 9.9; there are very few data for

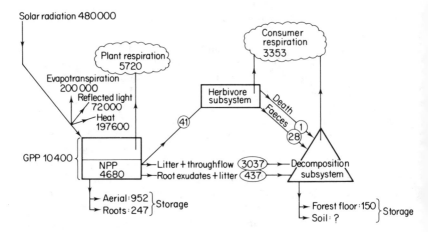

Fig. 9.9 Energy flow diagram for an undisturbed hardwood area in Hubbard Brook Forest, New Hampshire; values in kcal m^{-2} yr^{-1}. (Data from Gosz *et al.*[97])

the decomposers. Biomass was still being accumulated in this sub-climax forest, so that only 72% of NPP was added to the decomposition subsystem, 84% of this in the form of aerial litter.

Detailed information on energy flow is available for two British woodlands, especially through the herbivore subsystem and the decomposers, respectively. Data for **Wytham Wood** (Fig. 9.10a) were

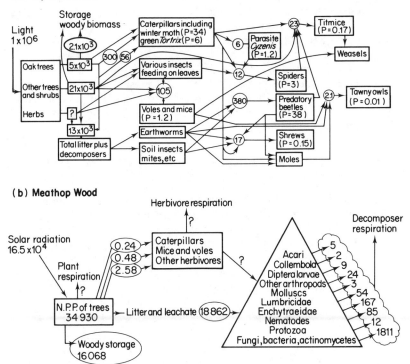

Fig. 9.10 Simplified energy flow diagrams for two English broadleaved sites (kJ m^{-2} yr^{-1}; values in boxes are for net production, those in circles are for energy input, and those in 'clouds' for respiration). **(a)** Wytham Wood, Oxford; there are no data for decomposers. **(b)** Meathop Wood, Cumbria; data are not available for carnivores. (From The Open University, *Energy flow through ecosystems* (S323 Unit 5: Whole ecosystems). © 1974, The Open University Press. With additional data for Meathop decomposers from Satchell, J. E. in Duvigneaud.[6])

largely derived from studies of population dynamics of certain herbivores and carnivores (see Sections 7.1 and 7.3), from which estimates were made for consumption and production. Consumption by caterpillars is equivalent to *c*.1.4% of the NPP of trees, but the quantitative importance of other herbivores was not assessed. Secondary production declines markedly as energy passes through the trophic web: 40 kJ m^{-2} yr^{-1} for *Tortrix* and *Operophtera* caterpillars, 1.2 for voles and mice, 0.17 for titmice and 0.01 kJ m^{-2} yr^{-1} for tawny owls which, with weasels, were the top carnivores. This value for owls represents 0.00004% of the NPP of trees and shrubs, compared with 50% going into the decomposition subsystem.

Studies at **Meathop Wood**, the I.B.P site in Cumbria, have concentrated on primary production and decomposition (Fig. 9.10b). Intake by herbivores was equivalent to 0.009% of the NPP of trees, indicating that this subsystem is less important than at Wytham. Annual increment represented 46% of NPP and input to the soil 54%. Assessments of respiration by decomposers indicate that enchytraeid worms are metabolically the most important group of litter and soil animals, but estimates of microbial activity are so liable to error that it has so far proved impossible to apportion energy flow between fungi and bacteria.

9.5 NUTRIENT CYCLING IN TEMPERATE, BOREAL AND TROPICAL WOODLANDS

The distribution of nutrients between the various components of a woodland ecosystem at a particular time varies with the species-composition and age of the wood, with soil type and with the individual elements. The fact that the major pools of available nutrients differ between biome types (Fig. 9.11) is of fundamental importance, not least in relation to exploitation by Man. In boreal forests, typified by evergreen conifers in far northern latitudes, the major pool is in slowly decomposing litter and humus. In tropical rain

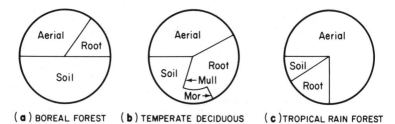

(a) BOREAL FOREST (b) TEMPERATE DECIDUOUS (c) TROPICAL RAIN FOREST

Fig. 9.11 Distribution of standing crop of total nitrogen between major aerial and underground pools in boreal, temperate and tropical zones. The bulk of the mineral nutrients in tropical rain forests is usually considered to be held in the vegetation, cf. **(c)** above. This broad generalization does not, however, apply to all nutrients in all tropical rain forests; potassium fits this model best in the tables given on pp. 27–80, UNESCO.[27] (From Swift, Heal and Anderson.[25])

forests, on the other hand, the bulk of nutrients is normally considered to occur in living vegetation, with minimal accumulation in soil and almost instantaneous uptake by autotrophs of nutrients released by leaching or rapid decomposition. Temperate woodlands represent an intermediate situation, commonly with about a third to two-thirds of the available total nutrients present in plant biomass, and with a diversity of possible pathways and rates of cycling.

Temperate broadleaved woodlands

Meathop Wood, Cumbria, can be taken as an example to illustrate some of the features characteristic of nutrient cycling in this type of woodland.[56] The distribution of major nutrients in plant biomass, litter and soil at Meathop, and the annual nutrient fluxes, are shown in Fig. 9.12. Details of gross uptake by plants are not available: *net uptake* is the sum of amounts retained plus those returned in litter or leachates. Nutrients are translocated to the most active, productive parts of the plant, such as photosynthetic tissues and young roots. In woody plants they also contribute to incremental growth, with higher concentrations in the sapwood and bark than in the heartwood. The concentration of elements in tree leaves is commonly 6–20 times greater than in wood of the same species, so that there is an inverse relationship between tissue durability and nutrient content per unit dry weight.

Seasonal variation in nutrient concentration is particularly noticeable in foliage. At Meathop, the calcium content of leaves continues to increase during the summer, being greatest at leaf-fall, whereas the other major elements are at their maxima in early or mid-summer, with much lower concentrations as the leaves senesce. Some of this reduction is caused by leaching, but in the main it results from cycling within the tree, involving translocation back from the leaves into long-lived tissues. These nutrients probably constitute a short-term store, in living wood, available for the next spring flush. This process of *conservation* is most marked in respect of nitrogen and phosphorus, whose contents in summer foliage exceed their annual net uptake by trees. In contrast, calcium may be present in excess of the requirements of the leaves, and is not conserved.

The most conspicuous input to the decomposition subsystem is *litter*. Non-leaf litter makes an appreciable contribution to the total nutrients in litter, especially in respect of nitrogen and phosphorus. The fall of budscales and catkins in spring, followed by peduncles of oak, accounts for the fact that in the nearby oakwood at Bogle Crag more phosphorus, and almost as much nitrogen and potassium, are added to the litter in the spring and summer as during the autumn. Significant contributions are also made by herbaceous litter, notably

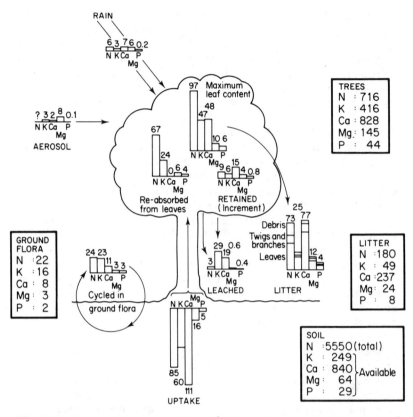

Fig. 9.12 Mean nutrient contents (kg ha^{-1}; in boxes) and nutrient fluxes (kg ha^{-1} yr^{-1}) in Meathop Wood, Cumbria; the canopy is dominated by oak, ash and birch, with an understorey of hazel and other shrubs, and a rich herb layer. A brown earth with mull humus, developed on glacial drift, has a pH of 4.1–7.5, depending on the depth of soil over the underlying Carboniferous Limestone. The mean annual rainfall is 1240 mm. Net uptake by trees is the sum of amounts in increment and those cycled in litter and leachates (e.g. for N, 85 = 9 + 73 + 3). See also Fig. 9.10. (Modified from Brown.[56])

nitrogen and potassium from bracken. (Elsewhere[86] it has been shown that spring-green plants can improve the seasonal availability of important ions to other species. When the leaves of *Allium ursinum* decay the large nitrate pool within them is immediately made available to summer-green plants without involving the action of nitrifying bacteria.)

Rainwater passing through the canopy (throughfall) and down the branches and trunks (stem flow) may become enriched in nutrients, as when bases are leached from the trees and herbs, or depleted, as with nitrogen and sometimes phosphorus at Meathop; such depletion may be caused by phylloplane microflora or leaf absorption.

Nitrogen and phosphorus are characterized by being tightly cycled, with minimal losses through leaching from the canopy or soil. Nitrogen input is supplemented by fixation of the gas in the phylloplane and soil, but there is evidence of phosphorus deficiency at Bogle Crag.

Nutrient cycles in other temperate woodland sites for which data are available show broad similarities to that at Meathop (Fig. 9.13; see also[51]). Although the absolute uptake of nutrients in less productive sites may be similar to or greater than that in richer areas, smaller proportions appear to go into incremental growth, so more is kept cycling.

Effects of herbivores

The *timing of herbivore activity* is as significant in nutrient cycling as it is in primary production (see Section 9.2). Defoliation of oaks by caterpillars such as *Tortrix viridana* occurs before nutrients are translocated out of the leaves, so preventing this important process of conservation. Complete loss of leaves at Meathop represents the removal of amounts of nitrogen and phosphorus, and to a lesser extent of potassium, equivalent to the requirements of incremental growth for four years. Lammas growth necessitates a further drain on reserves, creating a situation which is likely to be aggravated if defoliations occur in successive years. Fluxes of N, P and K from the canopy of a Danish beechwood were significantly raised after defoliation by caterpillars of *Dasychira pubibunda*, presumably through leaching from faeces and injured leaves;[170] similar increased losses from leaching occur in red pine (*Pinus resinosa*) defoliated by sawfly caterpillars (*Neodiprion sertifer*).[135] There is no evidence to support the idea that decomposition and mineralization are accelerated by the presence of caterpillar frass in the litter, which might otherwise provide some compensation by making nutrients more rapidly available to the plants. However, aphid honeydew seems to exert a stimulatory influence on decomposers.

Role of decomposers

Microorganisms are known to be essential in the *mineralization of necromass*, but it is difficult to quantify relationships, especially if detritivores are also involved.

The levels of certain elements are higher in fungi than in their litter substrates, and further concentration may occur in animals which feed on litter or fungi, the latter being a potentially rich source of nitrogen and, possibly, sodium and calcium. There is considerable

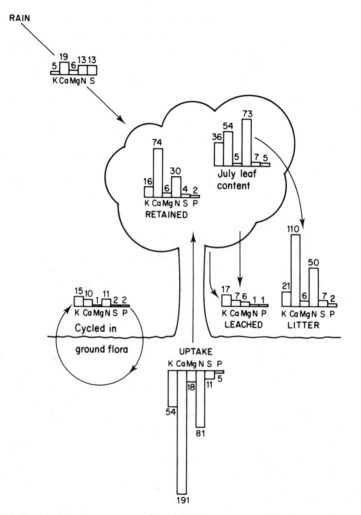

Fig. 9.13 Nutrient fluxes (kg ha⁻¹ yr⁻¹) in mixed oakwood at Virelles-Blaimont, Belgium. Details of species composition of this site are given in Fig. 9.1. (Modified from Froment *et al.*; in Duvigneaud.[6] © UNESCO 1971. Reproduced by permission of UNESCO.)

evidence for ***differential absorption of nutrients*** from ingested litter, the processing of large quantities of food, sometimes supplemented by coprophagy, being a possible means of concentrating scarce nutrients.[110] Although some mineralization occurs, as in the formation of ammonia as a nitrogenous excretory product in woodlice, many nutrients become *immobilized* for long periods in detritivores, for example calcium in cuticles and shells. Comminution of litter would be expected to result in increased susceptibility to leaching, and further losses of nutrients could follow if the assumed stimulation of microbial activity by detritivores (see Section 8.4) actually occurs. Whatever the reason, detritivores at Oak Ridge, Tennessee, increased the weight loss of *Liriodendron* litter by a third while halving caesium retention, compared to plots lacking animals.[242]

The balance between immobilization and mineralization is particularly important in respect of microbial decomposers. Catabolic breakdown of organic compounds releases energy for anabolic processes, which in turn require uptake of nutrients and their immobilization within decomposer tissues. Immobilization prevails so long as nutrients are in short supply, as often occurs with nitrogen and phosphorus during the initial stages of decomposition. Net mineralization of a particular nutrient usually occurs only when the ratio of carbon to that nutrient in the necromass falls below that of the tissues of the decomposers; for nitrogen, the critical value for C/N is about 25:1. Studies of nutrient release from decomposing leaves in Hubbard Brook Forest, New Hampshire, indicated that nitrogen, phosphorus and sulphur remained immobilized, and therefore unavailable to autotrophs, for at least a year after leaf fall, maximum release being possibly delayed until the following spring.[98] Similarly, maximum root growth in a *Liriodendron* forest at Oak Ridge occurred between January and March, this period of maximal uptake coinciding with minimal microbial immobilization. Conversely, losses to groundwater during periods of low uptake were minimized by high immobilization (Fig. 9.14). Further buffering of the system was provided by soil animals, which are thought by some authors to play an important part in regulating the balance between nutrient immobilization and release. Together, detritivores and microflora provide innumerable pools and pathways for the conservation and timely release of nutrients; this complexity may impart a characteristic stability to nutrient cycling in temperate woodlands. In forests generally, a significant proportion of the energy captured in photosynthesis is allocated to heterotrophs, thus ensuring that nutrients are effectively recycled, and so helping to maintain the high productivity of forest ecosystems.[242]

Uptake of nutrients from soil solution by trees (and probably many other autotrophs) often occurs by means of *mycorrhizas*, intimate associations of fungi and roots which are particularly important in less fertile soils (see Section 3.1). Many of the fungi involved are Basidiomycetes, often with conspicuous fruiting bodies, for example *Amanita muscaria*, the fly agaric, and various species of *Boletus*.

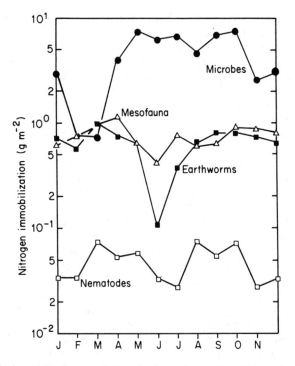

Fig. 9.14 Immobilization of nitrogen in decomposers in a *Liriodendron tulipifera* forest floor at Oak Ridge, Tennessee. The period of maximum root growth (January–March), when the roots absorb most nitrogen, coincides with minimal microbial immobilization. (From Ausmus, Edwards and Witkamp, in Anderson and Macfadyen.[1])

Hyphae spread out from the roots and permeate a greater volume of soil than the roots alone. The fungi also store nutrients which subsequently can be passed to the tree; this is especially significant with nutrients such as phosphorus, where availability in the soil solution is often low and varies seasonally. Although it has been claimed that mycorrhizal fungi act as decomposers,[238] most species seem to lack the necessary enzymes, and to depend on their higher-plant partner for carbon compounds. The amount of carbohydrate passed from tree to fungus may be equivalent to a tenth or more of the input to wood production, but this energy drain is presumably more than compensated by more efficient utilization of soil nutrients. Tree seedlings grow more quickly when infected with mycorrhizal fungi (Table 9.5) and are apparently less susceptible to pathogens. Recent work suggests that birch seedlings infected with

Table 9.5 Effects of mycorrhizas on growth of tree seedlings or cuttings (from Harley[107]).

	Growth in one season (g dry weight)	
	Non-mycorrhizal	Mycorrhizal
Pinus strobus	0.30	0.41
Eucalyptus pauciflora	3.3	6.2
Quercus robur	1.1	1.7

Amanita muscaria possess morphological features which may help to improve their water economy.[158] On the basis of such observations, attention is again being paid to the possibility of routinely infecting seedlings, especially if they are to be planted in sites to be afforested which lack the appropriate fungi.

Fertilizer applications

The nutrients most commonly supplied in fertilizers by foresters are nitrogen, phosphorus, potassium and calcium. Such applications are made in nurseries, to improve establishment and rate of development of new stands, or to promote the growth of older ones (in one case 90-year-old beech was shown to respond very positively to NPK fertilizer and lime). Higher responses are usually obtained on sites of lower quality (Fig. 9.15), but even on the better sites the improvement obtained normally justifies the cost of fertilizer application, which should be designed to ensure a suitable balance of nutrient elements.

In North America nitrogen is far more important in limiting tree growth than any other mineral nutrient.[4] This is as true for the northern hardwood forests as it is for Douglas fir in the Pacific Northwest. Western hemlock (*Tsuga heterophylla*), is, however, an example of a species whose growth is not normally improved by additional nitrogen. Nitrogen tolerant species—those with modest soil nitrogen requirements—(red and white oak, red maple and aspen) compete well on sites with low nitrogen status, while nitrogen demanders, such as the white ash, the basswood and the tulip tree (*Liriodendron tulipifera*), are at an advantage on soils with abundant nitrogen. Engelmann spruce responds vigorously to ammonium nitrogen but not to nitrate. At high latitudes and altitudes the amount of nitrogen available to trees is frequently low because so much is 'locked up' in the litter and organic matter on the forest floor.

Fertilizer applications influence many aspects of the forest ecosystem. Understorey plants and 'weed trees' often grow much more vigorously as a result, so that mechanical weeding or the application

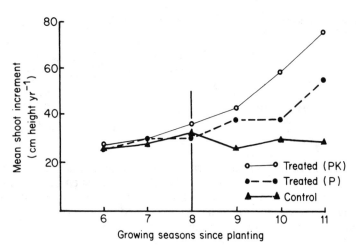

Fig. 9.15 Response of Sitka spruce (*Picea sitchensis*) to remedial addition of fertilizer in the autumn of 1973, eight years after planting. The single aerial applications to the trees, whose canopies had not closed, were at the rates of 375 kg unground phosphate rock per hectare (P), or this amount of phosphate together with 200 kg potassium chloride per hectare (PK). Control values are for trees grown for eleven years without this remedial fertilization. All trees were on unflushed deep peat in Galloway, Southern Scotland. The cost of the fertilizer application, in terms of 'years saved' before cropping, was more than recovered within three years of treatment. The same was true of Sitka spruce on a variety of other soils at various elevations in this area. (Redrawn from McIntosh, R. (1978). *Scottish Forestry*, **32**, 271–82; by courtesy of the Royal Scottish Forestry Society.)

of herbicides becomes necessary. Insect populations are affected in complex ways, as are the pattern of disease in forest trees and the development of mycorrhizas. With young stands in particular the increase in total leaf biomass, and consequently in transpiration, may be sufficient to reduce run-off into streams. The major consequence of the entry of fertilizer into aquatic systems associated with forests is *eutrophication*, in the sense of enrichment of waters and increased primary production. The respiratory requirements of associated microorganisms and other heterotrophs may lead to oxygen depletion, especially in the deeper regions of thermally stratified lakes.

Boreal forests

The concentration of nutrients in the needles of northern coniferous forests is lower than that in leaves of temperate or tropical species. Also, a greater proportion of most elements is translocated from the needles before they fall. Consequently the litter, which falls continually, is of low nutrient status, with high C/N and C/P ratios and a low level of water-soluble compounds. Rates of decomposition and mineralization are depressed by low temperatures, nutrient turnover being largely dependent on fungi and bacteria, mycophagous microarthropods and enchytraeids. Biostatic compounds such as resins act as further deterrents to decomposers. Organic matter accumulates on and in the soil, acting as the major nutrient pool in these forests (see Fig. 9.11), which often occur on nutrient-depleted podzols. Released nutrients are tightly cycled through mycorrhizas.

Tropical forests

It might be thought that the major input of nutrients to the forest floor of tropical rain forests would be as leachates from foliage, supplemented by rapid decomposition of litter. However, there is considerable variation between sites and between elements. A recent review[27] concludes that the relative input in the form of leachates ranges from less than a quarter for N, P and Ca, to over a half for K and Na. Leaching from the forest floor would remove nutrients beyond the reach of roots, or into drainage water, but in many of these forests there is a meshwork of mycorrhizal roots, which constitutes an absorptive barrier. When labelled nutrients were added to root mats in Amazonia, virtually none reached the mineral portion of the highly leached acidic soils on which the mats were perched.[223] Streams issuing from undisturbed forests of this kind are thus very low in nutrients, the efficiency of the root mats being comparable to that of an ionic resin column.

Rapid turn-over rates in the litter of tropical forests enable nutrients to be recycled more than once a year, thus helping to maintain high levels of primary productivity, favoured by climatic conditions. Productivity is, therefore, dependent on nutrient supplies, but these often come not from the soil, which is frequently depleted after thousands of years of leaching and uptake into plants, but from the trees themselves. The tightly regulated cycle, acting over many millennia, has enabled *trees* to *accumulate nutrient capital*. Nutrient conservation is particularly important in sites so poor in nutrients that primary production is lower than expected from the climate, for example dipterocarp forests on S.E. Asian white-sand soils.[123] High concentrations of *toxic compounds* in the leaves reduce losses of nutrients to herbivores, which would otherwise have to be made good from scarce supplies. Toxins may also have an adverse effect on decomposers, so that deep litter or even peat may accumulate, despite high temperatures and rainfall. Tropical rain forest on mineral deficient soils may be described as a 'counterfeit paradise', deceptive to the speculator in that interest on nutrient capital is not easily realized. There are, however, other tropical forests whose soils are quite rich in nutrients.

Disruption of nutrient cycling

The harvesting of trees and other forest plants by Man results in an important difference from the effects of forest fires or herbivore action: most of the harvested nutrients are removed from the ecosystem. The consequences of fires and harvesting also differ according to biome type and associated nutrient pools.

Fires in temperate woodlands may result in the addition of nutrient-rich ash to the soil pool, providing a seed bed for potential colonists, such as seeds from serotinous (resin-sealed) cones of jack pine (*Pinus banksiana*). On the other hand, ash may be blown away or removed in drainage water, depletion being further exacerbated if thin peaty soils are destroyed by fire. Depletions in harvested timber, particularly on nutrient-poor sites, may be partially rectified by the use of fertilizers, especially phosphorus and nitrogen, when replanting. The disruptive effects of clear felling were dramatically demonstrated at Hubbard Brook, New Hampshire, where all the vegetation in one watershed was felled and slashed but not removed.[145] Herbicides were applied for two years to prevent regrowth or colonization. Stream outflow from the cleared site during the following three years was about a third greater than from a comparable control watershed, largely because of a corresponding reduction in evapotranspiration (which normally equalled 41% of precipitation). Losses of major cations were markedly increased, while nitrate-nitrogen was also lost rather than gained by the system. These changes reflected greater concentrations in the soil solution, nutrients no longer being taken up by the vegetation. Nitrifying bacteria, which are normally inhibited in forest soils, increased appreciably, the resultant nitrate ions being readily leached, whereas previously ammonium ions had been absorbed by roots or adsorbed to soil colloids. Increasing acidity, resulting from decomposition of slash, reduced the base exchange capacity of the soil colloids, so facilitating the leaching of potassium, calcium and magnesium.

The vital link in the cycle can be restored by natural regeneration or by replanting, but in many tropical forests disturbance by Man has caused lasting damage to vast areas. Logging removes much of the accumulated nutrient capital, while clear felling to provide agricultural land has all too often resulted in soil erosion, top soil being washed away and silting up areas downstream. On the other hand, for thousands of years these forests supported shifting agriculture, based on the principle of slash and burn. Felling and firing patches of forest released nutrients to support food crops, but after a couple of years or so yields began to decline, the nutrient-retaining network of tree roots having been destroyed. The clearing was therefore abandoned and left fallow while the process was repeated several times elsewhere. Secondary succession gradually built up nutrient levels in the vegetation, but the fallow period was often measured in decades before sites could be profitably cleared again. However, human population pressure and the commercial exploitation of large areas, including conversion to plantations, have led to shorter and shorter fallow periods, with diminishing returns, compaction of soils and degeneration to scrub savanna. It has been estimated that 200 million people practise shifting cultivation over an area of 3 million km^2, and that this is currently the major cause of forest destruction. In an attempt to halt this decline, it has been proposed that cleared areas should be planted with forest trees and intercropped with food crops until the canopy closes, when further areas are cleared and planted. The continuing growth of the trees helps to restore fertility and to provide timber. This is the practice of *agrisilviculture*.

The replacement of vast areas of forest by grass for beef production, as in Amazonia, is a classic case of short-term exploitation which can lead only to degeneration in fertility. On the other hand, replacement by timber plantations, although disastrous from the point of view of community diversity, may improve fertility. In Brazil, where thousands of hectares of jungle have been cleared in the Jari project, it is claimed that the planting of *Gmelina arborea* (Malay bushbeech) has increased calcium levels in the topsoil, while the organic matter content of the soil has been raised by planting Caribbean pine (*Pinus caribaea*). It is, however, too early to assess the long-term effects of these plantations.

10

Woodland Management and Resource Potential

Forests and woodlands are complex renewable resources which can be exploited in a variety of ways, some very destructive. As the proportion of the world's land area covered by trees has shrunk the remaining forests have been increasingly subjected to multipurpose use. Forests may serve as water catchments, for recreation, for nature conservation, and for keeping game, as well as being sources of structural timber, paper, fuel and other products. Even when management objectives are reduced to the single requirement of timber production there are many alternatives from which to choose. Is the aim to achieve maximum timber production, perhaps to act as a strategic reserve, or maximum financial return? The fact that prices for timber fluctuate widely may largely determine when trees are felled by the small private owner, who often regards his trees more as a capital reserve than as a continuous source of income. At the other extreme the International Paper Company, which has developed fast growing 'supertrees' from the southern pines (e.g. *Pinus taeda*), affords an example of a large corporation with planned forest cropping programmes extending many decades into the future. The increasing demand for wood and the financial necessity to obtain a return on investment as soon as possible are both strong inducements to reduce the period between planting and felling; in future the number of trees in commercial forests allowed to reach beyond the age of sixty is likely to be low, apart from those in cold areas.

Many practical constraints reduce timber production to a level less than that theoretically possible for a given site. World demand for agricultural land has caused vast areas to be permanently deforested, and many forests are on relatively poor soils, have not been fertilized, and experience severe climates. This sometimes has advantages; slowly grown timber from northern forests often works better when planed or chiselled than that grown in warmer countries. Trees at higher latitudes are subjected to greater exposure, lower temperatures, and receive less light in winter, all of which lessen their productivity. Considerable capital investments in modern machinery, purchase of stock and construction of forest roads are required, while highly trained staff, fuel and fertilizers are expensive. Ethical problems may also be involved. Phosphates for food production are already in very short supply—is their use to increase timber production justified? Each forest is unique in the environmental, financial and even political conditions which must be considered by the forester managing it. The silvicultural system used (see Section 4.5), whether coppicing, clear cutting, shelter wood or selection, must be appropriate to the general management objectives. The most important decisions of all are the choice of trees to replant, and whether to maintain a complex forest with many species or a simple monoculture. Here a detailed knowledge of indigenous pests and diseases, and of potential exotic invaders, is most important, particularly with regard to planting pattern.

Even if the type of site and the tree species to be planted are fixed, the forester can greatly influence the form of the trees and the quality of the wood they produce. Such interactions between the forester's options and the quality of the crop (Fig. 10.1) are of crucial importance.

Clearly planning for future forests should be related to estimated demand for wood and forest products. In the Forestry Commission's review '*The wood production outlook in Britain*' (1977) it is forecast that by the year 2025 there will be a doubling in *Britain's annual consumption of wood*, currently running at 44 million cubic metres, of which 92% is imported. In order to reduce, albeit marginally, our dependence on overseas supplies, it has been proposed that indigenous resources should be increased, partially by improving yields from existing woodlands, but mainly by creating up to *1.8 million hectares of new plantations*. This option would almost double the wooded area of Britain, and would largely be carried out in low-grade areas of upland Scotland, with an estimated loss of about 2% to Britain's agricultural production. The impact on visual and recreational amenities is less easy to quantify. The wildlife potential of much of these uplands would be increased, especially if plantations establish a diversity of habitats and are interspersed with non-afforested areas. However, care would need to be taken in the case of certain plant communities such as those of peatlands, and of animals which are

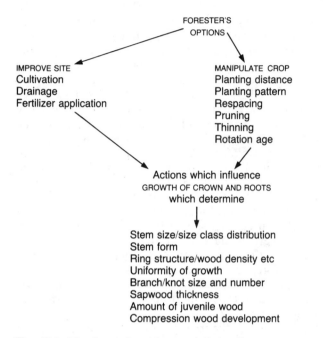

Fig. 10.1 The forester's options and their effects on tree growth and timber development. (From Brazier, J. D. (1979). Information Paper 12/79. Crown copyright, reproduced by permission of the Building Research Establishment, Princes Risborough Laboratory.)

confined to open moorland (e.g. large heather butterfly, golden plover and some birds of prey).

As the management of woodlands and forests becomes more intensive, and as ever more of the tree—roots, stump and bark, together with the mineral nutrients which it contains—is removed in forest products, so foresters require an increasingly accurate knowledge of the ecology of woodland processes. The same is true of those endeavouring to conserve woodlands of aesthetic and scientific value. Because of their complex structure and dynamic nature, woodland ecosystems will always pose management problems and provide a challenge to the ecologist.

Further Reading

1. ANDERSON, J. M. and MACFADYEN, A. (Eds) (1976). *The Role of Terrestrial and Aquatic Organisms in Decomposition Processes.* Blackwell Scientific Publications, Oxford.
2. ANDERSON, R. M., TURNER, B. D. and TAYLOR, L. R. (Eds) (1979). *Population Dynamics.* Blackwell Scientific Publications, Oxford.
3. CLAPHAM, A. R., TUTIN, T. G. and WARBURG, E. F. (1962). *Flora of the British Isles.* Second edition. Cambridge University Press.
4. DANIEL, T. W., HELMS, J. A. and BAKER, F. S. (1979). *Principles of Silviculture.* McGraw-Hill, New York.
5. DICKINSON, C. H. and PUGH, G. J. F. (Eds) (1974). *Biology of Plant Litter Decomposition.* Vols 1 and 2. Academic Press, London.
6. DUVIGNEAUD, P. (Ed.) (1971). *Productivity of Forest Ecosystems.* UNESCO, Paris.
7. ELTON, C. S. (1966). *The Pattern of Animal Communities.* Methuen, London.
8. EVANS, G. C., BAINBRIDGE, R. and RACKHAM, O. (Eds) (1975). *Light as an Ecological Factor, II.* Blackwell Scientific Publications, Oxford.
9. GODWIN, H. (1975). *The History of the British Flora.* Second edition. Cambridge University Press.
10. KARNOSKY, D. F. (1979). Dutch elm disease: a review of the history, environmental implications, control and research needs. *Environmental Conservation,* **6 (4),** 311–22.
11. KEBLE MARTIN, W. (1969). *The Concise British Flora in Colour.* Second edition. Ebury Press and Michael Joseph, London.
12. MANDAHL-BARTH, G. (1966). *Woodland Life.* Blandford Press, Poole, Dorset.
13. MAY, R. M. (Ed.) (1976). *Theoretical Ecology, Principles and Applications.* Blackwell Scientific Publications, Oxford.
14. MCCREE, K. J. (1973). A rational approach to light measurements in plant ecology. *Current Advances in Plant Science,* Commentaries in Plant Science No. 5, October 1973, 39–43.
15. MITCHELL, A. (1974). *A Field Guide to the Trees of Britain and Northern Europe.* Collins, London.

16. MORRIS, M. G. and PERRING, F. H. (Eds) (1974). *The British Oak*. B.S.B.I., E. W. Classey, Faringdon.
17. MORRIS, P. (Ed.) (1979). *The Natural History of the British Isles*. Country Life Books, Richmond upon Thames.
18. PEACE, T. R. (1962). *Pathology of Trees and Shrubs with special reference to Britain*. Clarendon Press, Oxford.
19. PENNINGTON, W. (1974). *The History of British Vegetation*. Second edition. English Universities Press, London.
20. RACKHAM, O. (1976). *Trees and Woodland in the British Isles*. Dent, London.
21. RACKHAM, O. (1980). *Ancient Woodland: its History, Vegetation and Uses in England*. Edward Arnold, London.
22. SOLOMON, M. (1976). *Population Dynamics*. Second edition. Studies in Biology, no. 18. Edward Arnold, London.
23. SPURR, S. H. and BARNES, B. V. (1980). *Forest Ecology*. Third edition. Wiley, New York.
24. STERN, K. and ROCHE, L. (1974). *Genetics of Forest Ecosystems*. Chapman and Hall, London.
25. SWIFT, M. J., HEAL, O. W. and ANDERSON, J. M. (1979). *Decomposition in Terrestrial Ecosystems*. Blackwell Scientific Publications, Oxford.
26. TANSLEY, A. G. (1939). *The British Islands and their Vegetation*. Cambridge University Press.
27. UNESCO (1978). *Tropical Forest Ecosystems*. UNESCO, Paris.
28. VARLEY, G. C., GRADWELL, G. R. and HASSELL, M. P. (1973). *Insect Population Ecology: an Analytical Approach*. Blackwell Scientific Publications, Oxford.
29. WOOD, R. F. (1974). *Fifty Years of Forestry Research*. H.M.S.O., London.

The Forestry Commission publishes, through H.M.S.O., a wide range of booklets, books, bulletins and reports on all aspects of forestry. Its annual reports on forestry research are useful guides to current trends. A recent book dealing with the classification of British woodlands is by G. F. Peterken (1981), *Woodland Conservation and Management*, Chapman and Hall, London.

References

30. ADAMSON, R. S. (1912). An ecological study of a Cambridgeshire woodland. *Journal of the Linnean Society (Botany)*, **40**, 339–87, Pl 12–17.
31. AMMAN, G. D. (1977). The role of the mountain pine beetle in lodgepole pine ecosystems: impact on succession. In *The Role of Arthropods in Forest Ecosystems*, MATTSON, W. J. (Ed.), pp. 3–18. Springer, New York.
32. ANDERSON, J. M. (1973). The breakdown and decomposition of sweet chestnut (*Castanea sativa* Mill.) and beech (*Fagus sylvatica* L.) leaf litter in two deciduous woodland soils. I and II. *Oecologia (Berlin)*, **12**, 251–74; 275–88.
33. ANDERSON, J. M. (1975). Succession, diversity and trophic relationships of some soil animals in decomposing leaf litter. *Journal of Animal Ecology*, **44**, 475–95.
34. ANDERSON, J. M. (1978a). Competition between two unrelated species of soil Cryptostigmata (Acari) in experimental microcosms. *Journal of Animal Ecology*, **47**, 787–803.
35. ANDERSON, J. M. (1978b). Inter- and intra-habitat relationships between woodland Cryptostigmata species diversity and the diversity of soil and litter microhabitats. *Oecologia (Berlin)*, **32**, 341–8.
36. ANDERSON, J. M. and BIGNELL, D. E. (1980). Bacteria in the food, gut contents and faeces of the litter-feeding millipede *Glomeris marginata* (Villers). *Soil Biology and Biochemistry*, **12**, 251–4.
37. ANDERSON, M. C. (1964a). Studies of the woodland light climate. I. The photographic computation of light conditions. *Journal of Ecology*, **52**, 27–41.
38. ANDERSON, M. C. (1964b). Studies of the woodland light climate. II. Seasonal variation in the light climate. *Journal of Ecology*, **52**, 643–63.
39. ARCHIBALD, J. F. and STUBBS, A. E. (1980). The effects of Dutch elm disease on wildlife. *Quarterly Journal of Forestry*, **74**, 30–7.
40. AUBRÉVILLE, A. (1938). La forêt coloniale: les forêts de l'Afrique occidentale français. *Annales Académie des Sciences coloniales, Paris*, **9**, 1–245.
41. AYENSU, E. S. (Ed.) (1981). *Jungles*. Book Club Associates, London.
42. BAINBRIDGE, R., EVANS, G. C. and RACKHAM, O. (Eds) (1966). *Light as an Ecological Factor*. Blackwell Scientific Publications, Oxford.
43. BAKER, H. G. (1973). Evolutionary relationships between flowering plants and

animals in American and African Tropical Forests. In *Tropical Forest Ecosystems in Africa and South America: a comparative review*, MEGGERS, B. J., AYENSU, E. S. and DUCKWORTH, W. D. (Eds), pp. 145–59. Smithsonian Institution Press, Washington.

44. BERTHET, P. (1963). Mesure de la consommation d'oxygène des Oribatides (Acariens) de la litière des forêts. In *Soil Organisms*, DOEKSEN, J. and DRIFT, J. VAN DER (Eds), pp. 18–31. North-Holland, Amsterdam.

45. BERTHET, P. (1967). The metabolic activity of Oribatid mites (Acarina) in different forest floors. In [181], pp. 709–25.

46. BEVAN, D. (1974). Control of forest insects: there is a porpoise close behind us. In *Biology in Pest and Disease Control*, PRICE JONES, D. and SOLOMON, M. E. (Eds), pp. 302–12. Blackwell Scientific Publications, Oxford.

47. BIRKS, H. J. B., DEACON, J. and PEGLAR, S. (1975). Pollen maps for the British Isles 5000 years ago. *Proceedings of the Royal Society of London, Series B*, **189**, 87–105.

48. BLACKMAN, G. E. and RUTTER, A. J. (1946). Physiological and ecological studies in the analysis of plant environment. I. The light factor and the distribution of the bluebell (*Scilla non-scripta*) in woodland communities. *Annals of Botany, New Series*, **10**, 361–90.

49. BLACKMAN, G. E. and RUTTER, A. J. (1954). *Endymion non-scriptus* (L.) Garcke. Biological Flora of the British Isles. *Journal of Ecology*, **42**, 629–38.

50. BOARDMAN, N. K. (1977). Comparative photosynthesis of sun and shade plants. *Annual Review of Plant Physiology*, **28**, 355–77.

51. BORMANN, F. H. and LIKENS, G. E. (1979). *Pattern and Process in a Forested Ecosystem*. Springer, New York.

52. BRASIER, C. M. (1979). Dual origin of recent Dutch elm disease outbreaks in Europe. *Nature, London*, **281**, 78–80.

53. BRASIER, C. M. and GIBBS, J. N. (1973). Origin of the Dutch elm disease epidemic in Britain. *Nature, London*, **242**, 607–9.

54. BRASIER, C. M. and GIBBS, J. N. (1975). Highly fertile form of the aggressive strain of *Ceratocystis ulmi*. *Nature, London*, **257**, 128–31.

55. BRAY, J. R. and GORHAM, E. (1964). Litter production in forests of the world. *Advances in Ecological Research*, **2**, 101–57.

56. BROWN, A. H. F. (1974). Nutrient cycles in oakwood ecosystems in N.W. England. In *The British Oak*, MORRIS, M. G. and PERRING, F. H. (Eds), 141–61. B.S.B.I., E. W. Classey, Faringdon.

57. BROWN, R. T. and CURTIS, J. T. (1952). The upland conifer-hardwood forests of northern Wisconsin. *Ecological Monographs*, **22**, 217–34.

58. BROWNE, F. G. (1968). *Pests and Diseases of Forest Plantation Trees: an annotated list of the principal species occurring in the British Commonwealth*. Oxford University Press.

59. BUNCE, R. G. H. (1977). The range of variation within the pinewoods. In *Native Pinewoods of Scotland*, BUNCE, R. G. H. and JEFFERS, J. N. R. (Eds), pp. 10–25. I.T.E., Cambridge.

60. BURNHAM, C. P. (1970). The regional pattern of soil formation in Great Britain. *Scottish Geographical Magazine*, **86**, 25–34.

61. BURNHAM, C. P. and MACKNEY, D. (1964). Soils of Shropshire. *Field Studies*, **2**, 83–113.

62. CLARK, F. E. (1967). Bacteria in soil. In *Soil Biology*, BURGES, A. and RAW, F. (Eds), pp. 15–49. Academic Press, London.

63. CLARK, J. (1961). Photosynthesis and respiration in white spruce and balsam fir. *New York State University College of Forestry Technical Publication 85*.

64. CLEMENTS, F. E. (1916). Plant Succession. An analysis of the development of vegetation. *Carnegie Institute Washington*, No. 242.

65. CLEMENTS, F. E. (1936). Nature and structure of the climax. *Journal of Ecology*, **24**, 252–84.
66. CONNELL, J. H. (1979). Tropical rain forests and coral reefs as open non-equilibrium systems. In [2], pp. 141–63.
67. CONWAY, G. (1976). Man versus pests. In [13], pp. 257–81.
68. COOPER, W. S. (1913). The climax forest of Isle Royale, Lake Superior, and its development. I. *Botanical Gazette*, **55**, 1–44.
69. COUSENS, J. (1974). *An Introduction to Woodland Ecology*. Oliver & Boyd, Edinburgh.
70. CROCKER, R. L. and MAJOR, J. (1955). Soil development in relation to vegetation and surface age at Glacier Bay, Alaska. *Journal of Ecology*, **43**, 427–8.
71. CROMPTON, E. (1962). Soil formation. *Outlook on Agriculture*, **3**, 209–18.
72. DARLINGTON, A. (1974). The galls on oak. In [16], pp. 298–311.
73. DAUBENMIRE, R. (1952). Forest vegetation of Northern Idaho and adjacent Washington, and its bearing on concepts of vegetation classification. *Ecological Monographs*, **22**, 301–30.
74. DAUBENMIRE, R. (1966). Vegetation: identification of typal communities. *Science*, **151**, 291–8.
75. DEMPSTER, J. P. (1975). *Animal Population Ecology*. Academic Press, London.
76. DE SILVA, B. L. T. (1934). The distribution of 'Calcicole' and 'Calcifuge' species in relation to the content of the soil in calcium carbonate and exchangeable calcium, and to soil reaction. *Journal of Ecology*, **22**, 532–53.
77. DICKINSON, C. H. and PREECE, T. F. (Eds) (1976). *Microbiology of Aerial Plant Surfaces*. Academic Press, London.
78. DIXON, A. F. G. (1970). Quality and availability of food for a sycamore aphid population. In *Animal Populations in relation to their Food Resources*, WATSON, A. (Ed.), pp. 271–87. Blackwell Scientific Publications, Oxford.
79. DIXON, A. F. G. (1971). The role of aphids in wood formation. I and II. *Journal of applied Ecology*, **8**, 165–79; 393–9.
80. DIXON, A. F. G. (1977). Aphid ecology: life cycles, polymorphism and population regulation. *Annual Review of Ecology and Systematics*, **8**, 329–53.
81. DIXON, A. F. G. (1979). Sycamore aphid numbers: the role of weather, host and aphid. In [2], pp. 105–21.
82. EDWARDS, C. A. and HEATH, G. W. (1963). The role of soil animals in breakdown of leaf material. In *Soil Organisms*, DOEKSEN, J. and DRIFT, J. VAN DER (Eds), pp. 76–84. North-Holland, Amsterdam.
83. ELLENBERG, H. (1978). *Vegetation Mitteleuropas mit den Alpen*. Second edition. Ulmer, Stuttgart.
84. ELTON, C. S. (1927). *Animal Ecology*. Sidgwick & Jackson, London.
85. ELTON, C. S. (1958). *The Ecology of Invasions by Animals and Plants*. Methuen, London.
86. ERNST, W. H. O. (1979). Population biology of *Allium ursinum* in northern Germany. *Journal of Ecology*, **67**, 347–62.
87. EVANS, G. C. (1972). *The Quantitative Analysis of Plant Growth*. Blackwell Scientific Publications, Oxford.
88. EVANS, G. C. (1976). A sack of uncut diamonds: the study of ecosystems and the future resources of mankind. *Journal of Animal Ecology*, **45**, 1–39.
89. EVANS, G. C. and COOMBE, D. E. (1959). Hemispherical and woodland canopy photography and the light climate. *Journal of Ecology*, **47**, 103–13.
90. FLOWERDEW, J. R. and GARDNER, G. (1978). Small rodent populations and food supply in a Derbyshire ashwood. *Journal of Animal Ecology*, **47**, 725–40.
91. FORD, E. D. and NEWBOULD, P. J. (1977). The biomass of ground vegetation and its relation to tree cover through a deciduous woodland cycle. *Journal of Ecology*, **65**, 201–12.

92. FRYDMAN, I. and WHITTAKER, R. H. (1968). Forest associations of southeast Lublin province, Poland. *Ecology*, **49**, 896–908.

93. GARDNER, G. (1977). The reproductive capacity of *Fraxinus excelsior* on the Derbyshire limestone. *Journal of Ecology*, **65**, 107–18.

94. GARRETT, S. D. (1951). Ecological groups of soil fungi; a survey of substrate relationships. *New Phytologist*, **50**, 149–66.

95. GAUSE, G. F. (1934, reprinted 1964). *The Struggle for Existence*. Hafner, New York.

96. GIMINGHAM, C. H. and BIRSE, E. M. (1957). Ecological studies on growth-form in bryophytes. I. Correlations between growth-form and habitat. *Journal of Ecology*, **45**, 533–45.

97. GOSZ, J. R., HOLMES, R. T., LIKENS, G. E. and BORMANN, F. H. (1978). The flow of energy in a forest ecosystem. *Scientific American*, **238(3)**, 92–102.

98. GOSZ, J. R., LIKENS, G. E. and BORMANN, F. H. (1973). Nutrient release from decomposing leaf and branch litter in the Hubbard Brook Forest, New Hampshire. *Ecological Monographs*, **47**, 173–91.

99. GRADWELL, G. R. (1974). The effect of defoliators on tree growth. In [16], pp. 182–93.

100. GRIME, J. P. (1966). Shade avoidance and shade tolerance in flowering plants. In [42], pp. 187–207.

101. GRIME, J. P. (1979). *Plant Strategies and Vegetation Processes*. Wiley, New York.

102. GRIME, J. P. and LLOYD, P. S. (1973). *An Ecological Atlas of Grassland Plants*. Edward Arnold, London.

103. GRUBB, P. J. (1977). The maintenance of species-richness in plant communities: the importance of the regeneration niche. *Biological Review*, **52**, 107–45.

104. HAMILTON, G. J. and CHRISTIE, J. M. (1971). Forest Management Tables (metric). *Forestry Commission Booklet, No. 34*, H.M.S.O., London.

105. HARDING, D. J. L. (1967). Faunal participation in the breakdown of cellophane inserts in the forest floor. In *Progress in Soil Biology*, GRAFF, O. and SATCHELL, J. E. (Eds), pp. 10–20. North-Holland, Amsterdam.

106. HARDING, D. J. L. and STUTTARD, R. A. (1974). Microarthropods. In [5], pp. 489–532.

107. HARLEY, J. L. (1971). *Mycorrhiza*. Oxford Biology Reader 12, Oxford University Press.

108. HARPER, J. L. (1977). *Population Biology of Plants*. Academic Press, London.

109. HARPER, J. L., LOVELL, P. H. and MOORE, K. G. (1970). The shapes and sizes of seeds. *Annual Review of Ecology and Systematics*, **1**, 327–56.

110. HASSALL, M. (1977). Consumption of leaf litter by the terrestrial isopod *Philoscia muscorum* in relation to food availability in a dune grassland ecosystem. *Ecological Bulletins. Stockholm*, **25**, 550–3.

111. HAYES, A. J. (1979). The microbiology of plant litter decomposition. *Science Progress, Oxford*, **66**, 25–42.

112. HEAL, O. W. and MACLEAN, S. F. (1975). Comparative productivity in ecosystems—secondary productivity. In *Unifying Concepts in Ecology*, VAN DOBBEN, W. H. and LOWE-MCCONNELL, R. H. (Eds), pp. 89–108. W. Junk, Wageningen.

113. HOPKINS, B. (1965). *Forest and Savanna*. Heinemann, London.

114. HORN, H. S. (1971). *The Adaptive Geometry of Trees*. Princeton University Press, New Jersey.

115. HORN, H. S. (1975). Forest Succession. *Scientific American*, **232(5)**, 90–8.

116. HUBBELL, S. P. (1980). Seed predation and the coexistence of tree species in tropical forests. *Oikos*, **35**, 214–29.

117. HUDSON, H. J. (1968). The ecology of fungi on plant remains above the soil. *New Phytologist*, **67**, 837–74.

118. HUGHES, A. P. (1959). Effects of the environment on leaf development in *Impatiens parviflora* DC. *Journal of the Linnean Society* (*Botany*), **56**, 161–5.

119. HUNT, D. J. and HAGUE, N. G. M. (1974). The distribution and abundance of *Parasitaphelenchus oldhami*, a nematode parasite of *Scolytus scolytus* and *S. multistriatus*, the bark beetle vectors of Dutch elm disease. *Plant Pathology*, **23**, 133–5.

120. HUTCHINGS, M. J. and BARKHAM, J. P. (1976). An investigation of shoot interactions in *Mercurialis perennis* L., a rhizomatous perennial herb. *Journal of Ecology*, **64**, 723–43.

121. IVERSEN, J. (1941). Landnam i Danmarks Stenalder. En pollenanalytisk Undersøgelse over det første Landbrugs Indvirkning paa Vegetationsudviklingen. *Danmarks Geologiske Undersøgelse*, RII, No. 66.

122. JANZEN, D. (1971). Seed predation by animals. *Annual Review of Ecology and Systematics*, **2**, 465–92.

123. JANZEN, D. (1974). Tropical blackwater rivers, animals and mast fruiting by the Dipterocarpaceae. *Biotropica*, **6**, 69–103.

124. JANZEN, D. (1975). *Ecology of Plants in the Tropics*. Studies in Biology, no. 58. Edward Arnold, London.

125. JANZEN, D. (1976). Why do bamboos wait so long to flower? In *Tropical Trees: Variation, Breeding and Conservation*, BURLEY, J. and STYLES, B. T. (Eds), pp. 135–9. Academic Press, London.

126. JANZEN, D. (1979). How to be a fig. *Annual Review of Ecology and Systematics*, **10**, 13–51.

127. JAYNES, R. A., ANAGNOSTAKIS, S. L. and VAN ALFEN, N. K. (1976). Chestnut research and biological control of the chestnut blight fungus. In *Perspectives in Forest Entomology*, ANDERSON, J. F. and KAYA, H. K. (Eds), pp. 61–70, Academic Press, New York.

128. JENIK, J. (1979). *Pictorial Encyclopedia of Forests*. Hamlyn, London.

129. JENSEN, V. (1974). Decomposition of angiosperm tree leaf litter. In [5], pp. 69–104.

130. JONES, E. W. (1945). The structure and reproduction of the virgin forest of the North Temperate Zone. *New Phytologist*, **44**, 130–48.

131. JONES, E. W. (1959). *Quercus* L. Biological Flora of the British Isles. *Journal of Ecology*, **47**, 169–222.

132. KÄÄRIK, A. A. (1974). Wood. In [5], pp. 129–74.

133. KALLIO, P. (1975). Kevo, Finland. In *Structure and Function of Tundra Ecosystems*, ROSSWALL, T. and HEAL, O. W. (Eds), *Ecological Bulletins*. Stockholm, **20**, 193–223.

134. KERSHAW, K. A. (1973). *Quantitative and Dynamic Plant Ecology*. Second edition. Edward Arnold, London.

135. KIMMINS, J. P. (1972). Relative contributions of leaching, litter fall and defoliation by *Neodiprion sertifer* (Hymenoptera) to the removal of cesium-134 from red pine. *Oikos*, **23**, 226–34.

136. KING, C. M. (1980). The weasel *Mustela nivalis* and its prey in an English woodland. *Journal of Animal Ecology*, **49**, 127–59.

137. KIRA, T. (1975). Primary production of forests. In *Photosynthesis and Productivity in Different Environments*, COOPER, J. P. (Ed.), pp. 5–40. Cambridge University Press.

138. KITAZAWA, Y. (1971). Biological regionality of soil fauna and its function in forest ecosystem types. In [6], pp. 485–98.

139. KLOMP, H. (1966). The dynamics of a field population of the pine looper, *Bupalus piniarius* L. (Lep., Geom.). *Advances in Ecological Research*, **3**, 207–305.

140. KREBS, C. J. (1978). *Ecology: the Experimental Analysis of Distribution and Abundance*. Second edition. (First edition, 1972). Harper & Row, London.

141. KURCHEVA, G. F. (1960). Role of invertebrates in the decomposition of oak litter. *Soviet Soil Science*, **4**, 360–5.

142. LARCHER, W. (1975). *Physiological Plant Ecology*. Springer, Berlin.

143. LA ROI, G. H. (1967). Ecological studies in the boreal spruce-fir forests of the North American taiga. I. Analysis of the vascular flora. *Ecological Monographs*, **37**, 229–53.

144. LEE, K. E. and WOOD, T. G. (1971). *Termites and Soils*. Academic Press, London.

145. LIKENS, G. E., BORMANN, F. H., JOHNSON, N. M., FISHER, D. W. and PIERCE, R. S. (1970). Effects of forest cutting and herbicide treatment on nutrient budgets in the Hubbard Brook watershed ecosystem. *Ecological Monographs*, **40**, 23–47.

146. LIVINGSTON, R. B. and ALLESSIO, M. L. (1968). Buried viable seed in successional field and forest stands, Harvard Forest, Massachusetts. *Bulletin of the Torrey Botanical Club*, **95**, 58–69.

147. LLEWELLYN, M. (1972). The effects of the lime aphid, *Eucallipterus tiliae* L. (Aphididae) on the growth of the lime *Tilia* × *vulgaris*. I. *Journal of applied Ecology*, **9**, 26–82.

148. LLEWELLYN, M. (1975). The effects of the lime aphid, *Eucallipterus tiliae* L. (Aphididae) on the growth of the lime *Tilia* × *vulgaris*. II. *Journal of applied Ecology*, **12**, 15–23.

149. LUXTON, M. (1972). Studies on the oribatid mites of a Danish beech wood soil. I. Nutritional biology. *Pedobiologia*, **12**, 434–63.

150. LUXTON, M. (1979). Food and energy processing by oribatid mites. *Revue d'écologie et de biologie du sol*, **16**, 103–11.

151. MACARTHUR, R. H. and WILSON, E. O. (1967). *The Theory of Island Biogeography*. Princeton University Press, New Jersey.

152. MACFADYEN, A. (1961). Metabolism of soil invertebrates in relation to soil fertility. *Annals of applied Biology*, **49**, 216–19.

153. MACFADYEN, A. (1963). The contribution of the microfauna to total soil metabolism. In *Soil Organisms*, DOEKSEN, J. and DRIFT, J. VAN DER (Eds), pp. 3–17. North-Holland, Amsterdam.

154. MADDEN, J. L. (1977). Physiological reactions of *Pinus radiata* to attack by woodwasp, *Sirex noctilio* F. (Hymenoptera: Siricidae). *Bulletin of Entomological Research*, **67**, 405–26.

155. MADGE, D. S. (1965). Leaf fall and litter disappearance in a tropical forest. *Pedobiologia*, **5**, 273–88.

156. MANN, K. H. (1967). The approach through the ecosystem. In *The Teaching of Ecology*, LAMBERT, J. M. (Ed.), pp. 103–11, Blackwell Scientific Publications, Oxford.

157. MARTIN, M. H. (1968). Conditions affecting the distribution of *Mercurialis perennis* L. in certain Cambridgeshire woodlands. *Journal of Ecology*, **56**, 777–93.

158. MASON, P. A., PELHAM, J. and LAST, F. T. (1977). Stem anatomy and sheathing mycorrhizas in the *Betula verrucosa-Amanita muscaria* relationship. *Nature, London*, **265**, 334–5.

159. MAY, R. M. (1976). Patterns in multi-species communities. In [13], pp. 142–62.

160. MEIDNER, H. and SHERIFF, D. W. (1976). *Water and Plants*. Blackie, London.

161. MELLANBY, K. (1968). The effects of some mammals and birds on regeneration of oak. *Journal of applied Ecology*, **5**, 359–66.

162. MILLAR, C. S. (1974). Decomposition of coniferous leaf litter. In [5], pp. 105–28.

163. MONTEITH, J. L. (1973). *Principles of Environmental Physics*. Edward Arnold, London.

164. MUELLER-DOMBOIS, D. and ELLENBERG, H. (1974). *Aims and Methods of Vegetation Ecology*. Wiley, London.

165. MUKERJI, S. K. (1936). Contributions to the autecology of *Mercurialis perennis* L. *Journal of Ecology*, **24**, 38–81.

166. NEWBOULD, P. J. (1967). *Methods for Estimating the Primary Production of Forests*. Blackwell Scientific Publications, Oxford.

167. NICHOLSON, P. B., BOCOCK, K. O. and HEAL, O. W. (1966). Studies on the

decomposition of the faecal pellets of a millipede (*Glomeris marginata* (Villers)). *Journal of Ecology*, **54**, 755–66.

168. NIELSEN, B. OVERGAARD (1977). Beech seeds as an ecosystem component. *Oikos*, **29**, 268–74.

169. NIELSEN, B. OVERGAARD (1978). Above ground food resources and herbivory in a beech forest ecosystem. *Oikos*, **31**, 273–9.

170. NILSSON, I. (1978). The influence of *Dasychira pubibunda* (Lepidoptera) on plant nutrient transports and tree growth in a beech (*Fagus sylvatica*) forest in southern Sweden. *Oikos*, **30**, 133–48.

171. O'CONNOR, F. B. (1964). Energy flow and population metabolism. *Science Progress, Oxford*, **52**, 406–14.

172. OLMSTED, N. W. and CURTIS, J. D. (1947). Seeds of the forest floor. *Ecology*, **28**, 49–52.

173. OVINGTON, J. D. (1965). *Woodlands*. English Universities Press, London.

174. PACKHAM, J. R. (1978). *Oxalis acetosella* L. Biological Flora of the British Isles. *Journal of Ecology*, **66**, 669–93.

175. PACKHAM, J. R. (1979). Factors influencing the growth and distribution of the Wood Sorrel (*Oxalis acetosella*) on the Long Mynd, Shropshire. *Caradoc and Severn Valley Field Club*, Occasional paper No. 3, 1–14.

176. PACKHAM, J. R. and WILLIS, A. J. (1976). Aspects of the ecological amplitude of two woodland herbs, *Oxalis acetosella* L. and *Galeobdolon luteum* Huds. *Journal of Ecology*, **64**, 485–510.

177. PACKHAM, J. R. and WILLIS, A. J. (1977). The effects of shading on *Oxalis acetosella*. *Journal of Ecology*, **65**, 619–42.

178. PARDÉ, J. (1980). Forest-biomass. *Forestry Abstracts*, **41**, 343–62.

179. PERRINS, C. M. (1980). The great tit, *Parus major*. *Biologist*, **27**, 73–80.

180. PETERMAN, R. M., CLARK, W. C. and HOLLING, C. S. (1979). The dynamics of resilience: shifting stability domains in fish and insect systems. In [2], pp. 321–41.

181. PETRUSEWICZ, I. (Ed.) (1967). *Secondary Productivity in Terrestrial Ecosystems*. Polish Academy of Sciences, Warsaw.

182. PETRUSEWICZ, K. and MACFADYEN, A. (1970). *Productivity of Terrestrial Animals— Principles and Methods*. Blackwell Scientific Publications, Oxford.

183. PFISTER, R. D., KOVALCHIK, B. L., ARNO, S. F. and PRESBY, R. C. (1977). *Forest habitat types of Montana*. United States Department of Agriculture Forest Service General Technical Report INT-34. Intermountain Forest and Range Experimental Station, Ogden, Utah.

184. PHILLIPSON, J. (1971). *Methods of study in Quantitative Soil Ecology: Population, Production and Energy Flow*. Blackwell Scientific Publications, Oxford.

185. PHILLIPSON, J., PUTMAN, R. J., STEEL, J. and WOODELL, S. R. J. (1975). Litter input, litter decomposition and the evolution of carbon dioxide in a beech woodland— Wytham Woods, Oxford. *Oecologia (Berlin)*, **20**, 203–17.

186. PIGOTT, C. D. (1975). Natural regeneration of *Tilia cordata* in relation to forest-structure in the forest of Białowieza, Poland. *Philosophical Transactions of the Royal Society, B*, **270**, 151–79.

187. PIGOTT, C. D. and TAYLOR, K. (1946). The distribution of some woodland herbs in relation to the supply of nitrogen and phosphorus in the soil. *Journal of Ecology*, **52** (Supplement), 175–85.

188. POPE, D. J. and LLOYD, P. S. (1975). Hemispherical photography, topography and plant distribution. In [8], pp. 385–408.

189. PROCTOR, M. and YEO, P. (1973). *The Pollination of Flowers*. Collins, London.

190. PUGH, G. J. F. (1974). Terrestrial Fungi. In [5], pp. 303–36.

191. RACKHAM, O. (1975). *Hayley Wood, its History and Ecology*. Cambridgeshire and Isle of Ely Naturalists' Trust, Cambridge.

192. RAUNKIAER, C. (1934). *The Life Forms of Plants and Statistical Plant Geography*. Clarendon Press, Oxford.

193. REYES, V. G. and TIEDJE, J. M. (1976). Ecology of the gut microbiota of *Tracheoniscus rathkei* (Crustacea, Isopoda). *Pedobiologia*, **16**, 67–74.

194. RISHBETH, J. (1963). Stump protection against *Fomes annosus*. III. Inoculation with *Peniophora gigantea*. *Annals of applied Biology*, **52**, 63–77.

195. RISHBETH, J. (1976). Chemical treatment and inoculation of hardwood stumps for control of *Armillaria mellea*. *Annals of applied Biology*, **82**, 57–70.

196. RODIN, L. E. and BAZILEVICH, N. I. (1967). *Production and Mineral Cycling in Terrestrial Vegetation*. Oliver & Boyd, Edinburgh.

197. ROHMEDER, E. (1967). Beziehungen zwischen Frucht-bzw. Samenerzeugung und Holzerzeugung der Waldbäume. *Allgemeine Forstzeitschrifte*, **22**, 33–9.

198. RUSSELL, E. W. (1973). *Soil Conditions and Plant Growth*. Tenth edition. Longmans, London.

199. RUSSELL, R. S. (1977). *Plant Root Systems: their Function and Interaction with the Soil*. McGraw-Hill, London.

200. SALISBURY, E. J. (1916a). The Oak-Hornbeam woods of Hertfordshire. I & II. *Journal of Ecology*, **4**, 83–117.

201. SALISBURY, E. J. (1916b). The emergence of the aerial organs in woodland plants. *Journal of Ecology*, **4**, 121–8.

202. SALISBURY, E. J. (1920). The significance of the calcicolous habit. *Journal of Ecology*, **8**, 202–15.

203. SALISBURY, E. J. (1924). The effects of coppicing as illustrated by the woods of Hertfordshire. *Transactions of the Hertfordshire Natural History Society and Field Club*, **18**, 1–21.

204. SALISBURY, E. J. (1925). The vegetation of the Forest of Wyre: a preliminary account. *Journal of Ecology*, **13**, 314–21.

205. SALISBURY, E. J. (1942). *The Reproductive Capacity of Plants*. Bell, London.

206. SALISBURY, F. B. and ROSS, C. W. (1978). *Plant Physiology*. Second edition. Wadsworth Publishing Company, Belmont, California.

207. SATCHELL, J. E. (1967). Lumbricidae. In *Soil Biology*, BURGES, A. and RAW, F. (Eds), pp. 259–322. Academic Press, London.

208. SATCHELL, J. E. and LOWE, D. G. (1967). Selection of leaf litter by *Lumbricus terrestris*. In *Progress in Soil Biology*, GRAFF, O. and SATCHELL, J. E. (Eds), pp. 102–19. North-Holland, Amsterdam.

209. SCHULZE, E. D. (1970). Der CO_2-Gaswechsel de Buche (*Fagus silvatica* L.) in Abhängigkeit von den Klimafaktoren im Freiland. *Flora, Jena*, **159**, 177–232.

210. SCHULZE, E. D. (1972). Die Wirkung von Licht und Temperatur auf den CO_2-Gaswechsel verscheidener Lebensformen aus der Krautschicht eines montanen Buchenwaldes. *Oecologia (Berlin)*, **9**, 235–58.

211. SCHULZE, E. D., FUCHS, M. I. and FUCHS, M. (1977a). Spatial distribution of photosynthetic capacity and performance in a mountain spruce forest of Northern Germany. I. Biomass distribution and daily CO_2 uptake in different crown layers. *Oecologia (Berlin)*, **29**, 43–61.

212. SCHULZE, E. D., FUCHS, M. and FUCHS, M. I. (1977b). Spatial distribution of photosynthetic capacity and performance in a mountain spruce forest of Northern Germany. III. The significance of the evergreen habit. *Oecologia (Berlin)*, **30**, 239–48.

213. SEEGER, M. (1930). Erfahrungen über die Eiche in der Rhinehene bei Emmendingen (Baden). *Allgemeine Forst-u. Jagdzeitung*, **106**, 201–19.

214. SERNANDER, R. (1936). The primitive forests of Granskär and Fiby: a study of the part played by storm-gaps and dwarf trees in the regeneration of the Swedish spruce forest. *Acta Phytogeographica Suecica*, **8**, 1–232. (English summary, pp. 220–7.)

215. SHAW, M. W. (1974). The reproductive characteristics of oak. In [16], pp. 161–81.

216. SHIMWELL, D. W. (1971). *The Description and Classification of Vegetation*. Sidgwick & Jackson, London.

217. SOUTHERN, H. N. (1970). The natural control of a population of tawny owls (*Strix aluco*). *Journal of Zoology, London*, **162**, 197–285.
218. SOUTHWOOD, T. R. E. (1973). The insect/plant relationship—an evolutionary perspective. In *Insect/Plant Relationships*, VAN EMDEN, H. F. (Ed.), pp. 3–30. Blackwell Scientific Publications, Oxford.
219. SOUTHWOOD, T. R. E. (1976). Bionomic strategies and population parameters. In [13], pp. 26–48.
220. SOUTHWOOD, T. R. E. (1977). Habitat, the templet for ecological studies? *Journal of Animal Ecology*, **24**, 337–65.
221. SPENCER, D. A. (1964). Porcupine population fluctuations in past centuries revealed by dendrochronology. *Journal of applied Ecology*, **1**, 127–49.
222. SPRUGEL, D. G. (1976). Dynamic structure of wave-regenerated *Abies balsamea* forests in the north-eastern United States. *Journal of Ecology*, **64**, 889–911.
223. STARK, N. M. and JORDAN, C. F. (1978). Nutrient retention by the root mat of an Amazonian rain forest. *Ecology*, **59**, 434–7.
224. STREET, H. E. and ÖPIK, H. (1976). *The Physiology of Flowering Plants*. Second edition. Edward Arnold, London.
225. SWIFT, M. J. (1976). Species diversity and the structure of microbial communities in terrestrial habitats. In [1], pp. 185–222.
226. SWIFT, M. J. (1977). The ecology of wood decomposition. *Science Progress, Oxford*, **64**, 179–203.
227. SYDES, C. and GRIME, J. P. (1981). Effects of tree leaf litter on herbaceous vegetation in deciduous woodland. I and II. *Journal of Ecology*, **69**, 237–48; 249–62.
228. TANTON, M. T. (1965). Acorn destruction potential of small mammals and birds in British woodlands. *Quarterly Journal of Forestry*, **59**, 230–4.
229. TRANQUILLINI, W. (1979). *Physiological Ecology of the Alpine Timberline*. Springer, Berlin.
230. TRIBE, H. T. (1957). Ecology of microorganisms in soils as observed during their development upon buried cellulose film. In *Microbial Ecology*, WILLIAMS, R. E. O. and SPICER, C. C. (Eds), pp. 287–98. Cambridge University Press.
231. VARLEY, G. C. (1970). The concept of energy flow applied to a woodland community. In *Animal Populations in relation to their Food Resources*, WATSON, A. (Ed.), pp. 389–405. Blackwell Scientific Publications, Oxford.
232. WAREING, P. F. and PHILLIPS, I. D. J. (1978). *The Control of Growth and Differentiation in Plants*. Second edition. Pergamon Press, Oxford.
233. WATT, A. S. (1919). On the causes of failure of natural regeneration in British oakwoods. *Journal of Ecology*, **7**, 173–203.
234. WATT, A. S. (1923). On the ecology of British beechwoods with special reference to their regeneration. Part I. *Journal of Ecology*, **11**, 1–48.
235. WATT, A. S. (1925). On the ecology of British beechwoods with special reference to their regeneration. Part II, Sections II and III. *Journal of Ecology*, **13**, 27–73.
236. WATT, A. S. (1947). Pattern and process in the plant community. *Journal of Ecology*, **35**, 1–22.
237. WAY, M. J. (1977). Pest and disease status in mixed stands vs. monocultures; the relevance of ecosystem stability. In *Origins of Pest, Parasite, Disease and Weed Problems*, CHERRETT, J. M. and SAGAR, G. C. (Eds), pp. 127–38. Blackwell Scientific Publications, Oxford.
238. WENT, F. W. and STARK, N. (1968). Mycorrhiza. *Bioscience*, **18**, 1035–9.
239. WHITTAKER, R. H. (1975). *Communities and Ecosystems*. Second edition. Collier Macmillan, London.
240. WHITTAKER, R. H. and MARKS, P. L. (1975). Methods of assessing terrestrial productivity. In *Primary Productivity of the Biosphere*, LIETH, H. and WHITTAKER, R. H. (Eds), pp. 55–118. Springer, New York.

241. WILLIS, A. J. (1973). *Introduction to Plant Ecology*. Allen & Unwin, London.
242. WITKAMP, M. and AUSMUS, B. S. (1976). Processes in decomposition and nutrient transfer in forest systems. In [1], pp. 375–96.
243. WOOD, T. G. (1971). The effects of soil fauna on the decomposition of *Eucalyptus* leaf litter in the Snowy Mountains, Australia. In *Organismes du Sol et Production Primaire, Proc. 4th Coll. Soil Zool.*, pp. 349–58. I.N.R.A., Paris.
244. WOOD, T. G. and SANDS, W. A. (1977). The role of termites in ecosystems. In *Production Ecology of Ants and Termites*, BRIAN, M. V. (Ed.), pp. 245–92. Cambridge University Press.
245. WOOLHOUSE, H. W. (1978). Light-gathering and carbon assimilation processes in photosynthesis; their adaptive modifications and significance for agriculture. *Endeavour, New Series*, **2**, 35–46.
246. YOUNG, J. E. (1975). Effects of spectral composition of light sources on the growth of a higher plant. In [8], pp. 135–60.

Index

Bold numbers refer to pages containing a definition.

Abies (Fir) 27, 28, 29, 43, 46, 68, 76–8, 93, 156, 215
A. balsamea 73, 112, 115, 158
Acer 88, 100, 109, 110, 120–2, 129, 137, 154, 185, 208
Actinomycetes 4, 128, 145
Adelgids 155, 156, 218
Agrisilviculture 241
Allelopathy 3
Allium ursinum (ramsons) 81, 102, 103, 232
Alnus (Alder) 4, 65, 102, 128, 129, 136
Amanita muscaria (fly agaric) 235
Anemone nemorosa (wood anemone) 6, 8, 39, 81, 84, 89, 101, 140
Annual rings 113, 216, 217, 219
Aphids 156, 169, 171, 218, 219, 220, 221
    effects on production 218
Apodemus sylvaticus (woodmouse) 19, 92, 163, 174, 175, 176
Armillaria mellea (honey fungus) 12, 149, 194
Aspect societies 6, 99–103
Assimilation efficiency (A/C) 220, 226
Aureobasidium pullulans 145, 189, 190

Bacteria
    as pathogens 145, 150
    in decomposition 15, 194, 201, 202, 203, 240
Bamboos 93, 95, 97
Barro Colorado, Panama 180
Base exchange 57, 240
Basidiomycetes 161, 189, 190, 192, 194, 195, 235
Beech snap 147
Beetles 150–1, 157–61, 195
Betula (birch) 2, 3, 16, 43, 49, 89, 90, 100, 130, 134, 135, 146, 225
Białowieża Forest, Poland 120–5
Biological (life form) spectra 22, 26–30
Biomass **207**, 209, 210, 215
Biomass accumulation ratio (B:P) 211
Blean Woods, Kent 198, 200
Bradfield Woods, Suffolk 139
Brown earths (soils) 58, 61, 66
Brunchorstia destruens (*Crumenula pinea*) 148

Bryophytes 6, 17, 30, 140–2
Bupalus piniaria (pine looper) 158, 163, 167–9, 170

CAI (Current annual increment) **211**
Calcicole **82**
Calcifuge **82**
Calcium 64, 82, 232, 234, 237
Calluna vulgaris (heather) 65, 66, 70, 82
Cannock Forest, Staffs. 159, 160
Carpinus betulus (hornbeam) ii, 93, 101, 120–5, 137, 142, 208
Castanea sativa (sweet chestnut) 87, 100, 140, 149, 193, 197, 204, 223
C. dentata (American chestnut) 146–7
Caterpillars
    of moths 17, 156, 157, 164, 173
    of sawflies 218, 233
    effects on production 216, 217
    and nutrient cycling 233
Cellophane 187
Ceratocystis 150–3, 194
Chaddesley NNR, Worcs. 156, 216
Chamaephytes 23, 24, 26–8
Charcoal 110, 138, 141, 142
Chasmogamy **101**
Chilterns, England 125–7
Chondrostereum purpureum 149
Choristoneura fumiferana (Spruce budworm) 158, 168, 170
Circaea lutetiana (enchanter's nightshade) 39, 83, 90, 127
Clear cutting (clear felling) 104, 240
Cleistogamy **101**, 102
Clethrionomys glareolus (bank vole) 19, 92, 163, 174, 176
Climatic optimum 135, 136
Climax **109**, 110, 111, 116, 127, 180
C/N ratio 14, 15, 30, 185, 235, 239
Comminution 59, **183**, 202, 235
Community structure 146, 155, 178, 179, 182
Compensation point, light **43**, 44
Competition 5, 67–70, 85, 109, 116, 117, 168, 176, 192, 196, 201
Competitive exclusion **116**
Conopodium majus (pignut) 8, 101

Conservation 143, 243
Conspecifics **95**, 180
Consumption
    of leaves 216
    of litter 226
    of wood by Britain 243
Continuum concept 75, 76
Control of pests and diseases 148–9, 152, 159
Coppicing 104, 105, 139–43
Coprophagy 201, **226**
Cordon sanitaire 152
Coriolus versicolor 149
Corydalis cava (hollow corydalis) 101
Corylus avellana (hazel) 27, 88, 102, 104, 126, 133–5, 156, 208
Crataegus monogyna (hawthorn) 125–7
Cryptococcus fagi 147
Cryptophytes 24
Cyclic change 110–16
Cyzenis albicans 164, 166–7

Day length 9, 89, 100
Decomposers 11, 12, 183
Decomposition 14–16, 183–96
    of broadleaves 190
    of needles 189
    of wood 193
    rates 202
Defensive compounds 3, 156, 157, 185, 193, 194, 239
Defoliation 156, 158, 159, 216, 233
Dendrochronology 2, 113, 127, 134
Dendroctonus 158, 161, 179
Density dependence **166**, 171–7
Deschampsia 44, 45, 65, 70, 82, 83
Detritivores 183, 184, 204
    distribution 197
    diversity 196
    earthworms 15, 185, 204, 226
    enchytraeids 15, 189, 193, 204, 227, 230, 239
    millipedes 201, 204
    mites 15, 187, 188, 189, 193, 197, 199, 201, 226, 227
    molluscs 187, 199, 226
    springtails 15, 187, 190, 203, 204, 206, 226
    succession 193
    woodlice 199, 201, 204, 226, 234
Devensian (= Weichselian) glacial 134, 135
Diapause **9**, 171, 197
Dichogamy **87**
Digestive enzymes 145, 187, 192, 195, 197–99
Digitalis purpurea (foxglove) 89
Dipterocarps 95, 97, 239
Diseases of trees 146–53
Diversity 78–83, 131, 139, 145, 179–82, 196–7
Dominance 75, 76, 180
Dormancy 100
Drainage 47, 62
Drepanosiphum platanoidis (sycamore aphid) 156, 169, 171, 218, 220

Drought 16, 47, 78, 131, 149, 151
Dryas 128, 129, 135
Dutch elm disease 150–3, 178

Ecesis **108**
Ecosystems **9**–14
Ecotone **77**
Elatobium abietinum (green spruce aphid) 171, 218
Elm decline 135, 138
Endemic populations 158
Endothia parasitica 146–8
Endymion non-scriptus (bluebell) 6, 8, 39, 81, 83, 101–103, 140
Energy flow 1, 10
    through animals 220, 227
    through ecosystems 228–30
    through microflora 227
Enoicyla pusilla 203, 206
Epilobium angustifolium (fireweed, rosebay willowherb) 17, 82, 89, 140
Ercall, Shropshire 6, 66
Erosion 4, 106, 240
Erwinia nimipressuralis 150
Eucallipterus tiliae (lime aphid) 171, 219, 221
Eucalyptus 2, 22, 98, 150, 204
Evaporation, potential **47**
Evapo-transpiration 6, 7, 240

Fagus sylvatica (common beech) 4, 16, 43, 49, 54, 55, 67, 68, 81, 90, 94, 95, 100, 111, 114, 118, 119, 125–7, 147, 154, 157, 173, 180, 204, 208–9, 219, 233
Fertilizers 237, 238, 243
Fiby forest, Sweden 110, 112, 113
Field layer 5, 232
Fire 2, 15, 16, 98, 110, 116, 159, 179, 240
    and nutrients 240
    serotiny 179, 240
Flandrian events 133–9
Flushing **9**, 166
Fomes annosus (*Heterobasidion annosum*) 148–9, 194
Food web 12
Forester's maturity 211, 213
Fraxinus excelsior (common ash) 24, 26, 46, 81, 87, 88, 90, 94, 100, 104, 119, 137, 149, 156
Frost 93, 99, 100
Fungi
    as pathogens 146–9, 150–3, 189
    as saprophytes 189, 190, 194, 195, 233
    of phylloplane 145, 190
Funnel cells 39, 41

Galeobdolon luteum see *Lamiastrum galeobdolon*
Galls 155
Gamlingay Wood, Cambs. 139
Gap regeneration 107, 111, 117, 118
Geophytes 23, 24, 28, 44

Germination requirements 89
Glacial moraine 110, 112, 127, 128
Glaciation 132–6
Glacier bay, Alaska 127, 128
Gleying 58–60
Glomeris marginata (pill millipede) 201, 206
Gmelina arborea 241
Grazing chain 12, 144
Gut contents 196, 197, 200

Ham Street NNR, Kent 142
Hayley Wood, Cambs. 63, 64, 139, 141, 217
Hedera helix (ivy) 7, 24, 89
Heliophytes (sun plants) **37**, 84
Helophytes 23
Hemicryptophytes 23, **24**, 28, 44
Herbivores **11**, 79, 144, 154, 233
Hestehaven (Danish IBP) 222
Holcus mollis (creeping soft-grass) 66, 81
Honeydew 145, 156, 233
Hubbard Brook Forest 221, 228, 235, 240
Hydrologic cycle 6, 7, 10
Hypovirulence 147–8

Ilex aquifolium (holly) 22
Immobilization **13**, 235
Impatiens parviflora (small balsam) 34, 41, 42
Index of similarity 28, 74, 75

Juniperus 125–7, 130

K (carrying capacity) 18, 19
Kampfzone 77
Key-factor analysis **162**–6, 173, 176
Kingley Vale, Sussex 126, 127
Krummholz 77
K selection 18–21, 176

LAI (leaf area index) **37**, 46, 129
Lamiastrum galeobdolon (yellow archangel) 7, 9, 39, 40, 81, 102, 123, 140
Lammas growth 156, 216, 233
Landnam clearances 138
LAR (leaf area ratio) **37**
Larix (larch) 24, 43, 99, 100, 149, 209, 218
Leaching 13, 16, 204, 239, 240
Leaf arrangement 42, 43, 46, 128–31
Leaf miners 156, 220
Leaf size classification **24**, 25
Leafy phase 7, 37
Life forms 22–30, 79
Life tables 162, 164
Light 33, 34, **35**–46
    diffuse (skylight) **33**, 36
    direct (sunlight) **33**, 36
    phase **36**
Liriodendron tulipifera 104, 185, 235, 237
Litter 14, 33, **183**
    and nutrients 231
    and plant diversity 80–81
    components 223

fall 222–3
turnover 225
Litter bags 203
Lumbricus terrestris 15, 185, 226
LWR (leaf weight ratio) **37**, 42
Lymantria dispar (gypsy moth) 157

Macrophytophagous **196**
Madingley Wood, Cambs. 36–8
MAI (mean annual increment) **211**
Mammals
    damaging trees 98, 109, 154, 220
    effects on production 220
    population dynamics 174–5
Management 104–7, 242–4
Masting 4, 87, 93, 118, 173, 177, 219
Meathop Wood, Cumbria (British I.B.P.) 222, 227, 229, 230, 231
Mercurialis perennis (dog's mercury) 8, 34, 82–5, 90, 101, 125, 127, 142
Microarthropods (e.g. mites and springtails) 189, 203, 204, 227, 239
Microflora 195, 199, 227, 235
Microhabitat 192, 193, 197
Microphytophagous **196**, 199
Mineralization **13**, 233, 235
Models, simulation 1, 168
Moder 59
MOF (mixed oak forest) 133–5
Monocarpy 4, 93
Monoclimax **109**
Monolayer trees 46, 128–31
Mor 15, 59, 63, 189, 204
Mull 15, 59, 63, 133, 204
Multilayer trees 46, 128–31
Mustela nivalis (weasel) 12, 167, 174–5
Mycorrhizas 5, 64–5, 77, 235, 237, 239
Myxomatosis 127, 178

Necromass 13, **183**, 193, 221, 233
Nectria coccinea 147, 218
Niche **116**, 180, 196, 197
Nitrogen 14, 30, 156, 169, 171, 185, 230–3, 235, 237, 240
Normal forest 107
Nutrient(s)
    and heterotrophs 233, 235
    concentrations 230–2
    conservation 231, 238, 239
    cycles in boreal forests 230, 238
    cycles in tropical forests 230, 239
    cycling 1, 10, 13, 230
    immobilization **13**, 235
    in litter 231
    mineralization **13**, 233

Oak wilt (*Ceratocystis fagacearum*) 153
Old field successions 128–31
Operophtera brumata (winter moth) 156, 163, 164, 165, 173, 216, 220, 229, 230
Opportunist species 17, 175

Optimum temperature   32, 44
Oribatid mites (Cryptostigmata)   188, 189,
    193, 197, 198, 201, 202, 226
Osmotic phenomena   49–51
Oxalis acetosella (wood sorrel)   9, 39–41,
    43–5, 49, 81, 84, 85, 101, 102, 111, 114, 123

Palatability   3, 185
Palynology (pollen analysis)   **133**
Panolis flammea (pine beauty)   159
Parasitism   79, 145, 152, 167, 171
Parus major (great tit)   9, 163, 172
Peniophora gigantea   148
Pests of trees   150, 152, 154, 155, 158, 159
Phanerophytes   22–**24**, 28
PhAR (photosynthetically active
    radiation)   **31**, 33, 34, 42, 46
Phenology   6–9, 34, 101–3, 156–7, 197
Phenotypic plasticity   **39**, 42
Phosphate   65, 243
Phosphorus   231–3, 235, 237, 240
Photography, himispherical   38
Photosynthesis   31–4, 53–5, 131
    gross   **32**
    net   **32**
Phylloplane   **145**
Phytochrome   31
Phytoclimate   26
Picea   43, 119, 149
P. abies (Norway spruce)   49, 54, 55, 68, 93,
    99, 120–2, 125, 133, 214, 223
P. sitchensis (Sitka spruce)   47, 62, 73, 127,
    128, 238
Pine looper   see *Bupalus piniaria*
Pinus   2, 47, 62, 73, 77, 90, 93, 100, 119, 131,
    148, 149, 154, 158–60, 179, 185, 240, 241,
    242
P. contorta (lodgepole pine)   52, 62, 73, 77,
    128, 158, 159, 179
P. sylvestris (Scots pine)   4, 15, 22, 27, 43,
    47, 49, 62, 68, 93, 104, 106, 125, 137, 158,
    189, 209, 223, 225
Piptoporus betulinus   146
Plagioclimax   **109**, 124
Plagiothecium undulatum   6
Plasticity, phenotypic   39, 42
Poa trivialis   81
Podzol   57, 58, 66, 189, 239
Pollarding   105
Pollen   87, 88, 132–8
Pollination   87, 88
Polycarpy   4
Polyclimax   **109**
Population dynamics of animals   18–21,
    162–78
Populus (poplar)   129
Potassium   230, 232, 234, 237, 238
Predation   166, 174, 177–8
Primaeval forest   107
Primula elatior (oxlip)   82, 83, 141
Primula vulgaris (primrose)   140

Production
    biomass ratio (P:B)   211
    commercial   211
    effects of herbivores   216, 218
    gross primary (GPP)   **211**
    net primary (NPP)   **210**
    primary   11
    secondary   13, 220, 227, 230
Protection forests   4
Pseudotsuga menziesii (Douglas fir)   2, 73, 76,
    78, 93, 209, 214
Pteridium aquilinum (bracken)   66, 80, 82, 85,
    140
Pupal surveys   159
PWP (permanent wilting percentage)   **48**
Pythium   146

Quercus (oak)   17, 52, 88, 89, 90, 100, 130,
    135–7, 149, 155, 185, 204, 215
Q. cerris (Turkey oak)   155
Q. petraea (sessile oak)   88, 93, 94, 141, 209
Q. robur (English oak)   8, 68, 88, 90, 91, 93,
    104, 119–26, 157, 164, 203, 208, 217

Rabbits   127, 178
Ranunculus ficaria (lesser celandine)   8, 39,
    101
Redox potential   **83**
Regeneration   16
    and intermediate disturbance   181
    gap   117, 118
    requirements   117
Regulation of populations   **166**, 177
Rendzina   7, 57, 58
Resistance to disease   150, 153
Resource, renewable   4, 139, 242
Respiration rates   32, 203, 227
R/FR ratio   31, 35
RGR (relative growth rate)   **37**, 42
Rhizobium   4, 145
Rhizomorphs   **149**
Rhizoplane   **145**
Ribes   119, 120
RLGR (relative leaf growth rate)   **37**
Root   4, 5, 64–8
    nodules   4
    /shoot ratio   42
    systems   67, 68
Rots
    butt   148
    heart   195
    root   148
    white, brown, soft   194, 195
r-selection   18–21
Rubus (bramble)   66, 80, 111, 114, 118, 140,
    154

Salix (willow)   87, 128, 129, 149, 154
Sambucus nigra (elder)   3, 82, 90
Sanicula europaea (wood sanicle)   82, 125,
    127, 142
Saprophytes   12, 145, 190

Sawflies 218, 233
Sciophytes (shade plants) 37, 84
Scolytus spp. 150–3
Scrub species 126
Seed
    buried 118–20
    dispersal 26, 90, 91
    predation 86, 97, 180, 219
    shadow 181
    size 89, 90
    tree system 106
Selection systems 104–6
Semelparous **20**, 95
Senescence 107, 111, 145, 170, 190, 213
Sequoia sempervirens (coastal redwood) 2,
    47, 90, 104, 131, 133, 209
Sequoiadendron giganteum (big tree) 2, 47,
    90, 131
Seral woodlands 120–32
Sere **109**, 127
Shade 33–46, 139, 140
    plants 37, 39–46
Shelterwood 104, 106
Shifting agriculture 240
Shredding 105
Silvicultural systems 104–7, 243
Sirex noctilio (wood wasp) 160
SLA (specific leaf area) **37**, 40, 42
Sloths 221
Soil 56–70, 80, 83
    organisms 184
    pH 30, 57, 63, 66, 68–70, 82, 128, 129, 142,
        190
Solling Plateau (German I.B.P.) 43, 45, 54–5
South Downs, England 125–7
Species richness 116–20
Spore dispersal 192, 202
Spruce budworm 158, 168, 170
Stand cycle 111, 213
Steady state forest 115, 116
Stomatal frequency 41, 42
    index 37, 42
Storm gap structure **110**, 112, 113, 116
Strategies
    deciduous/evergreen 53–5
    digestive 198
    K- 18–21
    pollinator 96
    r- 18–21
    reproductive 86, 157
Stratification **5**, **93**
Strix aluco (tawny owl) 19, 163, 176, 229
Substrate groups 192
Succession 108–37, 145
    degradative **187**, 191–6
    old field 128–31
Sugar fungi 187, 192
Sugar maple (*Acer saccharum*) 109, 110, 129
Sun plants 4, 37, 39–46
    flecks **33**, 34, 44

Symbiosis 4, 145, 199

Taiga **71**–5, 212
Taxus baccata (yew) 16, 90, 125, 126, 149, 157
Temperature 32, 47, 166, 172
    optimum 44
Tension zones **71**, 74
Termites 194, 199, 206, 227
Territory 154, 173, 177
Therophytes 24, 28
Tilia 61, 87, 93, 104, 136, 237
T. cordata (small leaved lime) 120–5, 136, 225
Tomicus piniperda (pine shoot beetle) 159,
    160
Top height **214**
Tortrix viridana (green oak roller) 156, 157,
    163, 166, 173, 216, 229, 230
Transpiration 49–53, 160
Treelines 77, 78
Tsuga 53, 73, 76, 109, 110, 127, 128, 133, 237
Tyloses 150

Ulmus (elm) 2, 17, 93, 100, 104, 120, 149,
    151–3, 178
ULR (unit leaf rate) **37**, 42
Umbra of leaf 130, **131**
Urtica dioica (stinging nettle) 24, 82, 124

Vaccinium (bilberry) 65, 66, 80, 82
Viola 101, 127
Virelles-Blaimont (Belgian I.B.P.) 7, 208
Viruses 149, 169

Water 46–53
    balance 49
    conservation 50, 51
    field capacity 47
    interception 6
    logging 83
    potential (ψ) 48
    runoff 6
    stemflow 6, 7, 232
    through-fall 7, 232
Wave regeneration **114**–16
White-sand soils 158, 239
Wildwood 107, 136, 137
Winter moth see *Operophtera brumata*
Wood quality 243–4
Wood sorrel see *Oxalis acetosella*
Wyre Forest 53, 68, 141
Wytham, Berks 163, 164, 172–5, 217, 222,
    225, 229

Yellow archangel see *Lamiastrum
    galeobdolon*
Yield class **214**, 215

Zonation **71**–8

English a   processes   ganisms

Ash, common *Fraxinus excelsior*
Bank vole *Clethrionomys glareolus*
Beech, common *Fagus sylvatica*
Big tree, Wellingtonia *Sequoiadendron giganteum*
Bilberry *Vaccinium myrtillus*
Birch *Betula*
Birch-bracket *Piptoporus* (= *Polyporus*) *betulinus*
Bluebell *Endymion non-scriptus* (= *Hyacinthoides non-scripta*)
Coastal redwood *Sequoia sempervirens*
Creeping soft-grass *Holcus mollis*
Dog's mercury *Mercurialis perennis*
Douglas fir *Pseudotsuga menziesii*
Dutch elm disease *Ceratocystis ulmi*
Elm, wych *Ulmus glabra*
Enchanter's nightshade *Circaea lutetiana*
Fir *Abies*
   Grand fir *A. grandis*
   Silver fir *A. alba*
Fly agaric *Amanita muscaria*
Great tit *Parus major*
Green oak roller *Tortrix viridana*
Gypsy moth *Lymantria dispar*
Hazel *Corylus avellana*
Hawthorn *Crataegus monogyna*
Heather, ling *Calluna vulgaris*
Hemlock, eastern *Tsuga canadensis*
Hemlock, western *T. heterophylla*
Holly *Ilex aquifolium*
Honey fungus *Armillaria mellea*
Hornbeam *Carpinus betulus*
Ivy *Hedera helix*

Knopper gall *Andricus quercus-calicis*
Lesser celandine *Ranunculus ficaria*
Lime, hybrid *Tilia* × *europaea*
   large-leaved *T. platyphyllos*
   small-leaved *T. cordata*
Lime aphid *Eucallipterus tiliae*
Oak, English (pedunculate) *Quercus robur*
   sessile (durmast) *Q. petraea*
Oribatid mites Cryptostigmata
Oxlip *Primula elatior*
Pill millipede *Glomeris marginata*
Pine, Corsican *Pinus nigra*
   lodgepole *P. contorta*
   Monterey *P. radiata*
   Scots *P. sylvestris*
Pine beauty *Panolis flammea*
Pine looper *Bupalus piniaria*
Pine shoot beetle *Tomicus piniperda*
Primrose *Primula vulgaris*
Ramsons (wild garlic) *Allium ursinum*
Spruce, Norway *Picea abies*
   Sitka *P. sitchensis*
Spruce budworm *Choristoneura fumiferana*
Stinging nettle *Urtica dioica*
Sycamore *Acer pseudoplatanus*
Sycamore aphid *Drepanosiphum platanoidis*
Tawny owl *Strix aluco*
Tulip-tree, tulip poplar *Liriodendron tulipifera*
Weasel *Mustela nivalis*
Winter moth *Operophtera brumata*
Wood mouse *Apodemus sylvaticus*
Wood sorrel *Oxalis acetosella*
Yellow archangel *Lamiastrum galeobdolon* (= *Galeobdolon luteum*)